TEACHING STRATEGIES FOR NEURODIVERSITY AND DYSLEXIA IN ACTOR TRAINING

Teaching Strategies for Neurodiversity and Dyslexia in Actor Training addresses some of the challenges met by acting students with dyslexia and highlights the abilities demonstrated by individuals with specific learning differences in actor training.

The book offers six tested teaching strategies, created from practical and theoretical research investigations with dyslexic acting students, using the methodologies of case study and action research. Utilizing Shakespeare's text as a laboratory of practice and drawing directly from the voices and practical work of the dyslexic students themselves, the book explores:

- the stress caused by dyslexia and how teachers might ameliorate it through changes in their practice
- the theories and discourse surrounding the label of dyslexia
- the visual, kinesthetic, and multisensory processing preferences demonstrated by some acting students assessed as dyslexic
- acting approaches for engaging with Shakespeare's language, enabling those with dyslexia to develop their authentic voice and abilities
- a grounding of the words and the meaning of the text through embodied cognition, spatial awareness, and epistemic tools
- Stanislavski's method of *units and actions* and how it can benefit and obstruct the student with dyslexia when working on Shakespeare
- *Interpretive Mnemonics* as a memory support and hermeneutic process, and the use of color and drawing towards an autonomy in live performance

This book is a valuable resource for voice and actor training, professional performance, and for those who are curious about emancipatory methods that support difference through humanistic teaching philosophies.

Dr. Petronilla Whitfield is Associate Professor in Voice and Acting at the Arts University Bournemouth, UK. She holds a PhD in Arts Pedagogy from Warwick University and an MA in Voice Studies from the Royal Central School of Speech and Drama. Trained originally as an actor at Arts Educational Schools, she was a professional actor for twenty years. She has taught voice and acting at leading British actor training institutions and universities for eighteen years.

TEACHING STRATEGIES FOR NEURODIVERSITY AND DYSLEXIA IN ACTOR TRAINING

Sensing Shakespeare

Petronilla Whitfield

Routledge
Taylor & Francis Group

NEW YORK AND LONDON

First published 2020
by Routledge
52 Vanderbilt Avenue, New York, NY 10017

and by Routledge
2 Park Square, Milton Park, Abingdon, Oxon, OX14 4RN

Routledge is an imprint of the Taylor & Francis Group, an informa business

© 2020 Taylor & Francis

Library of Congress Cataloging-in-Publication Data
Names: Whitfield, Petronilla author.
Title: Teaching strategies for neurodiversity and dyslexia in actor
    training : sensing Shakespeare / Petronilla Whitfield.
Description: New York : Routledge, 2019.
Identifiers: LCCN 2019016473 | ISBN 9781138311817 (hardback)
    | ISBN 9781138311848 (paperback) | ISBN 9780429458590
    (ebook)
Subjects: LCSH: Acting—Study and teaching. | People with
    disabilities and the performing arts.
Classification: LCC PN2075 .W45 2019 | DDC 792.02/807—dc23
LC record available at https://lccn.loc.gov/2019016473

ISBN: 978-1-138-31181-7 (hbk)
ISBN: 978-1-138-31184-8 (pbk)
ISBN: 978-0-429-45859-0 (ebk)

Typeset in Bembo
by Swales & Willis Ltd, Exeter, Devon, UK

DEDICATION

I dedicate this book to my students with dyslexia whose work lies at the center of this study. You have taught me so much, and your generosity in sharing your working methods will help to teach others. Your resourceful talents, courage, and tenacity in overcoming your obstacles and working with your dyslexia have inspired me and will inspire others who follow in your footsteps.

You have gone on to become professional actors, a theatrical agent, a casting director, television and theatre producers, a drama teacher for children with autism, a leader of drama in a special school for children excluded from mainstream education, amongst other interesting and valuable careers. I am proud of your achievements.

CONTENTS

ILLUSTRATIONS

Figures

Table

FOREWORD

As trainers and coaches of actors, we have for several years eagerly followed the progress of Dr. Petronilla Whitfield's research with acting students at the Arts University Bournemouth. While the dyslexic students and professionals we have encountered have brought abundant talent, insight, and persistence to their processes, we have observed that they have often experienced high levels of stress and anxiety when working on dramatic text. This can be exacerbated when working on Shakespeare. Unfamiliar vocabulary and unusual syntax that can be challenging for anyone can become particularly daunting for dyslexics. While many teachers have experienced this and perhaps attempted to mitigate it individually, the specific needs of dyslexic acting students have not always been recognized and addressed within the academy as a whole.

Not only does good pedagogy require that attention be paid to the needs of all students, but the British Equality Act of 2010 also places an obligation on organizations to make reasonable adjustments for people with recognized disabilities. In response to these mandates, Dr. Whitfield designed her research to explore what adjustments to her teaching methods were needed to overcome the disadvantage that dyslexia placed on her students at all levels of dramatic text work, from cold reading through to performance, and particularly with Shakespearean language. The result is a timely and important contribution not only to the field of actor training, but professional theatre in general.

Dr. Whitfield has brought together a detailed consideration of current thinking on dyslexia from a multiplicity of perspectives with rigorous and systematic action research involving both theory and practice. She has tested the efficacy of several methods of actor training in facilitating dyslexic students' work on Shakespearean text and used critical reflection to spur innovation and invite further research. In doing so, she has not only created a valuable resource for teachers and coaches, she has modeled a process of practical research into an area of actor training that historically has not had enough investigation. It is an implicit call to action to all of us who wish to make our teaching and coaching more effective, inclusive and empowering.

David Carey
Resident Voice and Text Director
Oregon Shakespeare Festival

Rebecca Clark Carey
Head of Voice and Text
Oregon Shakespeare Festival

ACKNOWLEDGMENTS

I am grateful to the Arts University Bournemouth for awarding me a Research Fellowship to write this book. Thank you to Professor Emma Hunt for her support for my work in developing inclusivity in teaching and learning. My special thanks to my research supervisor Professor Jonothan Neelands, who supervised my PhD thesis which forms the basis of this book. I should also like to thank David Carey for his encouragement of my work and writing by being the first to publish my research about my teaching of Shakespeare and dyslexic acting students when he was an editor at *Voice and Speech Review* in 2009. I also thank him for his excellent teaching as course leader on the MA Voice Studies at the Royal Central School of Speech and Drama, when I trained as a voice teacher in 2001, and where the roots of this book began. My deep thanks to Professor Nicola Shaughnessy and Associate Professor Stephen Purcell, examiners of my PhD dissertation, for wholeheartedly supporting my study and highlighting its potential for publication. My sincere gratitude to Dr. Rachel Moseley, Senior Lecturer in Psychology, who generously gave up her time on several occasions to share her scientific publications, advise, and read my paragraphs on neural reuse and embodied cognition in Chapter 3, clarifying the scientific details. A warm thank you must go to Professor Ross Prior for his recognition of the need for a scholarship of teaching and learning in actor training, and his interest and inclusion of my work in his edited book (referenced below). I am also hugely grateful to Professor Rod Nicolson for sharing his expertise in dyslexia, giving his attention to some of the early stages of my research, and explaining his understanding of my dyslexic students' methods from his perspective of psychology and knowledge about dyslexia. I am grateful to Dr. Achille Pasqualotto for his curiosity about my dyslexic students' working methods, and for sharing his research findings regarding the brain's plasticity and multisensory processing. I am indebted to Professor

Andrew Belser for his valuable feedback on the first draft of this book, who read every chapter, and offered such helpful comments and advice. At Routledge, I must thank Senior Editor Stacey Walker for her interest and recognition of the need for such a book, and Editorial Assistant Lucia Accorsi, who offered steadfast guidance throughout my writing of the book. A mention must go to other colleagues at the Arts University – my sincere thanks to Professor Rachel Worth for early discussions, Valerie Lodge for her sustained support from the beginning, and Professor Mary Oliver for understanding my task and guarding my time to do it.

A heartfelt thank you must go to my two children and my partner, who have tolerated a preoccupied mother and family member throughout the years of my studies and writing of this book.

Finally, I am indebted to my dyslexic acting students, whose work is central to this book, which is why I have dedicated this book to them.

Some of the material that is included in this book has appeared in parts in published journal articles and an edited book. My thanks to the editors of Intellect Books and at Taylor & Francis for giving permission to include sections taken from:

Whitfield, P. (2009). Shakespeare, pedagogy and dyslexia. *In:* Cooke, R. (ed.) *The Moving Voice: The Integration of Voice and Movement. The Voice and Speech Trainers Review*, 6:1, 254–262. Published online in *Voice and Speech Review*, 2013. Available from: https://doi.org/10.1080/23268263.2009.10767576. Accessed 7 May 2019.

Whitfield, P. (2015). Towards an emancipatory praxis of pedagogy: supporting acting students with dyslexia when working on Shakespeare. *Voice and Speech Review*, 9:2–3, 113–138.

Whitfield, P. (2016). A facilitation of dyslexia through a remediation of Shakespeare's text. *Research in Drama Education: The Journal of Applied Theatre and Performance*, 21:3, 385–400.

Whitfield, P. (2017). The Micro Grasp and Macro Gestus strategy as a facilitation of dyslexia in actor training: reconstructing the written text when performing Shakespeare. *Theatre, Dance and Performance Training*, 8:3, 329–347.

Whitfield, P. (2018). Entanglement in Shakespeare's text: using interpretive mnemonics with acting students with dyslexia. *In:* Prior, R. (ed.) *Using Art as Research in Learning and Teaching*. Bristol, UK: Intellect Books, pp. 181–198.

PART I

The Background to the Investigatory Practice

1

INTRODUCTION

This book places the individual with dyslexia at the heart of its investigative practice. Its study has originated through an interactive dialogue spanning many years with a growing community of acting students with specific learning differences, particularly those with dyslexia. It is written using the subjective voice of the 'I' in directly sharing my experiences, research, and learning with other teachers, exploring how changes in pedagogy and curriculum can alter individuals' achievements and views about themselves. Its topic has arisen from requests for help from many of the acting students I have worked with over the years, and continue to work with. In every institution I have taught in, these requests and accompanying signs of distress are discernible in certain teaching situations, across cohorts and subject areas. This cry for help arises from the presence of dyslexia, with its associated characteristics and sometimes overlapping learning differences within a range of circumstances produced within actor training. These signals of distress are frequently explicit, rupturing the flow and progression of work within the received practices of the status quo. Sometimes the signs are suppressed, yet the indicators of stress and discomfort remain palpable, and are heard very loudly by those who pay attention. Many teachers, especially in the environment of actor training, experience this sense of disquiet in certain situations within their everyday teaching practice (Leveroy 2012, 2013a, 2013b, 2015; Oram 2018a, 2018b). Historically, these requests for help have remained unanswered, ignored, misunderstood, or been considered too complicated and challenging to address. Occasionally, teachers have attempted to help, using improvised ideas or re-asserting traditional techniques pulled from their teaching toolkit. However, such techniques remain transitory, and are usually not evaluated (by peers or students) nor disseminated. They have not emerged from a long-term study into the situation nor extensive research into dyslexia itself nor the causes of the distress.

Frequently, those who struggle have been blamed, in a variety of ways, for the reasons for and results of their discomfort. The studies in this book focus on a selection of individuals who are labeled as possessing a disability. An educational psychologist has assessed them all as dyslexic.

The Personal Voice

In writing this book, I speak from a perspective gained through my own training and twenty years' experience as a professional actor, and eighteen subsequent years as a teacher of voice, acting, and more recently, academic writing (in both drama schools and university settings). Moreover, it is important to disclose myself as a member of the neurodiverse group. My wish to highlight the vulnerable status of those with a specific learning difference is influenced by my own assessed disability. Although I do not have dyslexia, I have been assessed by an educational psychologist as having a specific learning disability (SpLD) in the form of dyscalculia. Dyscalculia is a difficulty with understanding numbers, counting and matters of 'numerosity' (Department for Education & Skills 2004: 20). My dyscalculia lends me an empathy and concern for those with the apparent blocks caused by dyslexia. I can identify with their feelings of humiliation, discomfort, fear, confusion, and frustration, situated in an environment where the majority can do it, but the minority cannot, despite their possession of other abilities.

Questions Surrounding Terminology of Neurodiversity and Difference

In considering what might be termed as normative or neurotypical, the term 'neurodiversity' attempts to describe those who might be considered as different. Neurodiversity is an umbrella term grouping together a range of profiles which are also labeled as specific learning difficulties/disabilities or development disorders, such as dyslexia, dyspraxia, dyscalculia, attention deficit disorder, and Asperger's Syndrome (Palfreman-Kay 2005). In a definition of neurodiversity, Grant states:

> Neurodiversity is present when an exceptional degree of variation between neurocognitive processes results in noticeable and unexpected weaknesses in the performance of some everyday tasks when compared with much higher performances on a subset of measures of verbal and/or visual abilities for a given individual. Neurodiversity is a positive statement of differentiation, for while it explicitly refers to individuals whose everyday ways of thinking and behaving differ in certain key aspects from the majority of people, it rejects the assumption that these differences are dysfunctional and are to be 'cured'. Instead, there is a societal obligation that others make suitable adjustments and accommodations to enable inherent potential to be fully realized.
>
> (Grant 2009: 35)

Terminology is a contested area and provokes differing opinions. Although labels can be informative, the particular words used can reveal underlying attitudes. In a medical model of diagnosis, the label of 'learning difficulty/disability' is said by some to place the responsibility of addressing the difficulty or abnormality with the individual, while an identification of a 'learning difference' indicates that teaching must be adjusted. The social model of disability maintains that many of the problems experienced by those with intellectual disabilities are not caused by the intellectual disability itself, but by 'problems of access, support, community participation and acceptance' due to a 'disabling society that threaten the very existence of people who are cognitively different to the mainstream' (Goodley 2014: 7). However, some people prefer the term 'disability' to describe their experience, as they feel that their struggles are palpable in comparison to others' abilities, and what they experience feels like a disability to them (Pollak 2005: 4).[1]

In considering the wider meaning of the word 'neurodiversity', it is evident that all human beings are neurodiverse as we all have differing brains, bodies, lives, and experiences. The term 'neurodiversity' attempts to move away from presenting people with specific learning difficulties and developmental disorders as people with problems towards seeing them as a distinctive group of learners with different ways of learning (Palfreman-Kay 2005). According to Ross Cooper (an academic and university teacher who is dyslexic), labeling some people as neurotypical and others as neurodiverse highlights society's intolerance of differences and their discrimination against neurodiversity (Cooper 2006). Conversely, the educational consultant Thomas Armstrong embraces the term, calling for 'a new field of neurodiversity', rejecting more negative language in describing brain diversity (Armstrong 2010: xi, 3). He quotes Harvey Blume as one of the first people to use the word 'neurodiversity' in a published article in *The Atlantic* in 1998, saying: 'neurodiversity may be every bit as crucial for the human race as biodiversity is for life in general. Who can say what form of wiring will prove best at any given moment?'

Significantly, in his critical disability studies, Goodley has inserted a slash into the word dis/ability, highlighting the dualistic significations within it. He maintains that ableism, disablism, ability, and disability can only be understood 'simultaneously in relation to each other. The slashed and split term denotes the complex ways in which opposites bleed into one another' (Goodley 2014: xiii). The descriptions of the work in this book by those who have been designated as having a 'learning disability' demonstrate that dis/ability has counter-sides: the disability can reveal another dimension of a burgeoning ability when liberated to work through diverse channels.

Studying Dyslexia through Cross-disciplinary and Interdisciplinary Sources

In order to engage with the extensive body of research surrounding dyslexia, and with a range of theories which might offer explanations about experiences

in working with dyslexia, it has become necessary for me to step outside performance discourse and cross into areas such as psychology, science, education, and
literary theory. Reconnaissance within the familiar territories of acting methodologies and the various strands of pedagogy for actors has not rendered sufficient
specialized knowledge to answer my questions about the teaching of those with
specific learning disabilities/differences and dyslexia. The studies I describe in this
book are therefore cross-disciplinary and interdisciplinary, where the research
perspectives extrapolated from diverse fields have enabled my broader understanding of the impediments and strengths presented by dyslexia.

The subject of dyslexia has not been much investigated nor written about in
relation to pedagogical choices and inclusivity in actor training, and this may be
because it is extremely challenging in many ways. (The theories and characteristics of dyslexia are outlined in detail in Chapter 4.) The unresolved arguments
around the nature of dyslexia, despite years of extensive research in several fields,
reveal what a convoluted area it presents in practice. It is significant that much of
the literature about dyslexia contains a frequent reiteration of the words 'difficult',
'problem', and 'complex', both in describing the experience of the individual
with dyslexia and that of the researcher attempting to comprehend or find trust-
worthy answers in the scientific findings and arguments. Indeed, the dyslexia
specialists and psychologists Rod Nicolson and Angela Fawcett remark: 'If it
were not the case that dyslexia is both prevalent and debilitating , a researcher
might be excused for choosing a more convenient research area, one not con-
founded by so many uncontrollable factors' (Nicolson & Fawcett 2010: 13).

It has become evident to me that in actor training environments, it is commonplace to encounter individual students who have difficulty in reading without
effort, and physically articulating and processing speech sounds and language.
This can occur in conjunction with other characteristics, such as distractibility,
disorganization, anxiety, physical awkwardness, and memory challenges, despite
their possession of literacy, intrinsic motivation, athletic movement skills, acting talents, intelligence, and abilities. The obstacles blocking some individuals
with dyslexia from being able to contribute freely to sessions using text raise
pedagogical problems for the teacher, especially located within the larger student
cohort. The teacher often lacks the expertise to support the individual, increasing
a depression of ability in the student, which consequently promotes feelings of
inadequacy in the teacher.

In gathering my research and practice together in this book, my intention is to
share my experiences and to help guide the reader through some of the dyslexia
research, particularly in relation to actor training. Many of the dyslexia investigations concentrate on schoolchildren rather than on higher education students
in their study of artistic practices and performance. The scientific theories and
research findings involving dyslexia and the brain are often complex, but I have
found some to be extremely helpful in gaining insight about the experiences of
acting students with dyslexia. In making direct links with the science and the

processes of reading and acting, the perspectives I take can speak to others who work in similar environments. This focus can assist in answering questions that arise in our practice, helping to tackle the specialized demands of actor training in higher education and performance when working with dyslexic students.

Overview of the Book

This book argues for the necessity of a critical and reflective teaching praxis, and offers tested teaching strategies to facilitate inclusive and equitable approaches. The book's study is focused primarily on a range of individuals assessed as dyslexic in an actor training environment (although the suggested ideas have the potential to serve a variety of cognitive styles across subject discipline areas). Recognizing the challenges presented by dyslexia for many individuals, the research enquiries described within this book explore the visual, kinesthetic, and multisensory processing preferences demonstrated by some acting students assessed as dyslexic, specifically when working with classical texts such as Shakespeare. The body of research and the teaching strategies are produced from empirical evidence accumulated through observations, discussions, and practical trials with acting students with dyslexia, using the methodologies of case study and action research, underpinned by scientific theory. This research includes some of the work carried out in my six-year doctorate study in the areas of voice, reading, and the acting of Shakespeare when working with acting degree students with dyslexia (Whitfield 2015). Throughout the investigations, Shakespeare's text is utilized as a laboratory of study and practice.

Structure of Part I: Chapters 1–5

Part I of the book presents the background context underlying the practical explorations which are described in Part II.

Chapter 1 draws attention to the stress experienced by acting students with dyslexia, discussing the meaning of neurodiversity and the socio-cultural ideas surrounding labels such as difference and disability. Chapter 2 considers the facilitation of the acting student with dyslexia within the wider context of accepted pedagogical practices in actor training. Questioning what the overall aims might be when training acting students in higher education environments, a critical focus is given to the repetition of conventional practices which are teacher- or method-led, rather than responsive to students' needs. Chapter 3 describes a key transformative experience for student and teacher in a devised performance of a Shakespeare sonnet by an acting student with dyslexia. His breakthrough in overcoming his dyslexia is analyzed, drawing from theories of cognitive science, embodied cognition, and extended mind theory. Chapter 4 focuses on dyslexia, the arguments surrounding it, and the effect of dyslexia on acting students within the environment of actor training. Chapter 5 presents the underlying principles of working on Shakespeare which guide the author's practice. The rationale for using Shakespeare as a research laboratory in which to trial strategies of facilitation for those with dyslexia is made explicit. This includes what dyslexic students find difficult about Shakespeare and how Shakespeare's image-rich and action-based language can free those with dyslexia. The technical processes of how we read and the need for the actor's communication of the self in reading is analyzed, along with how dyslexia can impede this self-authorship.

Structure of Part II: Chapters 6–14

Part II presents the practical investigations in the study, interlinked with the underpinning theory. The research participants with dyslexia are introduced, including a close examination of their difficulties and strengths, with a description and analysis of their devised methods into the text. Six teaching strategies are offered, emerging out of six action research trials with the participants that aim to assuage their challenges and enhance their abilities. There are also examples of work where the strategies tested have not been successful, with an analysis of why they failed. The implementation, practice, and findings of six action research cycles are examined separately at each stage. Chapters that discuss the underlying theory informing the physical work precede the practice-based chapters.

In Chapter 6, the research methodology, ethics, setting, and the participants and material are outlined. Chapter 7 examines the proposition that for some acting students identified as dyslexic, a visual construct approach assists them in accessing the content of Shakespeare's text. Chapter 8 includes a case study observation where three research participants share their visually led methods in interacting with their mental images arising from the text. The first Action Research (Cycle One) is embarked on, involving the anchoring of the text through an aurally received rendition of a Shakespeare sonnet and the research participants drawing a response. Teaching Strategy One is trialed and its outcome discussed. Chapter 9 explores the historical background of Stanislavski's work with Shakespeare, and the origins behind a Cicely Berry approach to the text. It questions the efficacy in using Stanislavski's method of actions when working on Shakespeare's text for acting students with dyslexia. This method is compared with Cicely Berry's approach to actioning the images inherent in the words of the text. Chapter 10 includes Action Research Cycle Two and Teaching Strategy Two, with trials of entering, analyzing, and comprehending Shakespeare's text using a Stanislavski-inspired *Units and Action* sequence of stages in accessing all that might be mined from the text. Chapter 11 introduces a new set of participants. Action Research Cycle Three and Teaching Strategy Three are embarked upon. Drawing from Charles Peirce's theory of semiotic signs and David McNeill's labeling of gesture types, an identification of the gesture, its referent, and how it is embodied related to the significance of meaning found in the text is given primary focus. The difficulty with this work for the participants with dyslexia is described and considered.

Chapter 12 presents three participants' varying creations of a visual analogue of the written text, revealing their individual methods as successful compensatory strategies in circumventing their dyslexia. In Chapter 13, the work with the acting students with dyslexia continues into the Voice Story-telling unit. Action research (Cycle Four) involves the trial of a devised pedagogical strategy (Strategy Four), comprised of aspects of acting techniques merged with reading comprehension theory. I introduce the *Micro* and *Macro* approach as a tool to identify, anchor, and elaborate elements in the text into performance. Describing research trials with the dyslexic acting students, the study recounts the development of Teaching Strategy Four. This method progresses into a performance of Shakespeare's *Venus and Adonis*, employing the strategy to stabilize the text, enhance communication, support memory, and develop innovative performance (Action Research Cycle Five and Teaching Strategy Five). In Chapter 14, the findings of the study are introduced, and Action Research Cycle Six and Teaching Strategy Six are offered, which combine a study of Shakespeare's sonnets with the VARK learning styles framework. There is a description of the strategy's trialed outcome in student performance and recommendations for research-led teaching.

The chapters of this book are meant to be read sequentially. Each chapter progresses from the other in its content, practice, learning, and construction of ideas. However, the book's content can also be dipped into according to the interests of the reader.

Note

1 The UK Equality Act (Office for Disability Issues 2010) labels dyslexia as a learning disability (Brunswick 2012: 4), and the International Dyslexia Association also labels dyslexia as 'a specific learning disability that is neurobiological in origin' (International Dyslexia Association 2018). The American Psychiatric Association's *Diagnostic and Statistical Manual* (DSM 5) identifies it as a disorder (McLoughlin & Leather 2013: 7). Hendrickx (2010: 20) labels dyslexia as a difficulty, stating that the word 'disability' only describes individuals with an IQ level of 70 or below. The various theories and definitions of dyslexia and the contested labels of identification are presented in more detail in Chapter 4.

References

Armstrong, T. (2010). *The Power of Neurodiversity*. Boston, MA: Da Capo Press.

Brunswick, N. (2012). *Supporting Dyslexic Adults in Higher Education and the Workplace*. Oxford, UK: Wiley-Blackwell.

Cooper, R. (2006). *Neurodiversity and Dyslexia: Challenging the Social Construction of Specific Learning Difficulties*. London: South Bank University. Available from: http://outsidersoftware.co.uk/wp-content/uploads/2017/03/Neurodiversity-and-Dyslexia-Challenging-the-social-construction-of-specific-learning-differences.pdf. Accessed 7 May 2019.

Department for Education & Skills (2004). *A Framework for Understanding Dyslexia*. London: Department for Education & Skills.

Goodley, D. (2014). *Dis/Ability Studies*. London: Routledge

Grant, D. (2009). The psychological assessment of neurodiversity. *In*: Pollak, D. (ed.) *Neurodiversity in Higher Education*. Chichester, UK: Wiley-Blackwell, pp. 33–62.

Hendrickx, S. (2010). *The Adolescent and Adult Neuro-diversity Handbook*. London: Jessica Kingsley.

International Dyslexia Association (2018). Definition of dyslexia. Available from: https://dyslexiaida.org/definition-of-dyslexia/. Accessed 7 May 2019.

Leveroy, D. (2012). Dyslexia and sight-reading for actors. *In*: Dunt, S. (ed.) *Music, Other Performing Arts and Dyslexia*. Bracknell, UK: British Dyslexia Association, pp. 89–106.

Leveroy, D. (2013a). Enabling performance: dyslexia, (dis)ability and 'reasonable adjustment'. *Theatre, Dance and Performance Training*, 4:1, 87–101.

Leveroy, D. (2013b). Locating dyslexic performance: text, identity and creativity. *Research in Drama Education: The Journal of Applied Theatre and Performance*, 18:4, 374–387.

Leveroy, D. (2015). A date with the script: exploring the learning strategies of actors who are dyslexic. *Theatre, Dance and Performance Training*, 6:3, 307–322.

McLoughlin, D. & Leather, C. (2013). *The Dyslexic Adult*, 2nd ed. Chichester, UK: Whurr Publications.

Nicolson, R. & Fawcett, A.J. (2010). *Dyslexia, Learning and the Brain*. London: MIT Press.

Office for Disability Issues (2010). *Equality Act 2010*. London: Office for Disability Issues.

Oram, D. (2018a). Finding a way: more tales of dyslexia and dyspraxia in psychophysical actor training. *Voice and Speech Review*, 11:3, 276–294.

Oram, D. (2018b). Losing sight of land: tales of dyslexia and dyspraxia in psychophysical actor training. *Theatre, Dance and Performance Training*, 9:1, 53–67.

Palfreman-Kay. J. (2005). Institutional policy and neurodiversity in the post-16 sector. *In*: Pollak, D. (ed.) *Neurodiversity in FE and HE: Positive Initiatives for Specific Learning Difference*. Leicester, UK: De Montfort University, pp. 23–32.

Pollak, D. (ed.) (2005). Introduction. *Neurodiversity in FE and HE: Positive Initiatives for Specific Learning Differences*. Leicester, UK: De Montfort University, pp. 3–5.

Whitfield, P. (2015). *Towards Accessing Shakespeare's Text for Those with SpLD (Dyslexia): An Investigation into the Rationale for Building Visual Constructs*. PHD thesis, University of Warwick.

2

PEDAGOGY AND EDUCATION IN ACTOR TRAINING

Towards an Emancipatory Practice

Introduction

Some Key Pedagogical Questions

In actor training, the teaching of individuals with learning differences and dyslexia is situated within a rich confluence of practices, artistic expressions, cultures, and traditions. Some practitioners' systems have become firmly established as the leading methodologies for actor training in the field (especially those grounded in the European disciplines within Western traditions). Over the last century, these practitioners' ideas have been elaborated on, reiterated by teachers, directors, and practitioners, materializing into the customary systems of actor and voice training prevalent today. These methods form the foundational syllabus of the majority of programs in Western actor training. Although providing powerful vehicles for the languages and techniques of performance, certain modes of delivery in teaching these systems can leave some individuals struggling.

I begin with two pivotal statements made by two acting students assessed as dyslexic:

> For me, as a dyslexic, Shakespeare is very accommodating. It has taken me eleven years of struggle to come to realize, because of my dyslexia, I understand things through image and metaphor. Shakespeare's writing clicks in my head the way numbers click for a mathematician.
>
> *(Fred, acting student with dyslexia)*

> As soon as a text is presented to me, my guard instantly levers up due to fear and lack of confidence. I am instantly terrified I am going to embarrass

myself because of my reading ability and because I cannot analyze what I have read afterwards.

(Phoebe, acting student with dyslexia)

These statements encapsulate many of the issues explored within this book, and for those who teach, they generate both pedagogic possibilities and urgent questions. These re-occurring questions demand answers, and in doing so, open channels for discussion, reflection, and action amongst teaching communities. These questions include:

- How might we, as teachers, break away from teaching methods that reinforce the dominant, normative perspectives which privilege some 'ableist' groups over others?
- How do we ensure our teaching practices do not 'disable' those who process differently?
- How and why might we embrace an inclusive culture of supporting and exposing variation, diversity, and pluralistic abilities?
- What do we need to do to understand the specific needs of individuals (such as Fred and Phoebe quoted above) so we might free their capabilities?
- How might we scrutinize our own practice, ensuring that our values and pedagogical choices are ethical and socially just while fostering the potential abilities of every individual?

The Problems

Twelve years ago, when initially searching for advice on how I might draw from educational theory to improve my teaching, I uncovered barren ground. A search of the published literature in the world of performance training produces a plethora of books on practitioners' methods involving voice, movement, and acting, but there is a scarcity of material that centers on a critical analysis of the actual *pedagogy* of actor training. Nor are there many disseminations of personal teaching experiences describing changes of practices driven by problems, born out of research, underpinned by educational foundations. An exception to this is Stephen Wangh's *The Heart of Teaching* (2013), in which he similarly draws attention to the absence of pedagogical conversations in actor training and the lack of awareness of *why* we teach in certain ways. Offering a personal account of his teaching experiences with acting students, and recounting the 'unspoken travails of teaching' (ibid.: xiii), Wangh gives an honest examination of his successes in some student interactions and exercises, and his problems with others. He includes an analysis of why some 'lessons have gotten out of hand and we wonder what happened there?' (ibid.: 4).

Training as an actor is exacting and rigorous, requiring a mastery of skills, development of abilities, and transparency of personhood. It demands self-discipline, intrinsic motivation, and the capacity to draw deeply and openly on the psyche, emotions, imagination, prior education, and life experience. The task of teaching acting, voice, and performance is equally as challenging. The 'hard part of what we do', 'the paradoxes surrounding the power we teachers yield', the 'frustrations, obsessions and loneliness of the long-distance teacher', as acting instructor Stephen Wangh describes it, are not much debated nor reflected on in public domains nor in the literature (ibid.: xii, xiii, 4). In a discussion of the emotional and physical health of acting students, Prior et al. (2015: 68) liken actor training to the training of an athlete. Although a trained and articulate body is essential as an instrument of an actor's expression, considerable cognitive demands are also necessary (which are, of course, inextricably interwoven with the body). Such cognitive tasks make up an exhaustive list, but can include: comprehension and fluent communication of multifarious texts; a meticulous observation of the world and its people in order to re-enact them; an ability to remove habitual mannerisms and thought patterns of the self and adopt those of another; the study of language and sounds of speech, with an ability to consciously change one's vocal expression; dual-tasking; improvising; articulating ideas with clarity, and adapting to a variety of practitioners' methods. Finally, an exposition of work and personhood through performance can meet with fierce criticism from observers and teachers. This can place an individual in a vulnerable position, provoking high levels of anxiety.

Carving an Original Path: An Examined Pedagogy in Developing Teacher Identity and Research-based Teaching

Many of us, as teachers of acting and voice, are trained professional performers and teach our subject as we were taught it, at drama school, in the theatre, or in our teacher training. The received ideas and routines of others (often originating from traditions and cultures embedded many years ago) are regularly implemented and often unquestioned in their effectiveness in assisting (or undermining) a broad range of individual needs, or preferences of learning/cognitive styles (Waring and Evans describe cognitive styles as 'individual differences in cognition that help an individual to adapt to the learning environment'; 2015: 64). The curriculum in voice training and acting is commonly comprised of entrenched and repeated practitioner methods, albeit encompassing expert subject knowledge. This subject knowledge has generally been acquired by the teacher/performer through years of practical study and professional performance, and then further embedded when transferred to students. Paulo Freire criticizes the concept of what he has called a 'banking education', where the teacher possesses the 'cognizable object' and then deposits that object into the learner. The learner has to memorize the contents of the teacher's knowledge, but this does not produce a thinking for himself or herself, nor much critical reflection (Freire 1996: 61). Freire calls for a problem-posing education, wherein an intentionality and a *conscientization* (a critical awareness of one's self and behavior, and being conscious about the object in question) promotes a learning situation for all (ibid.: 60). Balk (1991, quoted in Prior et al. 2015: 65) stresses that acting students need to 'develop and expand their performing power on their own, and to be released from a dependency on authority figures within their subject' so they might learn through their own experiences.

Through the experience of developing my own teaching and independent thinking, I argue that teachers can also be released from a dependency on the replication of methods of the dominant figures in their specialist disciplines. Following the 'way to do it', as promulgated by a renowned practitioner as the authoritative voice of knowledge, creates a structure of habitual security for the teacher in repeating the established pathway of instructional language, method, value judgments, culture, and content. However, through examining their own practice, building on the knowledge and learning they already possess, considering the needs of the individuals they teach, and researching how they might improve and adapt their provision, teachers can cultivate their own voices and ideas. In doing so, teachers discover their own identity, in asking themselves: What kind of teachers are they? What knowledge do they value? What are their ethical stances? How do they position themselves as educators? Why do they teach that way? How are they serving the learners?

Integration of Educational Philosophy with Actor Training

Before I began to focus on my own teaching in a quest to improve my provision for students with dyslexia, I was not fully aware of the level of vulnerability surrounding many individuals with dyslexic difficulties. Initially, my methods of teaching Shakespeare replicated the procedures of those who had taught me, and whose books I had read. As Carr and Kemmis point out: 'much teacher action is the product of custom, habit [. . .] which constrain action in ways that the teachers themselves do not recognise' (1986: 189). I presumed that the more assiduously I duplicated the methods of those with an expertise in Shakespeare and voice, the better teacher I would be. Using a teacher-centered system, each student was expected to fit into a system that served the able majority. In a behaviorist[1] environment of utilizing a stimulus to provoke the expected response, the student would be awarded a judgment of 'right' or 'wrong', 'strong' or 'weak' for the outcome. I had little conception about how I might adjust my practice and assumptions based on an accommodation of, and knowledge about, learning differences and pedagogical theory, or that other ways of working might have cogency. I had little understanding about dyslexia.

In his study of acting teachers in actor training institutions, Ross Prior suggests that vocational actor training has 'shunned an examination of its own pedagogy, possibly in the belief that acting methodology and practical experience as an actor are alone sufficient' (2012: 91). He emphasizes that actor training concentrates on *methods* of acting, whereas areas concerning *how* to teach and to develop practice, and then to make that practice explicit, are under-researched. Prior sees this as problematic, as he believes that a lack of an explicitly articulated approach to learning means 'that trainer practice remains vulnerable to hit or miss approaches' (ibid.: xxi, 52, 219).

Teacher Aims, Values and Belief Systems: What Is the Purpose of Education in Actor Training?

This situation exposes a dichotomy for those of us who teach in the area of performance, and poses the question, what is the overall purpose of the education of acting students in higher education environments? Is the pedagogical role of teachers merely to confine themselves to training templates, aiming towards fulfilling an expected skill set for the professional performer, or might the education of the actor serve a wider, more holistic purpose? Should the role of educators also aim to nourish the selfhood and possibilities of all those they teach? By overlooking those who cannot function easily within conditioned models of processing, there is a danger that unique modes of expression, intelligence, or exceptional talents might remain undiscovered. Moreover, unhappy learning experiences, especially in those with SpLD and dyslexia, can have life-long negative effects, such as learned helplessness, depression, damaged self-concept, traumatic stress, and learned toxicity (Burden 2005: 20–33; Nicolson 2015: 75–76). Furthermore, in educating our students of acting, we are aware that the opportunities for secure employment for the professional actor are infrequent for the majority, and that the road to gaining employment is often littered with rejection, requiring resources of resilience, self-belief, and transferable skills (if moving into differing areas of employment). Therefore, as educationalists, there is a responsibility to promote personal growth, self-knowledge, and understanding of ability, as well as weaknesses, enhancement of confidence, well-being, and self-efficacy. (Philosopher Amartya Sen, in his promotion of the fulfillment of the capabilities of every individual towards their happiness and well-being, points out that 'well-being' describes a person's achievement, in how 'well' is their being, while the word 'advantage' denotes the opportunities that the individual has, especially compared to others; 1999: 3). The concept of self-efficacy originates from psychologist Albert Bandura's work, describing an individual's belief in their capability to achieve goals, tasks, and self-mastery, which can then affect their well-being, attainment, and feelings of self-worth (Bandura 1997).

I am not arguing for a lowering of standards, a diluting of specialist training, or for an 'anything goes' philosophy, but I am arguing for an emancipatory pedagogy towards a self-efficacy, based on humanist principles such as positive regard, promotion of self-worth (Rogers 1983), and Maslow's (1943) model of human needs and self-actualization. Maslow defines self-actualization as:

> the desire for self-fulfillment, namely the tendency for him [or her] to become actualized in what he [or she] is potentially. This tendency might be phrased as the desire to become more and more what one is, to become everything that one is capable of becoming.
>
> *(ibid.: 383)*

These aims require more than a repetition of training prototypes, replicated over the years.

Theories and Goals of Education and Pedagogy

Leach and Moon point out that the meaning of education is distinct from that of pedagogy. The word 'pedagogy' originally comes from the Greek word *paida-gogos*, meaning 'the leading of the child', and the word 'education' originates from the Latin word *educare*, meaning 'to bring up and to nourish' (Leach & Moon 2008: 4). Waring and Evans point out that the concept of pedagogy is complex, with numerous interpretations surrounding its definition. Although originally concerned with the teaching of children, the term is also used for teaching in higher education. Betham and Sharpe (2007, quoted in Waring & Evans 2015: 27) view 'pedagogy in the original sense of guidance to learn: learning in the context of teaching, and teaching that has learning as its goal'.

  In their book centering on socially just pedagogies in higher education, Walker and Wilson-Strydom define higher education as 'multi-dimensionally valuable [. . .] allowing people to grow, to be informed, to be articulate [. . .] to lead [. . .] flourishing lives' (2017: 9). They emphasize that universities should 'confront deep social cleavages around difference', arguing that chosen pedagogy practices can influence whether inequalities from outside institutions or inside institutions are reinforced or challenged (ibid.: 8). There are multiple theoretical perceptions concerning the concept of pedagogy and the function it serves in educational cultures. Bernstein has defined pedagogy as:

> a sustained process whereby somebody(s) acquires new forms or develops existing forms of conduct, knowledge, practice and criteria from somebody(s) or something deemed to be an appropriate provider and evaluator – appropriate either from the point of view of the acquirer or by some other body(s).
>
> *(Bernstein 2000: 78)*

This definition is rather rigid, and underplays constructivist views of the social and subjective building of knowledge. Although constructivism is a theory of learning and knowledge-building, its premise has also expanded to include a theory of teaching. In my studies of dyslexia, its effect on my students, and my devising of teaching strategies, constructivist learning, knowing, and teaching play a crucial role. It is also an essential stage in the research participants' construction of understanding about themselves, each other, their dyslexia, and how they might work most effectively. As both social and subjective constructivism are themes underpinning the work in this book, an overview of the principal theories of constructivism is presented in endnote 2 for those who wish to know more.[2]

Leach and Moon (2008: 144–155) assert that pedagogy should build the self-esteem and identity of learners. They divide the formation of identify into five attributes, as a key towards building self-esteem. These five attributes are essential elements for every individual, but are especially pertinent for the experience of dyslexic acting students, therefore a brief overview follows.

1) Voice – this is when individuals have a sense of their own agency and being in the world. They have a voice within the learning situation and feel they are listened to and respected. They have control over their activities and who they want to be.

2) Relationships – this is where there is a fostering of trust built between teacher and students, with empathy, understanding, and recognition of the emotional dimensions of learning.

3) Community – this is where individuals construct and discover their identity and where and how they fit within the group.

4) Language and the recognition that language and identity are interwoven – language, and how it used, enables thinking, builds relationships, transmits ideas and meaning, and forms a social identity.

5) Imagination – this is when individuals dream of expanded horizons, and think about how they are developing and where they would like to be. It also encapsulates areas such as creativity and art, all of which are fired by the imagination.

Searching for a Knowledge Base about SpLD (Dyslexia) in Actor Training

Several years ago, I recognized that Leach and Moon's five attributes of identity are often insecurely present or entirely absent within the dyslexic student's experience during class work. My subsequent investigations revealed very little published literature that included pedagogical understanding or inclusive initiatives for individuals with dyslexia within the educational context of actor training. (I am talking here about academic research and practical teaching in the areas of acting and voice training, not about learning support.) This motivated my pursuit of a six-year doctorate study of my acting students with dyslexia, which aimed to address this gap, and develop the capacity for more support in my own teaching (Whitfield 2015).

More recently, interest in this area has been growing and valuable research contributions have been published in the area of performance training and dyslexia by actor trainer Deborah Leveroy (2012, 2013a, 2013b, 2015). Daron Oram, Senior Lecturer in Voice, is focusing on his teaching of dyslexic and dyspraxic acting students and the problems they can meet with exercises in psychophysical work (Oram 2018a, 2018b). Dyslexia Coordinator Tanya Zybutz and Acting Teacher Colin Farquharson are also researching into supporting acting students with both dyslexia and dyspraxia (Zybutz & Farquharson 2016). In the USA, Rebecca Clark Carey (Voice and Text Director at the Oregon Shakespeare Festival Theatre) is investigating how she might create a more dyslexia-friendly working environment for professional actors with dyslexia (personal communication 2017).

Conclusion

In my search for a scholarship of teaching and learning, especially in facilitation of the needs of acting students with specific learning difficulties and dyslexia, I have uncovered a lack of reflective and critical awareness about pedagogical approaches, the use of educational theory in underpinning teaching methods, and how such philosophies can influence practice and enhance student progress and learning. There is scant articulation of teacher experience, enquiry, problems, or insights from which other teachers can learn and build their practice. Currently, as I write this book, there is only a very small body of research about dyslexia (and overlapping learning differences) in the fields of actor training. There are few recorded accounts of the voices of acting students with dyslexia, so that others might hear them, learn from them, and improve their provision. The work described in this book begins to fill those gaps.

Next Chapter

The next chapter describes a transformative breakthrough by an acting student with dyslexia in devising methods and performance of a Shakespeare sonnet. His innovative performance was an inspiring force, stimulating the questions, directions, and goals of my study into facilitating those with dyslexia in actor training. The chapter analyses his methods through theories of embodied cognition and neural reuse.

KEY POINTS OF CHAPTER 2

- The privileging of the neurotypical and able over the neurodiverse; the neglect of those with differences in learning and processing
- Training versus pedagogy – questions surrounding teaching cultures as reproduction, habit, and tradition

- A lack of educational theory, philosophy, or research underpinning pedagogical practice in actor training
- What is the purpose of actor training in higher education?
- The importance of teachers analyzing their aims and belief systems
- Theories of constructivism
- The five attributes of self-esteem
- The lack of published knowledge about dyslexia and inclusive actor training and teaching methods

Notes

1 Behaviorism is based on principles of stimulus and response, conditioning, and reinforcement of behavior through reward and punishment. It is teacher-led in activities where the teacher is in control of what is done, how it is done, and the expected behavior produced. It originates from the 19th century, with studies of animals' behavior controlled by certain conditions imposed on them to produce learned and repeated behavior. These methods have been transferred into teaching. Behaviorism as an approach to teaching is still commonly used today. Some of the principal theorists are Pavlov (1849–1936), Skinner (1904–1990), and more recently, Gagne (1916–2002). For more detail about behaviorism, see Bates (2016).

2 The first view of constructivism is of a social constructivism. This is where meaning and bodies of knowledge are built up during social interaction. These human constructs have been determined through history, politics, ideologies, application of power, religious beliefs, ideas, and preservation of status. Bredo (2000: 133) argues that some educational institutions display a kind of social constructivism that can make some students appear (or come to feel) intelligent or stupid by exercising limited definitions of what counts as knowledge.

The second view of constructivism is of a cognitive constructivism. This is when individuals actively construct their own subjective understandings and meanings through their life experiences and interactions with the outside world. As each individual has their own distinctive history and situated being in the world, it follows that their knowledge structure will be unique to them. Any new knowledge is not a replica of what is in the external world, nor received through a passive transmission from another, as the knowledge is built by the knower.

A constructivism theory of learning has its roots in the work of Piaget and Vygotsky (Bredo 2000: 133). Piaget claimed that when learners encounter an experience that contradicts their existing way of thinking, a state of *disequilibrium* is generated. Learners then change their thinking to re-establish equilibrium. By associating new information with ideas already known, they *assimilate* the new into their existing knowledge. Thus, in constructivist learning, knowledge is not absorbed as an objective thing that can be passed directly from teacher to student, or from student to teacher, but is scaffolded onto existing knowledge, skills, and expectations (Twomey Fosnot 1996: 14). At the center of Vygotsky's theory is the belief that the outside influence of culture and society forms and shapes the individual, rather than natural biological phenomena (Vygotsky 1987).

References

Bandura, A. (1997). *Self-efficacy: The Exercise of Control*. New York: W.H. Freeman.
Bates, B. (2016). *Learning Theories Simplified*. London: SAGE Publications.

Bernstein, B. (2000). *Pedagogy, Symbolic Control and Identity*. Lanham, MD: Rowman & Littlefield.

Bredo, E. (2000). Reconsidering social constructivism: the relevance of George Herbert Mead's interactionism. *In*: Phillips, D.C. (ed.) *Constructivism in Education*. Chicago, IL: University of Chicago Press, pp. 127–157.

Burden, R. (2005). *Dyslexia and Self-concept: Seeking a Dyslexic Identity*. London: Whurr Books.

Carr, W. & Kemmis, S. (1986). *Becoming Critical*. London: RoutledgeFarmer.

Freire, P. (1996). *Pedagogy of the Oppressed*. London: Penguin Books.

Leach, J. & Moon, B. (2008). *The Power of Pedagogy*. London: SAGE Publications.

Leveroy, D. (2012). Dyslexia and sight-reading for actors. *In*: Dunt, S. (ed.) *Music, Other Performing Arts and Dyslexia*. Bracknell, UK: British Dyslexia Association, pp. 89–106.

Leveroy, D. (2013a). Enabling performance: dyslexia, (dis) ability and 'reasonable adjustment'. *Theatre Dance and Performance Training*, 4:1, 87–101.

Leveroy, D. (2013b). Locating dyslexic performance: text, identity and creativity. *Research in Drama Education: The Journal of Applied Theatre and Performance*, 18:4, 374–387.

Leveroy, D. (2015). 'A date with the script': exploring the learning strategies of actors who are dyslexic. *Theatre, Dance and Performance Training*, 6:3, 307–322.

Maslow, A. (1943). A theory of human motivation. *Psychological Review*, 50:4, 370–396.

Nicolson, R. (2015). *Positive Dyslexia*. Sheffield, UK: Rodin Books.

Oram, D. (2018a). Finding a way: more tales of dyslexia and dyspraxia in psychophysical actor training. *Voice and Speech Review*, 11:3, 276–294.

Oram, D. (2018b). Losing sight of land: tales of dyslexia and dyspraxia in psychophysical actor training. *Theatre, Dance and Performance Training*, 9:1, 53–67.

Prior, R. (2012). *Teaching Actors*. Bristol, UK: Intellect Books.

Prior, R., Maxwell, I., Szabo, M., & Seton, M. (2015). Responsible care in actor training: effective support for occupational health training in drama schools. *Theatre, Dance and Performance Training*, 6:1, 59–71.

Rogers, C. (1983). *Freedom to Learn*. New York: Merrill.

Sen, A. (1999). *Commodities and Capabilities*. New Delhi, India: Oxford University Press.

Twomey Fosnot, C. (1996). *Constructivism Theory, Perspective and Practice*. New York: Teacher's College Press.

Vygotsky, L.S. (1987). *Mind in Society*. Cambridge, MA: Harvard University Press.

Walker, M. & Wilson-Strydom, M. (eds.) (2017). Thinking about the university context and socially just pedagogies. *Socially Just Pedagogies and Quality in Higher Education*. London: Palgrave Macmillan, pp. 3–19.

Wangh, S. (2013). *The Heart of Teaching*. Oxford, UK: Routledge.

Waring, M. & Evans, C. (2015). *Understanding Pedagogy*. London: Routledge.

Whitfield, P. (2015). *Towards Accessing Shakespeare's Text for Those with SpLD (Dyslexia): An Investigation into the Rationale for Building Visual Constructs*. PhD thesis, University of Warwick.

Zybutz, T. & Farquharson, C. (2016). Psychophysical performance and the dyspraxic actor. *Journal of Neurodiversity in Higher Education*, 2, 76–87.

3

DAVID – THE INSPIRATION AND INITIATOR OF MY STUDY

Introduction

It was the experience of working with David, a student assessed as dyslexic, which finally drove me into embarking on an investigation into how one might effectively enable acting students with dyslexia (Whitfield 2009). The task of attempting to facilitate David's capabilities (undermined by his dyslexia) and my witnessing of his metamorphosis into an authoritative performer had a tremendous impact on me. David is an individual who struggles to read a text line by line. During the Shakespeare unit, when reading aloud, the class would have to slow down considerably to accommodate his hesitant contribution. It would not have been appropriate to miss David out from reading with his fellow students, nor did he want to be. He was keen to meet the full experience of his actor training, and have parity with his fellows. Wishing to reflect the professional expectations of an actor and valuing shared experiential discovery with all of the class, I chose not to follow the often-recommended path with dyslexic students of giving him the text to study in advance. Familiarity with the text might ensure some comfort with the words, but spontaneous interpretation with the ensemble group in a shared discovery would be destroyed. Flushed pink with effort, David would stumble on nearly every sentence. Endeavoring to build his confidence, I would side coach as he tried to read. His acting ability could scarcely be glimpsed in the few times that he might manage to read a sentence without a block. Pronunciation and articulation of words also posed obstacles. Despite my guidance, he could not seem to adequately hear or retain my explanations. An expression of panic crossed his face as he wrestled with the words.

However, I noticed a significant improvement in his grasp of reading when we had worked on a Shakespeare text using the Cicely Berry-inspired deconstruction methods (Berry 1993: 149; Berry 2001: 99): the whole class of students reading the text round in a circle, word by word, then punctuation mark to punctuation mark, then sentence to sentence. This helped break it down for him so he could get an overall comprehension of the piece, although a discomfort and lack of fluency with words prevailed. Further progress developed when we physicalized the whole piece, sentence by sentence. As they spoke the text, each student used physical actions to express the core of meaning or feeling, as they saw it. Getting the words into his body/mind through the physical actions meant that suddenly David could read for about a paragraph without stumbling, and therefore had more freedom to exercise his acting instincts. However, once he stumbled on one word, his brief fluency crumbled and the former pattern returned.

David's Personal Breakthrough

I was therefore amazed by a performance David gave of a Shakespeare sonnet in a voice presentation assignment. The students had been asked to prepare and perform a Shakespeare sonnet in their chosen style, using whatever methods they wanted. David had chosen *Sonnet 17* as his performance piece.

> ### *Sonnet 17* (**Shakespeare 1997: 17**)
> Who will believe my verse in time to come,
> If it were filled with your most high deserts?
> Though yet, heaven knows, it is but a tomb,
> Which hides your life, and shows not half your parts:
> If I could write the beauty of your eyes,
> And in fresh numbers number all your graces,
> The age to come would say, 'This poet lies;
> Such heavenly touches ne'er touched earthly faces.'
> So should my papers (yellowed with their age)
> Be scorned, like old men of less truth than tongue,
> And your true rights be termed a poet's rage,
> And stretched metre of an antique song;
> But were some child of yours alive that time,
> You should live twice: in it, and in my rhyme.

David's interpretation was magnificent, in contrast to his previous efforts in class. He had concocted his own mode of performance, which appeared to be a kind of mind-map-in-action. David placed large cards all over the stage in set locations, with other cards deposited carefully in various pockets of his clothing. These cards had key words or phrases from the sonnet written on them, customized in design according to their meaning. As David spoke the sonnet, he ran to each appropriate card and held it up to the audience as he uttered each separate chunk of text. Moreover, he used the cards in a choreographed physical sequence to further inhabit Shakespeare's meaning.

For example, when Shakespeare had used the word *stretched*, David had a folded-up card with the word *stretched*, penned in elongated print, which he gradually revealed, extending in concertina-fashioned pleats, as he said the word (Figure 3.1). The word *heavenly* was written on a sign placed upstage and then, when spoken, was held high above David's head, whilst *earthly* was located and enacted downstage, on the floor (Figure 3.2). Antithesis was made distinct by variation used in graphic style; *heaven* was etched with a light-pressure pen, and in contrast, *tomb* was embellished in heavy, bold graphics. The phrase *not half your parts* was written on a half-shaded piece of paper, thereby signifying the *half*. For the phrase *hides your life*, David had folded a piece of paper in two, with the word *life* hidden within it. When speaking the phrase, David opened and closed the paper, briefly revealing and then hiding the word *life*, using swift hand movements. The words *beauty* and *graces* were words that David felt were written from Shakespeare's heart, therefore (he later explained to me) he decided to tuck them into his inner jacket pocket and produce them, as he spoke the words, as though 'from his heart'. During the words *live twice*, David presented a card with *live* written on it twice, on the front and back of the paper, which he flicked twice as he spoke the words. The word *scorned* was presented on a yellowed, aged piece of paper, as Shakespeare had stated that his words would be *yellowed with age*. The whole sonnet was performed in a semiotic dance of body, spoken word, and signifying cards. The written word signs appeared to be thoroughly grafted with David's visceral response, physically and symbolically in utterance. I was astonished by the strength of David's performance. Connecting to the audience

FIGURE 3.1 'stretched metre of an antique song'

FIGURE 3.2 'ne'er touched earthly faces'

members with deliberate eye contact, he delivered the sonnet with a freedom and assurance hitherto unseen in his work. As his teacher, I found myself riveted, and emotionally moved. His seemingly naïve but thickly layered communication revealed his comprehension of the words in tandem with a fluency and original performance style.

In attempting to understand its efficacy, I realized that David's method ran in parallel with Berry's method of the psycho-physical – *finding the action in the words* (Berry 2001: 73). Employing a highly visual focus, David was using his written words as a kind of physicalization, embodying Shakespeare's meaning through his signs which were skillfully maneuvered into expressing the content very exactly, living through his mapped visuospatial mental images. He was giving his imagery to the audience in a multisensory manner. It was led by the visual, but also worked kinesthetically and aurally. Reflecting on what I had witnessed, I tried to analyze what cognitive processes David had utilized, how he had unblocked his speaking of the text, and the function of his style of performance. I recognized that his methods were linked directly to his dyslexia, but the underlying reasons were beyond my learning at the time. However, I understood that in classes, when following the traditional reading text agenda, David's ability was hidden. However, when allowed to work in his chosen modalities, David had released his aptitude. In addition, it appeared that the dis/ability of dyslexia contributed to an engendering of an innovative performance style.

David's Process as Recorded in His Working Journal during the Shakespeare Unit

In an accompanying journal, David described his process towards creating his performance. I report this below in his own words.

1) Firstly, David writes:

> I read though [through] the sonnet, and read though [through] the sonnet and read it again and again. I wanted to make sure I knew what I was talking about and that I got the intention of the sonnet. The writer is so passionate and overwelmed [overwhelmed] by this person that if he writes about it the words could not support the reallity [reality] of the situation.

2) David then wrote the sonnet out on large white cards, in whole sentences, short phrases, or single words. He was imagining he was the author of the sonnet and trying to find the words to express himself. He says:

> The most improtant [important] elements of Shakespeare is the text, the words. And since the sonnet is partly about writing I wanted to do something physical were [where] I as a character would be in chaos, all over the place from the frustration but the words would keep the sanity in the peice [piece].

He then explored different ways of representing the meaning of the words, through drawing, graphic letter design on the cards, trying out differing actions with the cards, to embody what the speaker of the sonnet means. He comments that:

> I found that this method of writing things out, and finding the points in the sonnet that I wanted to emphorise [emphasize] with the white cards, this also help me understand the sonnet more deeply. I felt more connected to the text and started playing around with the idea, and how I could represent the words and their meaning until I thought it was ready for performance.

3) David then wrote the whole sonnet out again on A4 paper, line by line, leaving a space between each of the lines for additional explanations to be written underneath. He used different colors to denote information. The sonnet lines are written in black ink, and the meaning/paraphrase of these lines of text (as David understood it) is written in bright colors underneath the sonnet lines. Additionally, each section is then divided up by different-colored lines. Strong blue color is put over all the words that David had written on the cards and used in performance.

4) David has drawn a spatial map of the stage performance area on A4 paper in black ink, with the cards' positions placed on the paper, as on the stage area. His singular designs for each of the cards are included, with accompanying explanations for their design, movements, and the rationale for the area of the space they are placed in.

5) When rehearsing, David writes that he filmed himself. He explains:

> because my interupted [interpreted] piece used cards and signs I rehearsed the piece in front of a camera to help me gain confidence in presenting those signs without having to look at them, since I wanted my eyes and energy to be expressed towards the audience.

Embodied Cognition and Its Utility in Meaning-making: David's Process

The grounding of the written word through an embodied cognitive process is a continuing theme throughout the chapters of this book. Those of us in performance are familiar with the actor's exploration of physical actions to represent or inhabit meaning, motivation, psychological states, stimulate emotions, character creation, or to display aesthetic expression. Stanislavski understood that the body, mind, and meaning are inextricably linked. He instructed his actors that:

> things of the spirit are not sufficiently substantial. That is why we have recourse to *physical action* [his italics] [. . .] a small physical act acquires an enormous inner meaning; the great inner struggle seeks an outlet in such an external act.

(Stanislavski 1980: 148–149)

Recently, a rich body of published literature has emerged, linking cognitive theory, science, and embodied cognition with the world of performance (Blair 2008; Cook 2010; Kemp 2012; Shaughnessy 2013; Blair & Cook 2016). I too am drawing from a variety of perspectives in science and psychology in examining the role of embodied cognition, with a particular focus on how those with dyslexia might be harnessing it, towards accessing the written symbols of language and meaning.

The current interest in embodied cognition and symbols of language began in the 1990s (Sadoski 2017: 332). It has diverted the theorists of comprehension away from cognitive science theories, which argue that perception in any sensory modality is converted into abstract, amodal, and arbitrary mental symbols, similar to computer codes, where mental operations are carried out in this abstract code (Rumelhart 1990 and McClelland 2004, cited in Glenberg & Mehta 2008: 15). There is now an expanding body of scientists and psychologists who assert, through empirical studies, that cognition and comprehension are embodied and grounded through multisensory perception (Barsalou 1999; Johnson 1999; Wilson 2000; Gallese & Lakoff 2005; Pulvermüller 2008). A summary of embodied cognition is given by Thelan et al. (2001, quoted in Sadoski 2017):

> To say that cognition is embodied means that it arises from bodily interactions with the world. From this point of view, cognition depends on the kinds of experiences that come from having a body with particular perceptual and motor capacities that are inseparably linked and that together form the matrix within which memory, emotion, language, and all other aspects of life are meshed.

Meaning itself is not language, but it is communicated *through* language. In relation to the embodiment of language, letters, and words, de Vega et al. (2008: 435–436) specify that linguistic symbols, such as words, are arbitrary in that they do not resemble their referents and what they mean (except for examples of onomatopoeia). Words are abstract labels, and they are put into orders of units using patterns and principles. These make a symbolic system. However, de Vega et al. explain that linguistic symbols activate sensorimotor brain regions in a way that simulates the brain activity associated with the concept the word denotes. For example, the letters and word 'chair' do not capture what a chair actually is. One can only understand 'chair' through our sensory experience garnered through sitting in a variety of 'chairs'. The neural imprint of the physical/sensory stimulation associated with chairs is written into the brain's sensorimotor systems and thus activated by the concept of chair, or associations around 'chair' (Barsalou 1999).

The cognitive neuroscientist Friedemann Pulvermüller reports that action words can activate the sensorimotor brain regions typically involved in experiencing or interacting with that referent in the world. He specifies that the neurons responsive to the sound of words, those responsive to their visual word form, and those involved in articulating the word are interwoven with motor neurons which control movement in distributed brain circuits (thus named 'action perception circuits', for their role linking action-motor and perceptual brain regions). For example, the word 'kick' activates dorsal motor regions in the brain responsible for movement of the legs, 'pick' activates hand- and arm-related regions, and 'lick' activates the cortical motor map representing the tongue and lips (Pulvermüller 2008: 95–96). This is because action perception circuits in the brain develop from childhood experiences, where words tend to be learnt in the context of seeing, performing, or interacting with the object or action, such that brain activation in the core language regions occurs simultaneously with activity in sensorimotor areas. Due to principles of Hebbian (associative) learning, this 'coactivation of neurons in the articulatory motor and auditory sensory cortex results in 'a formation of cells assemblies mapping knowledge about actions and perceptions' (Moseley et al. 2016: 96). Once a collection of symbols has been acquired through this mapping of meaning through sensory perception, other associative words, their concepts, and their meaning can be understood through co-occurrence with each other, called 'correlation learning'. The process remains plastic throughout life, driven by neuronal activity (ibid.; Pulvermüller 2018).

David's Grounding of the Text through Epistemic Engineering, Epistemic Artefacts, and Epistemic Actions

The 'multidimensional contexts in which we remember, feel, think, sense, communicate, imagine and act [. . .] in rich ongoing interaction with our environments' have been discussed by many writers recently in the areas of cognition and performance (Tribble 2011, cited in Blair & Cook 2016: 131; Shaughnessy 2013; Blair & Cook 2016). However, with regard to circumventing certain challenges of dyslexia met in acting, David's idiosyncratic performance of the sonnet offers an excellent example of what philosopher Andy Clark calls *extended mind* and *extended cognition*. In *extended mind* theory, thinking and cognizing are not processes that remain inward and brainbound, separated from the world. There is an outward extension into the world built on a cycle of embedded perceptuo-motor capacities, which, Clark argues, enlarges the capability of the mind (2011: xxvi–xxvii). Clark maintains that cognizing includes 'tangles of feedback, feed-forward and feed-around loops', 'crisscross[ing] the boundaries of brain, body and world' (ibid.: xxviii). Here cognition permeates through the boundaries of the body organism into the environment, where non-biological artefacts become extended cognizing objects of the mind. Clark labels these tools as epistemic artefacts (*epistemic* meaning related to knowledge). These artefacts are spaces where we make meaning, develop our thoughts, receive feedback through the affordances they offer in a multi-perceptual loop, and store information to be accessed when we need it, supporting memory. Clark explains:

> Plastic human brains may [. . .] learn to factor the operation and information-bearing role of such external props and artefacts deep into their own problem-solving routines, creating hybrid cognitive circuits that are themselves the physical mechanisms underlying specific problem-solving performances.
>
> *(ibid.: 68)*

David's clever employment of his designed signs, their manipulation, and spatial stations demonstrates his construction of external *epistemic artefacts* as active agents in his thinking. This is not only extending his depth of understanding about the words of the sonnet, or a method of communication, but also a form of *engineering* in building a problem-solving method in bypassing aspects of his dyslexia. *Epistemic engineering*, Clark states, is when we change our environment or build physical constructions that transform problem spaces in ways that aid thinking and reasoning about some target (ibid.: 61–62). Those changed spaces can then feed back, driving new practices and realizations. A component of epistemic engineering includes information encoded in subsystems that can be more easily accessed, such as offloading key features onto the environment (ibid.: 69). David's devised performance activated a system spanning mind, body, and world in a distributed (spread across processes of attention, perception and memory) and situated cognition (interacting with the environment). His actions can be identified as *epistemic actions* (these are not to be confused with *pragmatic actions*, which simply achieve a practical goal, such as closing the door). Epistemic actions extract information, playing a role in problem-solving. The manipulation of physical objects/spaces/actions enables a thinking through, a seeing of possibilities, which might not have been visible without this process, thus working as constructors of knowledge (Kirsh & Maglio 1994, cited in May 2015: 59–60).

Memory Support

David's system can also be recognized as a memory storage system. The method of *Memory Loci* (location) or *Memory Palace* used by the early Greek philosophical schools is said to have been devised by the ancient Greek poet Simonides (Yates 1966: 17–19). Simonides created a system for memorizing where, in his imagination, he placed an object in different rooms of his imaginary palace. When he wanted to recall the objects, he could search through the imaginary rooms in his mind to find them. Classical orators, such as Cicero, to remember the long speeches they had to deliver, used this method as an aid (ibid.: 37). For David, running through his memory stations, positioned at certain places on the stage, triggered a stream of memories, each bout of particular memories attached to that place and the text that went with it. The system David created facilitated his episodic memory (past personal experiences) and semantic memory (recall of words) to enable his procedural memory (automatic procedures) in his speaking, acting, and remembering of the words and meaning that he had appropriated to the sonnet.

Neural Reuse and Multisensory Processing: A Positive Aspect of Dyslexia?

In returning to the ideas of difference and neurodiversity, the emerging experimental neuroscience concerning theories about neural reuse and neural overlapping is of relevance in considering David's novel performance ideas. Although, to my knowledge, there is as yet no scientific research that looks specifically at neural reuse/overlap and dyslexia, the principal theories might help to explain the attributed strengths, types of synesthesia, and visual and spatial preferences attributed to the presence of dyslexia (West 1997; Bacon & Handley 2010). As I am not a scientist nor a psychologist, I do not pretend to assert any definitive scientific claims. However, as a practitioner of the arts, I can draw from the findings of others, including in the fields of science and psychology, when they appear to bear a relationship with my own.

According to researcher Achille Pasqualotto, in the last few decades experimental psychology and neuroscience have begun to move away from an oversimplification of multisensory processing (Pasqualotto 2019). In particular, he states that there is a slow demise of the concept that external inputs are processed by distinct modules in the brain, and an acceptance of the concept that partially overlapped neural networks process external inputs. This has been shown through neuroimaging techniques (Anderson 2014: 4). Michael Anderson's theory of neural reuse (Anderson 2014) contends that particular parts/modules of the brain are not fixed in a singular function for carrying out specific tasks, but there is a multiple use and reuse of brain areas linked in neural networks, where a single region can be dynamically involved in different networks, depending on task demands. This can produce a diverse behavioral performance (Anderson 2016: 8; Pulvermüller 2018). Anderson underlines that the brain is a dynamic system in which function is continually changing to adjust to the situation. He specifies that seeing, touching, interacting with, and manipulating things are ways of thinking, explaining:

> We have achieved our cognitive capacities in part because we have found ways to reuse our physical capacities to augment our mental ones; in a process supported by neural reuse, we repurpose our behavioural routines in multiple circumstances for myriad cognitive ends.
>
> *(Anderson 2016: 9)*

Pasqualotto (2019) specifies that the brain is more engaged with multisensory processing for cognitive tasks than used to be understood, and this is only now being tracked through improved technology. He and other researchers have documented the interaction of the sensory regions during perceptual and cognitive tasks, showing that overlapping brain areas process information from different modalities (Pasqualotto 2016). As an example, Pasqualotto reports research showing the visual cortex being activated when blind people are carrying out physical tasks despite not being able to see. In an additional trial, when sighted people were blindfolded, in a short time it was recorded that their visual cortex became involved in tactile tasks, before the brain had time to build new pathways, therefore demonstrating that other areas of the brain are used in a variety of actions and thinking. Pasqualotto maintains that research has shown that the clusters of brain areas (or networks) that were thought to be unisensory are actually multisensory, and that sensory inputs conveyed by different sensory modalities are processed in parallel and influence one another (Pasqualotto & Proulx 2015; Pasqualotto et al. 2013). After reading about his research, I contacted Pasqualotto about my dyslexic students' methods of working through visual and kinesthetic modalities. Having read the descriptions of their methods and examined pictures of their work, he concluded:

> This process is possible because in the brain most neurons process information from more than one sensory modality (overlapped neural networks). It is remarkable that *because* of dyslexia these multisensory links become observable because individuals have to find another way to accomplish the task of learning their part.
>
> *(Pasqualotto, personal communication, 2018)*

Conclusion

There can be negative connotations around words that begin with 'dys' or 'dis' (such as the labels of dyslexia and disability) implying a state of being that is faulty (Goodley 2014). This example of David's methods in interacting with the written text into performance revealed his ability to powerfully engage with the words through alternative modes of extended cognition when free to engineer his own ways. This holds pedagogical significance as it demonstrates that inflexible, repeated teaching approaches can accentuate models of disability, whereas this emancipatory process uncovered a substantial ability in David's case. David's breakthrough was a revelation to me as his teacher. His work provided a springboard for my future investigations with other individuals with dyslexia, many of which are recorded in the practical investigations of work in Part II of this book.

Next Chapter

The next chapter outlines dyslexia, what it might be, how it is assessed, and how it can affect some acting students in their work.

KEY POINTS OF CHAPTER 3

- The initiator of the study – David – and his breakthrough towards a self-actualization
- Embodied cognition, extended mind theory, and grounded perception – what it is and how it became apparent in David's performance
- David's emancipation from his dyslexic difficulties, his connection with the words, and performance of the text released through epistemic engineering and employment of epistemic artefacts and epistemic actions
- Neural reuse and overlap, and their possible utilization demonstrated in those with dyslexia

References

Anderson, M.L. (2014). *After Phrenology: Neural Reuse and the Interactive Brain*. Cambridge, MA: MIT Press.

Anderson, M.L. (2016). Précis of *After Phrenology: Neural Reuse and the Interactive Brain*. *Behavioral and Brain Sciences*, 39, 127–128.

Bacon, A. & Handley, S. (2010). Dyslexia, reasoning and the importance of visual-spatial processes. *In*: Alexander-Passe, N. (ed.) *Dyslexia and Creativity*. New York: Nova Science Publishers, pp. 25–49.

Barsalou, L.W. (1999). Perceptual symbol systems. *Behavioural and Brain Sciences*, 22:4, 577–660.

Berry, C. (1993). *The Actor and the Text*. London: Virgin Books.

Berry, C. (2001). *Text in Action*. London: Virgin Books.

Blair, R. (2008). *The Actor, Image and Action*. London: Routledge.

Blair, R. & Cook, A. (eds.) (2016). *Theatre, Performance and Cognition*. London: Bloomsbury.

Clark, A. (2011). *Supersizing the Mind*. Oxford, UK: Oxford University Press.

Cook, A. (2010). *Shakespearean Neuroplay: Reinvigorating the Study of Dramatic Texts and Performance through Cognitive Science*. Basingstoke, UK: Palgrave Macmillan.

de Vega, M., Graesser, A., & Glenberg, A. (2008). Reflecting on the debate. *In*: de Vega, M., Glenberg, A., & Graesser, A. (eds.) *Symbols and Embodiment*. Oxford, UK: Oxford University Press, pp. 397–440.

Gallese, V. & Lakoff, G. (2005). The brain's concepts: the role of the sensory-motor system in conceptual knowledge. *Cognitive Neuropsychology*, 22:3/4, 455–479.

Glenberg, A. & Mehta, S. (2008). The limits of covariation. *In*: de Vega, M., Glenberg, A., & Graesser, A. (eds.) *Symbols and Embodiment*. Oxford, UK: Oxford University Press, pp. 11–32.

Goodley, D. (2014). *Dis/Ability Studies*. London: Routledge.

Johnson, M. (1999). *The Meaning of the Body*. London: Chicago University Press.

Kemp, R. (2012). *Embodied Acting: What Neuroscience Tells Us about Performance*. London: Routledge.

May, S. (2015). *Rethinking Practice as Research and the Cognitive Turn*. Basingstoke, UK: Palgrave Macmillan.

Moseley, R., Kiefer, M., & Pulvermüller, F. (2016). Grounding and embodiment of concepts and meaning: a neurobiological perspective. *In*: Coello, Y. & Fischer, M. (eds.) *Foundations of Embodied Cognition*. London: Psychology Press, pp. 101–122.

Pasqualotto, A. (2016). Multisensory integration substantiates distributed and overlapping neural networks. *Behavioral and Brain Sciences*, 39, 127–128.

Pasqualotto, A. (2019). Brain networks require a network-conscious psychopathological approach. *Behavioral and Brain Sciences*, 42, 30–31.

Pasqualotto, A. & Proulx, M.J. (2015). Two-dimensional rubber-hand illusion: the Dorian Gray hand illusion. *Multisensory Research*, 28, 101–110.

Pasqualotto, A., Finucane, C.M., & Newell, F.N. (2013). Ambient visual information confers a context-specific, long-term benefit on memory for haptic scenes. *Cognition*, 128, 363–379.

Pulvermüller, F. (2008). Grounding language in the brain. *In*: de Vega, M., Glenberg, A., & Graesser, A. (eds.) *Symbols and Embodiment*. Oxford, UK: Oxford University Press, pp. 85–116.

Pulvermüller, F. (2018). Neural reuse of action perception circuits for language, concepts and communication. *Progress in Neurobiology*, 160, 1–44.

Sadoski, M. (2017). Reading comprehension is embodied: theoretical and practical considerations. *Educational Psychology Review*, 30, 331–345.

Shakespeare, W. (1997). *Shakespeare Sonnets*. Ed. Duncan-Jones, K. London: Arden Shakespeare.

Shaughnessy, N. (ed.) (2013). *Affective Performance and Cognitive Science*. London: Bloomsbury.

Stanislavski, C. (1980). *An Actor Prepares*. London: Methuen Drama.

West, T. (1997). *In the Mind's Eye: Visual Thinkers, Gifted People with Dyslexia and Other Learning Difficulties, Computer Images and the Ironies of Creativity*. New York: Prometheus Books.

Whitfield, P. (2009). Shakespeare, pedagogy and dyslexia. *In*: Cooke, R. (ed.) *The Moving Voice: The Integration of Voice and Movement. The Voice and Speech Trainers Review*, 6, 254–262. Published online in *Voice and Speech Review*, 2013. Available from: https://doi.org/10.1080/23268263.2009.10767576. Accessed 7 May 2019.

Wilson, M. (2000). Six views of embodied cognition. *Psychonomic Bulletin and Review*, 9, 625–636.

Yates, F. (1966). *The Art of Memory*. London: Pimlico.

4

MATTERS OF DYSLEXIA

Introduction

I expect there are many teachers of voice and acting who are familiar with the following scenario. We have planned what we anticipate will be an exciting voice and text session for our students, built around igniting and relishing spontaneous responses to Shakespeare's words. Our session begins, and is starting to flow. The text is passed around individual to individual for their voiced and physical responses, developing momentum as the textual baton is shared. As it arrives at the next individual for their contribution, there is a sudden silence, and the impetus jolts and stops. The momentum is frozen and the energy in the room collapses. The individual whose contribution we wait for mutters: 'I'm sorry, I'm dyslexic.' We pause inwardly, gathering our teaching skills to the fore, and bounce back with full support. The dyslexic student's attempts to lift the baton and run with the text remain half-realized, staccato, and mumbled. We try harder to assist, side coaching with prompts of words and explanations of meaning and pronunciations, and the student becomes more anxious. An air of tension gathers in the room; there is a perceptible impatience permeating the atmosphere from the other students. The journey of discovery has been broken. Bearing pedagogical responsibility, we are aware of the discomfort the dyslexic student is experiencing and conscious of our inadequacy in effectively assisting. The other students become bored, and we move on, feeling an inner disquiet, uncertain about how to proceed.

I have observed repeatedly that the free expression of acting students with dyslexia can become severely restricted when interacting with written text. Reading a text aloud while being watched by teachers and peers is a highly visible activity, highlighting the possibilities of a perceived failure for those who carry painful memories from their school days. Being laughed at by peers, accused of being lazy, not trying, or trying too hard, and made to feel stupid by teachers are common experiences for those with dyslexia (McLoughlin & Leather 2013: 12–13). (One of my dyslexic students described vomiting with fear before going to school, and eventually not being able to attend at all. Others have broken down in tears as they re-told school incidents connected to their dyslexia, etched into their memory.) The example of my teaching experience I have related at the start of this chapter illustrates how the anxiety levels for those with dyslexia can be exacerbated by a teacher's presumption of students' skills within a public arena.

The Current Situation: Explanatory Context

At British drama institutions (in both conservatoires and universities), dyslexia is included under a generic title of 'specific learning difficulty' in student records, making statistics about students assessed as dyslexic unclear. In a recent conversation with the Student and Academic Service departments in four major drama schools in the UK, they reported that there are a number of dyslexic students in each cohort every year, and on some courses the numbers are increasing substantially (personal communications, 2015). I also questioned a small sample of voice and acting teachers conducting university acting courses in America, and they reported that they frequently teach students presenting with dyslexia or dyslexic characteristics in their classes every year. Responding to questions I put to them about their experience in teaching dyslexic acting students, they related that some individuals will try to hide their dyslexia, do not disclose it, and are reluctant to discuss it, as they believe there is a stigma in being identified as dyslexic (personal communications, 2018). Professor Hague, director of the BFA Performance course at Auburn University, Alabama, remarked: 'several of my students continue to struggle, particularly with heightened texts, and memorization. While I can give them some help in that process, in general I do not have the skills to address their particular challenges' (personal communication, 2018). Hague gives an overview of the situation from her perspective, saying:

> It is common to find dyslexic students in our classes. Instructors are not, in general, prepared to deal with the special needs of these students and there is a limited body of research on which to draw in order to facilitate and empower these actors when they come to us for training.

In the UK, the Centre for Educational Development, Appraisal and Research (part of the Faculty of Social Studies within the University of Warwick) in its *Dance and Drama Awards Strategic Review*, mentions that dyslexia (and dyspraxia) is the most 'common concern' in disability amongst the 'exceptionally talented' students who had won a scholarship for conservatoire performing arts training (Neelands et al. 2009: 4, 61). Montgomery (2003) has drawn attention to the need for specialist provision for those with 'double exceptionality', who are highly gifted, but with a disability (such as dyslexia). She argues that dyslexia is one of the most common forms of double exceptionality, and their abilities not being perceived and adequately catered for risks grave educational outcomes for talented dyslexics (ibid.: 43). Of course, not all individuals with dyslexia or specific learning differences are exceptionally talented, and a sample of dyslexic individuals will show a range of abilities and intelligence. However, as demonstrated by David's work described in Chapter 3 and by my research participants in the forthcoming chapters, many have distinctive abilities which might easily be disregarded in conventional teaching environments.

Teaching in Higher Education and Dyslexia

According to learning support lecturer David Pollak, the number of students assessed as dyslexic attending universities has increased enormously in the UK (Pollak 2013: 59). Education researchers Barbara Pavey et al. report that a study of undergraduate students in higher education carried out from 2003 to 2006 showed that those with dyslexia did not perform as well as non-dyslexic students, indicating that they may not achieve their potential (Mehaan, in Pavey et al. 2010: 30). Pollak (2013: 70) stresses that not only should support be delivered by a specialist teacher, but all staff should be dyslexia-aware. In the UK, several items of legislation have been put in place as guidance for higher education practice. The UK Disability Discrimination Act: Code of Practice Post-16, which also applies to higher education, states: 'An educator's duty to make reasonable adjustments is an anticipatory duty owed to disabled people and students at large' (Disability Rights Commission 2007: 227). The application of 'reasonable adjustments' means that any barriers which would disadvantage anyone with a disability should be removed, in the physical environment and through teachers' reviews of their practice. Such reasonable adjustments are not defined, but are left open for the educators to decide, according to their subjects, while still maintaining academic standards. The Code of Practice for the Assurance of Academic Quality and Standards in Higher Education in the UK requires that: 'The delivery of programmes should take into account the needs of disabled people or, where appropriate, be adapted to accommodate their individual requirements' (Quality Assurance Agency for Higher Education 1999, Section 3, Precept 10). Both of these requirements place responsibility for enabling those with specific learning disabilities/differences on the educator/teacher.

The Presence of Dyslexia

For some individuals, considerable hurdles are met when endeavoring to find their way into a text, along with other associated difficulties. The difficulties I describe are displayed in my research investigations and by the individuals I teach who have been assessed as dyslexic by an educational psychologist, either at university or at school before coming to university. These difficulties prevail despite undergoing reading practice in various forms in acting and voice classes over a two-year period or more. They reveal themselves across much of the syllabus of voice and acting when dealing with forms of language such as sight-reading, phonetics, accent study, public speaking, and articulation. They become particularly noticeable when working on Shakespeare, with the additional pressure of unusual language, accuracy of word, and heightened performance.

Specifically, I am referring to the act of reading classical text aloud, in a variety of situations, such as within the larger cohort of the class, in voice exercises, scene rehearsal, or alone in a tutorial situation. Moreover, these word difficulties can permeate *beyond reading*, into the *speaking* and *acting* of the text into performance, such as: the ability to process sounds received aurally, adapt an accent or one's speech from a habitual model, break out of embedded intonation patterns in the speaking of the text, dual-task through speaking the words while physically doing something else, remembering the meanings and pronunciations of words, and articulating the syllables within the word. Occasionally, additional words are inserted which are not present in the text, confusing meaning and the received rhythms and sound. It is apparent that some individuals have an inability to read aloud with a smooth, unbroken flow without regular hesitant stumbling and insecurity. They explain that sometimes this is because they have forgotten how to pronounce a word, do not recognize the word, do not understand the meaning of the word or the context, have to process the word letter by letter, the small words seem to swim about, the extraneous words randomly inserted into the text are voiced unconsciously, or the print appears as meaningless marks on the page. In some cases, they cannot explain or understand why they cannot read the words within the given situation. Some individuals appear to read aloud with fluency, but cannot absorb the content nor remember what they have read. Issues of anxiety regarding identity, achievement, and dwindling self-confidence accompany their efforts.

Positive Abilities

Conversely, I also notice that these individuals can have unique strengths and original approaches to the work that counter their difficulties, so that they often stand out within the student cohort. It is these strengths, striking and idiosyncratic in form, contrasting sharply with the difficulties, which are notable and intriguing. McLoughlin and Leather (2013: 14) include artistic ability and visuospatial skills as positive characteristics of dyslexia, but underline that this is speculation and anecdote, rather than being evidenced. Psychologist and dyslexia researcher John Everatt (1997) cites that Aaron and Guillemord (1993), Edwards (1994) and Vail (1990) have argued that dyslexics have superior visual skills. Everatt, in a controlled study, did not find proof of this, but did find that dyslexics had higher creativity scores compared with his non-dyslexic research participants (1997: 20).

In another study, John Everatt, Beverly Steffert, and Ian Smythe found that there was, 'evidence of greater creativity in tasks requiring novelty or insight and more innovative styles of thinking' (1999: 28). In their final discussion, they posit the possibility that those with dyslexia have had to develop creative skills to overcome their disabilities. Yoshimoto has also studied the talents of those with dyslexia, and he includes listening skills, expansive vocabulary, excellent general knowledge, problem-solving skills, creative thinking, and artistic talent (Yoshimoto, in Reid 2016: 249). (For further discussion and examples of the strong visuospatial abilities that those with dyslexia might possess, see Steffert 1996, cited in Mortimore 2003; West 1997; Davis 1997; Schneps 2014; and for reasoning and narrative skills, see Eide and Eide 2011).

What Is Meant by the Term Dyslexia?

The word 'dyslexia' comes from the Greek. *Dys* means difficulty, and *lexia* refers to words or language. A German physician, Rudolf Berlin, coined the term in 1887 to describe stroke patients who had lost their ability to read, but had not lost their vision, hearing, or any other cognitive skill. The label 'word blindness' then took over in the USA and the UK (led by a doctor called Morgan Pringle in 1896), when it was generally thought that the primary disability was a defect in visual memory. The first approach for the support of dyslexia was in 1937 by the neurologist Samuel Orton, who thought the problem was visual and named it 'strephosymbolia', meaning 'twisted symbol', due to some people with dyslexia reversing letters (Nicolson, in Elliott & Nicolson 2016: 9–10). The word dyslexia regained popularity when it was realized that not all individuals with dyslexia had visual difficulties. In the 1950s, dyslexia was thought to be a problem with phonological processing, viewing it through linguistic conditions rather than as a neurological problem. The introduction of functional magnetic resonance brain imaging can now show differences in the brain's activity of those with dyslexia, especially in the left hemisphere (Stein 2018: 313–314).

Currently, the labeling of an individual as 'dyslexic' is a contentious area. There is an unbounded discourse of theories and explanations for and against the concept and label. In spite of extensive research, the suggested causes, identification, and approaches of support for those identified as dyslexic remain diverse and sometimes conflicting (Nicolson & Fawcett: 2010: 1). The very existence of dyslexia as an identifiable construct is questioned by some professionals. Professor of education Julian G. Elliott and educational psychologist Simon Gibbs go so far as to describe the assessment of dyslexia as akin to reading one's horoscope, as there will be some elements that seem to fit (Elliott & Gibbs 2012). They contend that dyslexia is unscientifically proven, with much disagreement about who has or does not have dyslexia and what the criteria are for inclusion or exclusion (Elliott & Gibbs 2009: 116; Elliott & Grigorenko 2014). This lack of clarity, they believe, makes it problematic to address. In their estimation, there is no evidence that shows teaching methods which should favor one thing over another, and therefore focused instruction should apply to all who struggle with reading, assessed as dyslexic or not (Elliott & Gibbs 2009: 122; Elliott & Grigorenko 2014: 177). The report on dyslexia written for the UK Secretary of State by the educationalist Jim Rose attempts to address this argument, stating:

> Dyslexic difficulties are best thought of as existing on a continuum from mild to severe, rather than forming a discrete category. Until recently, a child was deemed to either have or not have dyslexia. It is now recognised that there is no sharp dividing line between having a learning difficulty such as dyslexia and not having it.
>
> *(2009: 34)*

Rod Nicolson and Angela Fawcett (psychologists with a research specialism in dyslexia) describe the complexity of defining the condition of dyslexia accurately, remarking that many definitions concentrate on reading difficulty, which is a learned skill affected by the literacy learning background, but could also be a symptom of other causes (2010: 33). They have outlined their own definition, which encapsulates what I have observed in the behavior and challenges of some of the dyslexic students in my classes, so I present it here:

> Developmental dyslexia is one of the developmental disorders characterised by impaired functioning of the procedural learning system. The key diagnostic indicator is impaired procedural learning in language areas, leading to specific difficulties in reading, writing and spelling. Early problems will emerge in terms of implicit awareness of phonological rules, but problems will also arise in learning other non-explicit linguistic regularities, including orthography and morphology. Phonological difficulties, motor difficulties, automatization difficulties and early speech difficulties occur in dyslexia, but these are not the defining characteristics of the disorder. Children with dyslexia will normally show dissociation between aspects of their procedural learning and those of declarative learning.
>
> *(ibid.: 221–222)*

Other definitions of dyslexia by the International Dyslexia Association and the British Dyslexia Association are given in endnote 1.[1]

Dyslexia (and its accompanying spectrum of characteristics) is observed in individuals across social class, levels of education, and languages. There is variation in how dyslexia is manifested in other languages with differing orthographies, such as in Arabic, Greek, or Chinese, or languages such as Italian that have a more direct link with the grapheme and its phonological sound than in English with its irregular spelling patterns. None the less, forms of dyslexia are found here too (see Brunswick et al. 2010).

Assessment of Dyslexia

Within my own teaching sphere, I have sometimes been puzzled by the shadowy line drawn between the dis/abilities of students who have been assessed by an educational psychologist as 'definitely dyslexic' or who tell me they have been told that they are 'border-line dyslexics' or 'not dyslexic enough'. None the less, I understand that it is important not to merge 'reading difficulty' and 'dyslexia' into a single phenomenon and that there are multiple dimensions to these terms.

An educational psychologist usually carries out a formal identification of dyslexia in higher education institutions. The common way of analyzing who is dyslexic uses an IQ test, the Wechsler Scales of Intellectual Abilities. This test is a series of measures of performance on a range of skills, including knowledge of vocabulary, mental arithmetic, three-dimensional thinking, and speed of copying symbols. As part of the assessment, the four index scores for verbal comprehension, working memory, perceptual organization, and processing speed are important. When all the scores are combined, an IQ measurement can be calculated. With dyslexia (or other learning difficulties), they are looking for what is called a 'spikey profile' or a discrepancy model. The discrepancy is when there are unexpected variations in scores. In a dyslexic's results, there might be high scores for verbal and reasoning skills, comprehension, and general knowledge, but surprisingly low scores for working memory and processing. David Grant (who is an educational psychologist) explains that to make a formal assessment of dyslexia, what is important is 'the extent of the discrepancy between the scores for reading and verbal reasoning, not the reading level itself' (2010: 33). He underlines that there are a variety of differing dyslexias, so there is no precise model of expectation. If the poor reading skills are because there is a lower cognitive ability, and not a specific learning disability, all of the scores would be more evenly balanced and generally below average. However, there is contention about this method of assessing dyslexia, as it is argued that reading and phonological skills are independent of general intelligence (Joshi & Aron 2008, in Reid 2016: 38). Reading ability and intelligence are hard to measure exactly, but the formal identification of dyslexia needs a cut-off point in percentile scores. As the assessment of intelligence and reading can be imprecise, the cognitive neuroscientist Mark Seidenberg (2017: 155) questions that a few points either way can make the difference in achieving a definitive identification of dyslexia or not. It is further argued that there are likely to be dyslexics who might have lower intelligence or come from poorly educated backgrounds, so the discrepancy in scores might not show and their dyslexia might be unnoticed. Assessment is further complicated by some people having other learning difficulties/differences along with dyslexia (sometimes referred to as comorbidity). These overlapping differences can include dyscalculia, dyspraxia, attention deficit disorder, Asperger's syndrome, and specific language disability. This therefore complicates deciphering what might be part of the dyslexia and what might be a feature of another overlapping condition (Thomson 2009: 17).

The Dominant Theories of Dyslexia

There are at least fifteen theories that attempt to explain the underlying causes of dyslexia, as presented in *A Framework for Understanding Dyslexia* (Department for Education & Skills 2004: 76–114), and several of these are discussed throughout this book. When thinking about the theories of dyslexia, they can be broken down into three levels of analysis (Frith 2002): the behavioral level (behavior which can be observed, like reading), the cognitive level (how the brain is processing things, like memory, language, learning), and the biological level (brain-based structure). Nicolson has included a genetic level, where dyslexia is passed down through the family genes (Elliott & Nicolson 2016: 25). Frith also includes environment (such as teaching and socio-cultural contexts) as connected to all three levels. Recognizing the disagreements about the causes of dyslexia, Frith links the levels together to construct a description of dyslexia, saying:

> Dyslexia is a neuro-developmental disorder with a biological origin, which impacts on speech processing with a range of clinical manifestations. There is evidence of a genetic basis and there is evidence of a brain basis, and it is clear that the behavioural signs extend well beyond written language. There may be different kinds of genes and different kinds of brain conditions that are [. . .] responsible for the dyslexia syndrome, but in each case the symptoms have to be understood within the cultural context.
>
> *(2002: 65)*

Pavey et al. point out that the debate around the theories of dyslexia is currently in flux, as research now encompasses foreign languages, genetics, and brain imaging. However, there are two theories that dominate the field: the phonological deficit and the cerebellar deficit hypothesis. A third theory, the magnocellular deficit hypothesis, is also prominent in the field.

An overview of these three theories of dyslexia is presented in endnote 2.[2] Readers are further guided by references to specialist literature if they wish to study the theories in more detail.

The Role of Working Memory, The Phonological Loop, and the Visuospatial Sketchpad

There is a widely held opinion amongst researchers that many of those with dyslexia have poor working and short-term memory (especially verbal rather than visual), which might be a contributory factor in their inability to read fluently (Gathercole & Packiam Alloway 2008: 29; Mortimore 2008: 102; McLoughlin & Leather 2013: 19). Working memory is said to be responsible for the temporary acquisition, storage, and manipulation of information, and acts as a 'translator between sensory input and long-term memory' (Fletcher-Janzen, cited in Dehn

2008: xiii). A familiarity with Alan Baddeley's model of working memory and its separate components (Baddeley 2007; Baddeley et al. 2015: 70–84) is advantageous for those who work with the voice, Shakespeare, and dyslexia; in particular the phonological loop (the memory store for words and sounds) and the visuospatial sketchpad (memory store for images). Thomson (2009: 172) stresses that the phonological loop is interesting to those studying dyslexia because of its relationship with language, reading, and speech.

See endnote 3 for details of Baddeley's model of working memory, phonological loop, and visuospatial sketchpad.[3]

An Ideographic, Evidence-based Approach for the Individual

Regardless of the controversy about the umbrella term 'dyslexia', Pavey et al. (2010: 6) insist that there are definitely some individuals for whom the skills of literacy are difficult and resistant to standard teaching, despite their possession of other abilities. Dyslexia consultant and psychologist David McLoughlin and researcher Carol Leather (2013: 2) propose that the appropriate questions should be asked to evaluate definitions, such as: Why do some people learn to read, but continue to find spelling difficult? Why do some people achieve good accuracy, but find it hard to retain what they read? Why do some people who master skills they found difficult to acquire, such as reading and spelling, report problems with organization and time management? Dyslexia researchers Rod Nicolson and Angela Fawcett (2010: 17) include: How can an otherwise high-achieving person be so impaired in learning to read? For voice and acting teachers working with adult students with text, these difficulties are often tangible, impacting on the teaching/working environment, content, and participants.

These questions draw attention to some of the puzzling factors facing those of us who teach individuals with dyslexia. Many of the intervention measures described in the literature on dyslexia center on children in elementary school settings, which increases the difficulty in finding applicable ideas to support adult students of acting. Additionally, the advice given to facilitate those with dyslexia in higher education is generic across disciplines, and therefore does not attend to the distinct demands of actor training, and the acting of Shakespeare in particular. In a critique of actor training and dyslexia, Leveroy (2013: 79) questions support methods that encourage the dyslexic learner to 'fit in' with established practices, rather than teachers changing their approaches. McLoughlin and Leather (2013: 9) emphasize that if specific needs are to be met, the teacher should use an 'ideographic', evidence-based approach. This, they stress, must involve research to attain an expertise about dyslexia, to fully understand the disadvantages suffered, and to develop an awareness of the individual preferences. In their collection of exercises for working on text in *The Verbal Arts Workbook*, voice practitioners David Carey and Rebecca Clark Carey (2010) make an important contribution to the field of actor training by giving the subject of dyslexia attention as a potential learning barrier. Carey and Clarke Carey declare that they have encountered dyslexia amongst acting students many times (ibid.: xviii). In their Introduction, they describe the condition and offer generic advice on how to manage it. Facilitative strategies are proposed, such as reading aloud with a partner, as described in the *paired reading exercise* in Reid (2016: 225–230) and in Whitfield (2009: 261). Other ideas are offered, such as receiving the text in advance of the class, larger font sizes, printing on colored paper, and using transparent colored overlays.

The use of colored overlays arises from the work of psychologist Helen Irlen (1991). She declares that those who have *scotopic sensitivity syndrome* (glare from the page, unstable print, visual stress) can be assisted by using colored overlays or tinted glasses when reading (Department for Education & Skills 2004: 64). It should be noted that not all of those with dyslexia have problems with visual stress, and that some people who are not dyslexic do. In my experience, some individuals with dyslexia report that colored overlays assist them in processing the words on the page, whilst others say they make no difference, or even hinder them. One of my research participants responded with angry frustration when colored overlays were offered, describing it as 'patronizing' that it was imagined that her difficulties could be so simplistically fixed by a colored filter. Another confessed that he had pretended that the overlays helped as he did not want to disappoint the teacher who had given them to him. Elliott and Grigorenko (2014: xv) claim that the use of tinted lenses or overlays has questionable validity and little empirical support. Singleton and Trotter carried out a test using colored overlays on university students which compared individuals who said they suffered visual stress with those that did not. They then divided the group into two: those with dyslexia and those without any reading problems. They found that only the individuals who were both dyslexic and reported that they experienced visual stress improved their reading rate with colored overlays (by 16 percent). The dyslexics who did not suffer visual stress only improved by 3 percent. In addition, the non-dyslexic students involved in the test still read much faster than the dyslexics did. The reading rate of the dyslexic group with high visual sensitivity using a colored overlay remained the same as the dyslexic group without visual stress (Reid 2009: 53). Singleton also highlights that some adults and children can be embarrassed about needing to use colored overlays (Reid 2009: 52) or wear colored glasses. Moreover, for the acting student, when endeavoring to read and act with freedom, coping with additional paraphernalia such as retaining the colored overlays in their position on the page can interfere with the flow of action, emotion, and thought. One dyslexic student reported that the colored lenses in her glasses assisted in stabilizing the text on the page, but then blocked her communication with other actors in a scene (due to their dark color) and hid her facial expressions.

Carey and Clark Carey's inclusion of the subject of dyslexia and advice for facilitation in their book is valuable in recognition of the difficulties faced by teachers and students in voice studies and actor training. However, there is still much more that can be done to enable the dyslexic student. Such provisions currently do not include teachers' reflection on their own contributions to the individual's experience through an analysis of the individual's difficulties and subsequent adaptation of their teaching content and approaches used. Such activity would demonstrate a deeper engagement with the special needs of the individual, leading to the ideographic, evidence-based approach recommended by McLoughlin and Leather.

The Ethics of Language and Terminology Used in This Book

Because the label 'dyslexia' can be used loosely to describe all sorts of reading weaknesses, it has been important to ensure that my research participants have been formally assessed as dyslexic by an educational psychologist. Regarding the terminology used to describe students with dyslexia, the dyslexia specialists Gavin Reid (2016), David Pollak (2009), and Tilly Mortimore (2008) have recommended using the term 'student with dyslexia' as an ethically acceptable title to describe the individuals I am concerned with (personal communication, January 2011). McLoughlin and Leather (2013: 6) reject the term 'people with' or 'people who have' dyslexia, as having medical connotations, and prefer to use the terms 'dyslexic people' or 'dyslexic'. The political arguments surrounding the use of the labels 'specific learning difficulties', 'disabilities', 'dis/abilities', or 'differences' have many perspectives, and the labels can be viewed as appropriate according to the situation and manner in which they are being used (Pollak 2009: 7). Having an assessed learning disability myself, I take full responsibility for deciding to use all of the labels variously throughout the book. This is a conscious decision in attempting to reflect the multi-layered factors involved in dyslexia, and the heterogeneous nature of neurodiversity.

Conclusion

The investigations recounted in this book do not seek to test the veracity of the diverse theories explaining dyslexia, nor to determine exactly which type of dyslexia my participants might present. Throughout my studies, I have observed that dyslexia is indeed a slippery concept, involving an assortment of shifting characteristics, proving difficult to demarcate. The unresolved arguments around the nature of dyslexia, despite years of extensive research in many areas, reveal what a convoluted area it presents in practice. However, that should not stop teachers searching for ways that may counter dyslexic difficulties, alleviate stress-inducing activities, and give attention to any accompanying strengths.

The Next Chapter

In the next chapter, I introduce the case for using Shakespeare as the working material in studying and assisting individuals with dyslexia. The assertion of the 'rules of the text' promulgated by some practitioners and attitudes behind the teaching of Shakespeare are discussed. The search for a freedom of the authentic self in reading capabilities, voicing, and articulation, within the boundaries of the classical language, is also given attention.

KEY POINTS OF CHAPTER 4

- An overview of the current numbers of those with dyslexia in actor training institutions in the UK, and the experience of some teachers in the US
- Higher education, codes of practice, and policy in teaching dyslexic students
- The effect of dyslexia on the individual, with the pressures of expectations in education
- What is dyslexia?
- How is dyslexia identified?
- Manifestation of dyslexia in reading, and effects on confidence
- Positive abilities in those with dyslexia
- The dominant theories of dyslexia
- Alan Baddeley's model of memory, the phonological loop, and the visuospatial sketchpad
- The need for an evidence-based ideographic approach to facilitate individuals with dyslexia
- The terminology used to describe individuals assessed as dyslexic

---

Notes

1 A number of definitions of dyslexia have been proposed. The International Dyslexia Association (2018) states:

> Dyslexia is a specific learning disability that is neurobiological in origin. It is characterized by difficulties with accurate and/or fluent word recognition and by poor spelling and decoding abilities. These difficulties typically result from a deficit in the phonological component of language that is often unexpected in relation to other cognitive abilities and the provision of effective classroom instruction. Secondary consequences may include problems in reading comprehension and reduced reading experience that can impede growth of vocabulary and background knowledge.

The British Dyslexia Association (2018) states:

> In 2009 Sir Jim Rose's Report on 'Identifying and Teaching Children and Young People with Dyslexia and Literacy Difficulties' gave the following description of dyslexia:

- 'Dyslexia is a learning difficulty that primarily affects the skills involved in accurate and fluent word reading and spelling.
- Characteristic features of dyslexia are difficulties in phonological awareness, verbal memory and verbal processing speed.
- Dyslexia occurs across the range of intellectual abilities.
- It is best thought of as a continuum, not a distinct category, and there are no clear cut-off points.
- Co-occurring difficulties may be seen in aspects of language, motor co-ordination, mental calculation, concentration and personal organisation, but these are not, by themselves, markers of dyslexia.
- A good indication of the severity and persistence of dyslexic difficulties can be gained by examining how the individual responds or has responded to well-founded intervention.'

In addition to these characteristics, the BDA acknowledges the visual and auditory processing difficulties that some individuals with dyslexia can experience, and points out that dyslexic readers can show a combination of abilities and difficulties that affect the learning process. Some also have strengths in other areas, such as design, problem solving, creative skills, interactive skills and oral skills.

2 The overview of the four dominant theories of dyslexia I give here is brief. Each theory includes a large body of research, description, and knowledge, and further specialized reading is advised to understand them fully. Other than the books already cited, for an overview of additional theories and the arguments for and against the concept of dyslexia, I recommend reading *Dyslexia: Developing the Debate* by Julian Elliott and Rod Nicolson (2016).

The phonological deficit theory: There is strong support for phonological deficit as a core explanation for dyslexia (Nicolson & Fawcett 2010: 21, Pavey et al. 2010: 88, Thomson 2009: 187, Hatcher & Snowling 2002: 67). Dyslexia researcher Maggie Snowling tells us that one of the most commonly reported difficulties that dyslexics struggle with is 'phonological awareness and limitations of verbal short-term memory' (1998: 6). She states that dyslexic children are slow to transfer from an orthographic visual stage into the alphabetic stage of reading. They have difficulty in processing, retaining, and decoding phonemes to graphemes in both spelling and reading. This core-deficit is retained into adulthood, especially with newly encountered words, phonological awareness and verbal short-term memory. In addition, there can be difficulties with rhyme, sound blending and naming speed. This poor recognition of sounds can affect the reading, speech pronunciation, syllabification skills and comprehension of the text (Thomson 2009: 183).

The cerebellar deficit hypothesis: There is an argument that the phonological deficit theory does not satisfactorily explain all of the problems presented by dyslexia, such as poor organization, concentration, distractibility (McLoughlin & Leather 2013: 22), learning and automatization difficulties (Nicolson & Fawcett 2010: 137), physical co-ordination, eye movement control in reading, and speech muscle control in speaking (Eide & Eide 2011: 25).

The cerebellar theory (which developed from the *automaticity deficit*) originates from Nicolson and Fawcett (2010; Nicolson 2015), who contend that an impairment of the cerebellum gives rise to difficulties in automatization of skills, phonological and motor skills, articulation of speech, and information processing speeds. It has been suggested by some that cerebellar deficits might be associative rather than causal (McLoughlin & Leather 2013: 19). The automaticity deficit states that those with dyslexia have difficulties in making skills automatic, which means they have to 'consciously compensate' (Nicolson 2015). Recently, Alvarez and Fiez (2018) have supported the *cerebellar deficit hypothesis*, and the role of the cerebellum with cortical systems known to be involved in reading, articulation, and automaticity of processes.

The magnocellular theory of developmental dyslexia: Some people with dyslexia complain that the words seem to move about on the page, and it has been shown in some research trials that when looking at a target, dyslexic children's eye fixations move around, out of control. It is therefore suggested that dyslexic children might have a problem with unstable visual perception resulting in difficulties with reading (Stein 2018: 316). It is argued that this may be due to an impaired development of magnocells (large neurons in the brain) that are responsible for the timing of sensory and motor events. Focusing on the words on the page in reading requires the capabilities of the magnocellular system, and weaknesses can lead to confusion of letter orders and a weak visual memory for the written word. It might be that the auditory system is also part of this, for example in hearing letter sounds, given the slower auditory processing often found in those with dyslexia (Department for Education & Skills 2004: 86). This theory is complicated in its use of scientific terms and understanding of neuroscience, such as the suggestion that the functions of the magnocellular system (which codes information about contrast and movement) might be weak, leading to a strengthening of the parvocellular system (which codes information about detail and color) in those with dyslexia. To fully engage with the ideas underlying this theory, further reading is recommended.

3   Baddeley's model has four components: the central executive, the phonological loop, the episodic buffer, and the visuospatial sketchpad,.

The central executive is the focal point of working memory. It can focus on important information while blocking out disruptions, dual-task by processing information and acting as a store, and has access to and from long-term memory (Dehn 2008:22). McLoughlin and Leather (2013: 21) assert that, in their experience, those with dyslexia show problems with the function of the executive in aspects of planning, sequences, attention, and finding it hard to change a habitual manner of doing things, such as a 'set' reading style. The central executive supervises two 'slave systems': the phonological loop and the visuospatial sketchpad, which are interconnected by the episodic buffer.

The phonological loop is supported by the left part of the brain and 'plays a crucial role in language processing, literacy and learning' (Baddeley 2007: 17; McLoughlin & Leather 2013: 20). It has two departments. One is a short-term store for words, numbers or sentences. However, its capacity is limited. It can hold the information there for only a few seconds before it decays. This is known as short-term memory. To 'catch' the information before it disappears, it has to be transferred into working memory before it can be placed into long-term memory. This 'catching' happens when the information seen is subvocalized, or vocalized – 'either works equally well' (Gathercole & Packiam Alloway 2008: 87) – in an articulatory rehearsal and transferred into a phonological code of phonemes or words. The phonological loop rehearsal can only hold a small amount of information at once before it is forgotten. Monosyllabic words can be remembered more easily than polysyllabic words, which take more time and effort in rehearsal articulation (Baddeley 2007: 9). Ideas, reasoning, and sense are then put together in the central executive area, which can then store them in long-term memory.

It is common that those with dyslexia have problems with working memory overload and phonological processing which lead to inaccurate and slower language-based learning (Eide & Eide 2011: 24–25). They can also have trouble with articulating words and possess a lack of awareness in how they make speech sounds (Griffiths & Frith 2002).

As there is no direct pathway between the phonological loop and the visuospatial sketchpad, *the episodic buffer* acts a boundary between the two. It can act as a temporary storage space for the multi-modal information from the two systems and long-term memory and combine them into representations to be stored in long-term memory (Mortimore 2008: 107; Dehn 2008: 25).

The visuospatial sketchpad stores short-term visual images of things, places, and manipulation of space and plays a key role in creating images (Dehn 2008: 19–22; Baddeley 2007: 63–101). The visuospatial sketchpad is activated in the right side of the brain

(McLoughlin & Leather 2013: 22), and as yet there has been limited research into its full role and capacity. It is thought that visual information can be stored independently in long-term memory, but that visual information is usually recoded into verbal information to put into the phonological store. As we gain language, we inevitably link words to our images, which then activate the phonological loop (Dehn 2008: 21).

When we are babies, we think in images as we have no language to name things, so the visuospatial sketchpad will be the main memory system (Mortimore 2008: 107). Gradually, lexical and semantic knowledge is built through listening to others, speaking and eventually, learning to read. The words are then mapped onto the image. The earliest record of written language is in picture form, but as communication became more precise, it was impossible to decipher an exact meaning from one picture, so gradually symbolic logograms were developed which evolved into the alphabet (Seidenberg 2017: 38–55).

References

Alvarez, T.A. & Fiez, J.A. (2018). Current perspectives on the cerebellum and reading development. *Neuroscience and Biobehavioral Reviews*, 92, 55–66.

Baddeley, A. (2007). *Working Memory, Thought, and Action*. Oxford, UK: Oxford University Press.

Baddeley, A., Eysenck, M.W., & Anderson, M.C. (2015). *Memory*, 2nd ed. London: Psychology Press.

British Dyslexia Association (2018). Defining dyslexia. Available from: www.bdadyslexia. org.uk/dyslexic. Accessed 7 May 2019.

Brunswick, N., McDougall, S., & de Mornay Davies, P. (2010). *Reading and Dyslexia in Different Orthographies*. London: Psychology Press.

Carey, D. & Clark Carey, R. (2010). *The Verbal Arts Workbook*. London: Methuen Drama.

Davis, R. (1997). *The Gift of Dyslexia*. London: Souvenir Press.

Dehn, M. (2008). *Working Memory and Academic Learning*. Hoboken, NJ: John Wiley & Sons.

Department for Education & Skills (2004). *A Framework for Understanding Dyslexia*. London: DfES.

Disability Rights Commission (2007). *Disability Discrimination Act 1995: Code of Practice Post-16*. London: The Stationery Office.

Eide, B. & Eide, F. (2011). *The Dyslexia Advantage*. London: Hayhouse.

Elliott, J.G. & Gibbs, S. (2009). Does dyslexia exist? *In*: Cigman, R. & Davis, A. (eds.) *New Philosophies of Learning*. Chichester, UK: Wiley Blackwell, pp. 115–130.

Elliott, J.G. & Gibbs, S. (2012). The dyslexia debate. *In*: Adey, P. & Dillon, J. (eds.) *Bad Education: Debunking Myths in Education*. Maidenhead, UK: Open University Press, pp. 263–278.

Elliott, J.G. & Grigorenko, E. (2014). *The Dyslexia Debate*. New York: Cambridge University Press.

Elliot, J.G. & Nicolson, R. (2016). *Dyslexia: Developing the Debate*. London: Bloomsbury.

Everatt, J. (1997). The abilities and disabilities associated with adult developmental dyslexia. *Journal of Research in Reading*, 20, 13–21.

Everatt, J., Steffert, B., & Smythe, I. (1999). An eye for the unusual: creative thinking in dyslexics. *Dyslexia*, 5:1, 28–46.

Frith, U. (2002). Resolving the paradoxes of dyslexia. *In*: Reid, G. & Wearmouth, J. (eds.) *Dyslexia and Literacy*. Chichester, UK: John Wiley & Sons, pp. 45–68.

Gathercole, S. & Packiam Alloway, T. (2008). *Working Memory and Learning*. London: SAGE Publications.

Grant, D. (2010). *That's the Way I Think*, 2nd ed. Oxford, UK: David Fulton.

Griffiths, S. & Frith, U. (2002) Evidence for an articulatory awareness deficit in adult dyslexics. *Dyslexia*, 8, 14–21.

Hatcher, J. & Snowling, M. (2002). The phonological representations hypothesis of dyslexia: from theory to practice. *In*: Reid, G. & Wearmouth, J. (eds.) *Dyslexia and Literacy: Theory and Practice*. Chichester, UK: Wiley, pp. 69–85.

International Dyslexia Association (2018). Definition of dyslexia. Available from: https:// dyslexiaida.org/definition-of-dyslexia/. Accessed 7 May 2019.

Irlen, H. (1991). *Reading by the Colours*. New York: Avery.

Leveroy, D. (2013). Enabling performance: dyslexia, (dis)ability and 'reasonable adjustment'. *Theatre, Dance and Performance Training*, 4:1, pp. 87–101.

McLoughlin, D. & Leather, C. (2013). *The Dyslexic Adult*, 2nd ed. Chichester, UK: Whurr.

Montgomery, D. (2003). *Gifted and Talented Children with Special Educational Needs: Double Exceptionality*. London: David Fulton.

Mortimore, T. (2003). *Dyslexia and Learning Style: A Practitioner's Handbook*. London: Whurr.

Mortimore, T. (2008). *Dyslexia and Learning Style*, 2nd ed. Chichester, UK: John Wiley and Sons.

Neelands, J., Lindley, R.M., Lindsay, G., Winston, J., Galloway, S., Kellgren, I., & Morris, M. (2009). *Dance and Drama Awards Strategic Review 2009: Final Report*. Warwick, UK: CEDAR Warwick Institute for Employment Research.

Nicolson, R. (2015). *Positive Dyslexia*. Sheffield, UK: Rodin Books.

Nicolson, R. & Fawcett, A. (2010). *Dyslexia, Learning and the Brain*. London: MIT Press.

Pavey, B., Meehan, M., & Waugh, A. (2010). *Dyslexia-friendly Further and Higher Education*. London: SAGE Publications.

Pollak, D. (ed.) (2009). *Neurodiversity in Higher Education*. Chichester, UK: Wiley Blackwell.

Pollak, D. (2013). Supporting higher education students who are dyslexic. *In*: Brunswick, N. (ed.) *Supporting Dyslexic Adults in Higher Education and the Workplace*. Chichester, UK: John Wiley & Sons, pp. 59–73.

Quality Assurance Agency for Higher Education (1999). *Code of Practice for the Assurance of Academic Quality and Standards in Higher Education, Section 3, Students with Disabilities*. Gloucester, UK: Quality Assurance Agency for Higher Education.

Reid, G. (2009). *The Routledge Companion to Dyslexia*. Oxford, UK: Routledge.

Reid, G. (2016). *Dyslexia a Practitioner's Handbook*, 5th ed. Chichester, UK: John Wiley.

Rose, J. (2009). *Identifying and Teaching Children and Young People with Dyslexia and Literacy Difficulties*. DCSF-00659-2009. Nottingham, UK: Department for Children, Schools and Families

Schneps, M.H. (2014). The advantages of dyslexia. *Scientific American*, 19 August. Available from: www.scientificamerican.com/article/the-advantages-of-dyslexia/. Accessed 7 May 2019.

Seidenberg, M. (2017). *Language at the Speed of Sight: How We Read, Why So Many Can't and What Can Be Done about It*. New York: Basic Books.

Snowling, M. (1998). Dyslexia as a phonological deficit: evidence and implications. *Child Psychology & Psychiatry Review*, 3:1, 4–11.

Stanovitch, K.E. (1988). Explaining the differences between the dyslexic and the garden-variety poor reader: the phonological-core variable-difference model. *Journal of Learning Disabilities*, 21:10, 590–604.

Stein, J.F. (2018). Does dyslexia exist? *Language, Cognition and neuroscience*, 33:3, 313–320.

Thomson, M. (2009). *The Psychology of Dyslexia*, 2nd ed. Chichester, UK: Wiley-Blackwell.

West, T. (1997). *In the Mind's Eye: Visual Thinkers, Gifted People with Dyslexia and Other Learning Difficulties, Computer Images and the Ironies of Creativity*. New York: Prometheus Books.

Whitfield, P. (2009). Shakespeare, pedagogy and dyslexia. *In*: Cooke, R. (ed.) *The Moving Voice: The Integration of Voice and Movement. The Voice and Speech Trainers Review*, 6, 254–262. Published online in *Voice and Speech Review*, 2013. Available from: https://doi.org/10.1080/23268263.2009.10767576. Accessed 7 May 2019.

5

SHAKESPEARE AS LABORATORY AND READER AS CREATOR

Introduction and Background Context

I begin with a summary of the historical context and assumptions that underpin my priorities in a training methodology for the acting student in the reading, speaking, and performance of Shakespeare. These perspectives formed the foundation of my practice prior to developing my work with the dyslexic students, and I acknowledge that some aspects of my approach to teaching Shakespeare are classically orthodox and Anglo-centric in nature. They are rooted in my working experiences as an actor with the Royal Shakespeare Company, with theatre directors Peter Hall (founder of the Royal Shakespeare Company) and his colleague John Barton (both students at Cambridge University, influenced by scholar and director George Rylands and literary critic F.R. Leavis and his close reading strategies), and the former voice director of the Royal Shakespeare Company, Cicely Berry (who originally trained at the Central School of Speech and Drama). In her comprehensive history about theory and practice in approaching Shakespeare, the Shakespeare academic Abigail Rokison (2009: 30) has highlighted the pervasive influence on much of the work that is created at the Royal Shakespeare Company as originating from the Royal Central School of Speech and Drama. My pedagogical syllabus is shaped by my training as a voice teacher at the Royal Central School of Speech and Drama, and in particular by the course leader at the time, principal teacher of voice, text and Shakespeare David Carey (now Voice and Text director at the Oregon Shakespeare Festival). Carey's own experience as a voice coach with the Royal Shakespeare Company and his scholarly knowledge of Shakespeare, vocal pedagogy, language, and teacher training has been an enormous influence on my development as a teacher and in my learning. Additionally, I have attended a variety of workshops led by vocal practitioners with a specialism in Shakespeare such as Andrew Wade, Patsy Rodenburg,

Lyn Darnley, Barbara Houseman, Bardy Thomas, Joanna Weir-Ouston, and Kristin Linklater. All of these teachers (except for Linklater and designated Linklater teacher Weir-Ouston) have been employed as voice coaches working alongside Cicely Berry at the Royal Shakespeare Company. Berry trained originally as a teacher at the Royal Central School of Speech and Drama, was employed at the Royal Shakespeare Company in the early 1970s, and has developed her idiosyncratic exercises on exploring Shakespeare's text through working with many of the Royal Shakespeare directors such as Trevor Nunn, Peter Brook, Terry Hands, John Barton, and Adrian Noble (ibid.: 50). She has disseminated her exercises and ideological views towards the voice and text in her numerous publications, which are established internationally as seminal working manuals for teachers, directors, and actors.

Moreover, my own experience as a professional actress in acting in Shakespeare's plays ensures that my understanding of the demands of the work also originates from my knowledge of the rehearsal processes, discovering what might be ascertained through the language, the characters' motivations, technical requirements in speaking the words, interaction with others in shared creation, and the communication of the text in professional performance. As a young actor at the Royal Shakespeare Company (and with the Peter Hall Company), I observed accomplished actors in their acting of Shakespeare. I watched and listened carefully to the directors, such as John Barton and Peter Hall, and voice director Cicely Berry guiding the actors and discussing the text with their specialized knowledge of Shakespeare. This learning has meant I have gained a deep awareness of the requirements in acting and speaking Shakespeare within this cultural context.

In my own training as an actor at a British conservatoire drama school in the 1970s, when working on Shakespeare's text, an emphasis was placed on a psychologically real approach, with a rejection of the perceived to be artificially mannered 'verse speaking declaimed style of the 1940s and 50s' (Martin 1991: 32). In accordance with the fashion of the time, I was instructed to disregard the poetic structure in which it was written and to utilize a prosaic style of communication, aiming for a feeling of inner conviction and naturalness, making no adjustment in my spoken style between a contemporary or classical text. According to the Shakespeare director Peter Hall and voice practitioner Patsy Rodenburg, a decline in specialized teaching of Shakespeare had become commonplace in some actor training institutions from the 1960s onwards, and concern had arisen about the lack of knowledge demonstrated by some young actors when joining the classical theatre companies (Hall 2003: 11; Rodenburg 2002: xii; Rokison 2009: 9). Peter Hall (the founder of the Royal Shakespeare Company) stated that the recognition of rhetorical device in Shakespeare's text was not being adequately taught in actor training, nor being passed down from experienced actors to younger actors in the dying repertory theatre system in the UK, where Shakespeare has become rarely performed. Since then, there has been an effort by Hall, Rodenburg, and Carey and Clark Carey (amongst others) to establish an actor's classical training foundational knowledge, which gives the acting student the 'basic tools to start work on Shakespeare' (Rodenburg 2002: xii; Carey & Clark Carey 2015). In order to inhabit both the language and the role presented in the text, the actor needs to communicate 'an understanding of the language and how it works' (Rodenburg 2002: 4). In conjunction with structural observation, the vocal delivery should encompass a corpus of technical skills in order to embody length of thoughts, communicate argument, support passionate feeling, and articulate the elaborate language. This requires physical training to build a dynamic breath support system underpinning vocal resonance and projection, a flexible vocal range to express the richness of heightened language, and a muscularity of articulation to enable clarity of word. Shakespearean scholar Abigail Rokison (2009: 37) has considered the impossibility of defining what might be identified as the authentic rendition of Shakespeare's text. She underlines that Shakespeare's text is not a single entity, but a body of writing that has become a 'multifarious beast' contributed to by copious editors throughout the ages, removed from the original author's intent. In the training I have received, authority is commonly given to Shakespeare as a single entity, and it is stressed that the first Folio is 'as close to Shakespeare as I can get' (Block 2013: xiii) and the 'purity of the Folio text [. . .] reveals the clues for the actor who can hear the shape of the original play' (Hall 2003: 22).

Hall deliberates that:

> Shakespeare's text is scored precisely, Shakespeare tells an actor quite clearly when to go fast, when to go slow, when to pause, when to come in on cue. He indicates which word should be accented and which word should be thrown away [. . .]. The actor's task is to engender a set of feelings which will make this textual shape, this end result the true one. This brings us closer to Shakespeare's meaning than any other form of analysis I know.
>
> *(2000: 41)*

This view of Shakespeare as author directing through the text can be appreciated if adopting the perspective of reader-response theorist Georges Poulet, who reflected on the remarkable transformation wrought through the act of reading. He suggested that the writer, emerging into a shared consciousness, impregnates the reader's mind. Poulet considers: '[t]his "I" who thinks in me [. . .] is the "I" of the one who writes the book [. . .] I am on loan to another, and this other thinks, feels and suffers within me' (1980: 45–46). The actor Simon Callow brings an additional perspective to Poulet's theory. In an actor's notes, he advises:

> you must look for the character located within yourself [. . .] another person is coursing through your veins, is breathing through your lungs, but of course, it's not. It's only you – another arrangement of you. Only then

will the energy spring from within, instead of being externally applied; only then will you have renewed the umbilical connection between the character and the author.

(1984: 166)

Questioning actors' methods of examining Shakespeare's text for so-called legitimate 'meanings', theatre arts scholar William. B. Worthen conveys bemusement about the reverential observance of 'an absent authority' in the 'ghostly presence of Shakespeare'. He queries why actors do not want to be driven by their own creations, rather than being 'released into a physical freedom in training, but restricted by the presence of the author' (Worthen 1996: 25; Worthen 1997: 140). For Worthen, the supposed significations promulgated as Shakespeare's meanings are not present in the text, but constructions of the individual's worlds through their own ways of reading, thinking, and acting within shared cultures. He proposes that in reifying Shakespeare, actors impoverish their own performance, turning away from admitting their own responsibility for their contemporary culture-making and critical activity (Worthen 1996: 12–25).

It is an actor's common practice to attempt to decipher the possible codes buried within a play text, to shape decisions of intricate detail on characterization, subtext, motivation, and style. As Rokison acknowledges, 'clearly the text and its form are the main tools of the Shakespearean actor and director' (2009: 3). Additionally, the authority given to Shakespeare and the text demonstrates an aesthetic literary sensitivity and appreciation for the ingenuity of the incredible language and poetic form displayed in Shakespeare's writing. Conversely, I also recognize and support the critical appraisal posed by Rokison when she highlights how many actors unquestionably accept and reiterate what Barton, Hall, or Berry (and others) proclaim as 'the rules about speaking Shakespeare' as a complete, non-negotiable authority (Rokison 2009: 13).

My syllabus in teaching second-year acting degree students the acting of Shakespeare over a nine-week term includes a practical exploration of different methods into accessing Shakespeare's text and his characters, performance of monologues, and assessed scenes. This acting work is supported by voice classes throughout the nine-week syllabus, focusing on Shakespeare's linguistic form married with ideas of truthful communication, and an assessed performance of Shakespeare sonnets. Through this syllabus, I aim to give each individual the tools to be employed as a professional actor in a classical theatre environment, and an acquisition of transferrable skills which might be further utilized in aspects of education, performance, and life. Although I teach the fundamentals of Shakespeare's structural form as one of the elements in the Shakespeare syllabus, this classical training does not preclude an engagement with less orthodox approaches and the freedom to embark into non-traditional postmodern performance. I am open to embracing contemporary explorations, world cultures, and technology where, in some instances, the text might play a secondary role to innovation in communication and performance style.

These contrasting opinions on what might or might not be embedded in the text offer possibilities of removing the restrictions set by others, so as to find a freedom for the individual within their speaking of the text. Worthen's arguments against adherence to specified rules inherent in the text present emancipatory possibilities for those who are overwhelmed by text-based instructions, fixed procedures, and producing expected outcomes.

Reading Shakespeare in the Contemporary Environment

The readability of Shakespeare for the contemporary young person can present uncharted terrain. At the beginning of the Shakespeare unit, my acting students commonly relate that their school experience of studying Shakespeare was boring and restricted in scope, and many of them found Shakespeare's writing incomprehensible. Amongst my acting students, some can read effortlessly, but still find Shakespeare's writing hard to grasp. Hall (2003: 10) deliberates that in another two hundred years, it is likely that Shakespeare will be 'only faintly visible' and will have to be translated, as our human circumstances, cultures, and language transform through the passage of time.

English scholar Simon Palfrey (2005: 24) ruminates on how Shakespeare's language remains strange and difficult no matter how familiar we become with it. Palfrey underlines that a word can have multiple meanings, but suggests that 'art is truest when it knows which one it wants' (ibid.: 20). Describing Shakespeare's language as 'at once overloaded and astonishingly rapid, giving the impression of a torrent of words [. . .] stuffed full with figurative expressions', Palfrey recognizes the difficulty for a reader, or audience, in absorbing all that is within Shakespeare's writing. He specifies that 'this can be annoying because his words are not offered as exquisite linguistic miniatures to be pored over [. . .] they are dramatic speeches, spoken in the course of unfolding action' (ibid.: 21). However, Palfrey underlines that through education, enjoyment arises from overcoming such resistances and an increased understanding.

The Rationale for the Focus on Shakespeare

It is regularly asserted that in an actor training syllabus, Shakespeare should play a central role as it can provoke a significant advance in student learning due to the requirements for intellectual, physical, and technical proficiencies (Berry 1993: 9; Hall 2003: 12; Rodenburg 2002: 14; Carey & Clark Carey 2010: xvi). I believe that Shakespeare's text is a superb tool to work with. His understanding of the human condition encapsulated within exquisite language can illuminate, excite, and nourish the mind and soul while engendering a physical impact. 'It makes me shake, this language,' muses the actor Ben Kingsley when delving into Shakespeare. 'It is so strong, that if I let it push me, it's like getting a little vial of something and whacking it into your arm. It works on you' (Kingsley, in Barton 1984: 60).

Moreover, the 'otherness' of Shakespeare's language uncovers a paradox in the work of those with dyslexia, in my experience. My annual teaching of the Shakespeare unit has revealed evidence that, for some of those with dyslexia, a confrontation with Shakespeare's text can initially block access to meaning and inhibit cognition and fluent reading, yet can also provoke a unique blossoming of artistic modalities. Although Shakespeare's language can initiate obstacles for those with dyslexia, his abundant word pictures and action-filled images, wrapped within metaphor, simile, and personification, can lead to interdisciplinary innovation in style.

In his creation of images, Shakespeare regularly transforms motionless or abstract ideas into verbal images of physical movement (Spurgeon 1935: 51). This 'action language' is illustrated in phrases such as 'make him bite the law by th'nose' (Claudio in *Measure for Measure*, Act III, Scene i), meaning to flout the law, or 'if I must die I will encounter darkness like a bride and hug it in my arms' (ibid.), where Claudio attempts to convince himself that he is psychologically ready to die. The animated word pictures not only stimulate the imagination and emotions, but also lend themselves to a vivid interpretation of the text through concrete embodiment.

However, in their study of changes in the brain when reading Shakespeare, psychologist James L. Keidel et al. (2013) have labeled Shakespeare's language as a 'neurological tempest' because of his surprising idiosyncrasies in syntax, grammar, and word order. In an investigation using functional magnetic resonance imaging to register what is happening in the brain, participants listened to sentences taken from *Othello*, such as Iago's line 'O, tis the spite of hell [. . .] to lip a wanton in a secure couch, and to suppose her chaste' (Act IV, Scene i). These lines contain two examples of the functional shift: the use of the noun 'lip' as a verb, meaning to kiss/copulate, and the use of the adjective 'wanton' as a noun to represent Desdemona (Keidel et al. 2013: 914). Keidel et al. found that Shakespeare's shift in grammar function triggers a surprise effect and an alteration in the neuroanatomical activation of brain hemispheres, demanding more work. Although the semantics and syntax are classically processed in the left hemisphere of the brain, when reading Shakespeare, Keidel et al. (2013) state that brain networks involved in processing the non-literal aspects of language are turned on in the right hemisphere of the brain. Interestingly, Maryanne Wolf (2008: 186) describes several studies that show dyslexics using more of the right side of the brain when reading than the left. Davis (2008: 267–268) emphasizes that Shakespeare's frequent shifts of grammatical function can excite the imagination, but also deviate from expectation and conventions: for example, where the adjective is energized into a verb, such as 'him have you *madded*' (Quarto 4.2, 40–44), or there is a change of a noun into a verb, as in 'Nay *godded* me indeed' (*Coriolanus* 5.3, 10–11). Davis suggests that such functional shifts produce 'a sudden electrical charge in the brain by [. . .] getting closer to the very roots of sudden mental-verbal formation [. . .] more primal in meaning-making' (2008: 267). Although such language adaptation is 'electrical' for some, for others who are less used to listening and reading in the Shakespearean style and cannot grasp the words, it can become nonsensical.

Shakespeare and Dyslexia

My annual teaching of the Shakespeare unit with second-year acting degree students has highlighted the considerable barriers dyslexic individuals can encounter, and that established approaches to working on Shakespeare make little provision for those with dyslexia who might function more effectively using modalities outside of conventional procedures. The unfamiliar language and multi-inferences of meanings inherent in Shakespeare's writing can interfere with the guessing of words or meaning, which is sometimes a survival tactic when reading used by dyslexic individuals. Furthermore, attempting to retain meaning, accuracy of word, and pronunciation in working memory, especially when reading aloud under observation by peers and teachers, can provoke extreme stress. In describing their reading experiences with Shakespeare, my dyslexic students have repeated statements such as: 'the more I panic the more I stumble', 'I need to practice it ten times before I am able to see the words', 'I cannot second guess this language', 'I can't remember how to pronounce it', 'I have to watch someone else do it first so I can remember it', and 'to me it is just black marks on the page' (research participants' comments, 2008–2016).

There are several prominent books that concentrate on an actor's approach to speaking Shakespeare. The majority of them center on meticulous observation of the language and its influence on acting choices. These books are indispensable resources of technical knowledge for actors who work with Shakespeare. However, for those with dyslexia, the books and their multifactorial techniques imparted about acting Shakespeare can trigger cognitive overload and anxiety in those that struggle with reading and the attendant difficulties that dyslexia contributes. An example of this emphasis on achieving accurate outcomes in reading is given by theatre director Adrian Noble (2010: 4–5). Noble specifies that in order to learn how to act the text, we have to 'learn how to read the text'. The 'rules' must be learnt; the 'do's and don'ts of the craft', which include the essential seven basic elements. These are:

- Apposition (the juxtaposition of words, phrases, and ideas)
- Metaphor (similes, comparisons)
- Meter and pulse
- Line endings (rhyme, alliteration, and assonance)
- Word play
- Vocabulary
- Shape and structure.

All of these are examples of an intellectual study of the form of the written word, with which the reader must become familiar in order to read a passage with effect, Noble advises. This advice is advantageous for those actors who possess erudite literacy abilities in grabbling with the word on the page. Sometimes, Noble includes a purely practical approach, as when instructing the reader to:

> follow the trail of the imagery. At first it is probably best to stress, or even over stress, the words [. . .] try to become more playful with the language. Imagine it's a ball thrown between the two of you, or it's a tennis match only with words.
>
> *(2010: 42)*

This is a developmental exercise for those who can abandon their thought processes to playful exploration, but for those who are struggling to catch the words, and therefore the metaphorical 'ball', while also attempting to remember the language 'rules', such tennis matches are ambitious, and the ball is likely to be dropped.

Dyslexia-friendly Instruction in Shakespeare

There is, however, one book on acting Shakespeare's text whose initial sixty-seven pages of exercises stand out as being dyslexia-friendly when put into practice. In *Freeing Shakespeare's Voice*, voice and acting practitioner Kristin Linklater takes a radically different approach to the text, stating, 'my guide to speaking Shakespeare is experiential rather than prescriptive' (1992: 1). When I have taught Linklater's exercise sequence based on Shakespeare's *Sonnet 65*, students with dyslexia become animated and more confident when speaking the text. In this exercise, Linklater does not introduce the text through literary rules, which must be understood, learned, and demonstrated. She guides the participant through the text in a sequence of progressive stages, encouraging an idiosyncratic, experimental response to the language. Gradually, through a sequential procedure, the phonemes and their sounds in the words are deconstructed and reconstructed, and then each word is singularly explored, building up into phrases and whole lines, until the sonnet is re-assembled. Layers of personal interpretation and imagery linked directly to the words are consciously accumulated. There is no danger that the participant might not be able to succeed with the task of absorbing or delivering Shakespeare's words, as each individual response, if coming from what Linklater has termed, the 'vertical plane' (the heart to the head), is deemed relevant (ibid.: 30).

It is beneficial for those with dyslexia to work in an environment where there is no right or wrong, and to explore the sounds which make up words: 'many poor readers – adults as well as children – experience problems in articulating phonemically complex or multi-syllabic words' (Beaton 2004: 101). In her description of what is imperative in speaking Shakespeare, voice coach Patsy Rodenburg identifies exactly what some dyslexics find hard to achieve, saying:

the whole of every word is important. You must speak the beginning, middle and end of each one, effortlessly – not swallowing word ends or skidding over multi-syllabic words. The physical nature of the word is the fabric of the play.

(2002: 72)

Linklater places an emphasis on the power of the visual sense, color associations, and the accuracy of the images connected with the words. She frequently suggests a realization of the text in terms of pictures or painting, underlining the effect on the actor when speaking Shakespeare (Linklater 1992: 33). She remarks:

Images are intrinsic to words [. . .]. Introduce the sense of sight to the meaning of a word and images will emerge and multiply. Images lead more directly, albeit more explicably, to emotion than logical reasoning does and the speaker of poetry can trust that such a deep instinctive connection is the wellspring for a true understanding of the text.

(ibid.)

In advocating learning skills for those with dyslexia, McLoughlin and Leather (2013: 127) recommend that tasks should be made manageable (to reduce the load on working memory and dual-tasking), multisensory (to increase the possibilities of learning), and memorable (to support recall). Reid (2003: 206) includes the practice of repetition and over learning. McLoughlin and Leather (2013: 118) also propose the utilization of visual images as an effective learning tool for those with dyslexia. Although Linklater has not aimed to especially support those with dyslexia, her breaking down of the sonnet into chunks, requiring both subvocalized and vocalized expression, the repetition of words, the provision of time, the utilization of motor movements, and inclusion of writing the words down, with an emphasis on the senses (especially the visual), encapsulate all of the recommended factors.

The Technical Process of Reading

According to Maryanne Wolf (Director of the Centre for Reading and Language Research at Tufts University), the brain was never meant to read, and reading was only invented a few thousand years ago (2010: 3). The concept of *neuronal recycling*, which is laid out in cognitive neuroscientist Stanislas Dehaene's book *Reading in the Brain* (2009), posits that a part of the brain's architecture that might originally have been devoted to a particular function can be recycled for another function, such as a cultural invention, which has moved away from being naturally found in nature, like the act of reading. Dehaene opines that an ancient function in the brain can be retrained or orientated into another function that is useful in the current cultural context. The original region or network of the brain cannot be too radically changed away from its original properties or use, but the new cultural learning can adapt around the original genetic bias. The new cultural invention has to find an ecological 'niche' in the brain where the original function can be modified for the new function (ibid.: 144–148). Therefore, a cultural act like reading has found a cerebral niche in the visual cortex, which has a primary purpose of seeing for survival, prior to the act of reading. Seidenberg (2017: 12–13) emphasizes the importance of reading for enhancing human cognition, our ability to thrive, and to record and communicate our knowledge with depth and quality. In attempting to define the act of reading, Wolf describes it as an 'almost instantaneous fusion of cognitive, linguistic, and affective processes; multiple brain regions; and billions of neurons' (2008: 145). (This description links with the ideas of neural reuse discussed in Chapter 3.)

Reading and the brain is an immensely complicated area, and much of it is highly scientific in nature. However, it is valuable for the voice or acting teacher to have some understanding of and familiarity with the dominant theories of reading. Therefore, overviews of the technical process of reading and the dominant theories of reading are supplied in end note 1,[1] where there are references to literature that specializes in the science of reading which can be scrutinized further for those who wish to know more.

Conclusion: The Actor's Presentation of the Authentic Self

Critically, the research investigations in this book do not focus on a strict adherence to the assigned 'rules of the text' to be extracted from a close study of Shakespeare's writing. This is not because I do not think they are important in the playing of Shakespeare, but because of their propensity to create more barriers for those with dyslexia. Consequently, much of my focus centers on a deep-seated component of what acting can entail, such as the 'confrontation and plumbing of the human potential' (Harrop 1992: 81). In an analysis of the psychology of acting, Harrop refers to acting as a search for the self through the playing of differing roles, possibly a testing out of many selves, with the merging of the 'I' of the character with the 'I' of the actor (ibid.: 27). He underlines that the actor's authenticity depends on the integrity of the performing self.

Ideas about the 'self' is an enormous topic, with multifarious theories analyzing what the self and authenticity of self might actually be.[2] I am including some ideas about selfhood here, which can only touch on a few of those viewpoints. For those who study voice and expressive human sound, the authentic, 'true' voice is deemed to originate from deep within the psyche and body, 'without artifice, [. . .] posturing [. . .] or masking' (Cooke 2009: 174). It is this authenticity of voice and integrity of self that I listen out for in the reading, speaking, and performance of my students with dyslexia. Acting practitioner Robert Benedetti usefully illuminates the term *authentic* for the actor, which assists in explaining my concern for those acting students with dyslexia where an expression of an autonomous 'I' can be impeded in their work. He explains:

> whatever 'style' of theatre you are engaged in, your work must be *authentic*. This word literally means *self-authorship*, or *to be the author of yourself* [. . .]. Your deepest task is to be *trans-formed*, to allow your total personal energies to flow into a new form [. . .] to [. . .] *re-author* yourself so as to serve a precise and meaningful artistic function within the demands of your play.
>
> *(Benedetti, cited in Worthen 1997: 95)*

Neuroscientist Antonio Damasio defines the sense of personhood as the *autobiographical self*, wherein the essence of an individual is built from their innate and acquired personality traits, intelligence, and memories of unique personal episodes set within their social and cultural experience. They thereby construct a picture of who they are and where they fit through these memories. This image of self can be remodeled according to their experiences and how they reconstruct them in autobiographical memory (Damasio 2000: 222–230). In *the looking glass theory of self* (Cooley 1902, in Hood 2012: 51), individuals search for confirmation of who they are through what the world reflects back to them, and the response of others to them. Such attentiveness to others' opinions can have a painful and negative influence for those with dyslexia when working in a public arena such as acting and reading in classes. Listening to their inner voice of self-criticism, they can often look to the external reflection of others as a judgment of their ability and value. Vannini and Franzese (2008), in an analysis of an authenticity of self, include people's emotional experiences of being true or untrue to themselves in relation to what their idea of their true self is. They underline that this is nuanced and bound up with aspects of identity, roles, values, and personal goals. They specify that there is a conflict between authenticity of self and a need for social approval. They also identify one aspect of self as involving deep psychological needs, internal feelings, desires, and spirituality (ibid.: 1624). It is this latter aspect that I am alert to, as expressed through the voice and speech in those with dyslexia, with an overall awareness of the holistic influences shaping their voices and communication.

The Following Chapters in Part II of the Book

This search for a freedom of personal response, in a transaction between the author (Shakespeare), the text (carrier of representative signs), the reader/actor (as author and creator), and finally the receiver (the audience), brought about through the lived experience of the words (especially in those with dyslexia), is the subject of the following chapters of this book. This is investigated through practical trials with acting students assessed as dyslexic, in their work on Shakespeare's text, as laid out in Part II.

KEY POINTS OF CHAPTER 5

- The foundational principles and practice in honoring the word, and technical skill underlying the training in Shakespeare
- The recent history of teaching Shakespeare in actor training in the UK
- Discussion surrounding the authority of Shakespeare as author and the rules of the text, versus the reader/actor as creator of the text
- The rationale for using Shakespeare as a practical research laboratory for those with dyslexia
- The grammatical shifts of language that Shakespeare uses, how his word use can surprise the reader and alter activation in the right and left hemispheres of the brain
- How we read – the technical process and the dominant theories of reading
- The actor's voicing of an authentic self, what that might mean, and a freedom of response to the text

---

Notes

1 A predominant theory regarding the reading process is the *Dual Route Approach* (Coltheart 2005: 8). This theory posits there are two routes in accessing the word: the *lexical* and *non-lexical*. The *lexical* route involves the reader recognizing the visual appearance of the word and then finding its representation stored in the lexical memory, with immediate access to its meaning and pronunciation. The *non-lexical* route means that readers build up the word through relating each grapheme to its phoneme (or cluster of letters), and thus finally, through the sounds of the word, arriving at its pronunciation and meaning (see Seidenberg 2017: 124–125).

Alternatively, another influential theory is the *Connectionist model* (Plaut 2005: 24–26). This theory attempts to depict the co-ordination of processes and representations involved in reading aloud, lexical tasks, and learning. The basic components are the three units of orthography (written form), phonology (spoken form), and semantics (meaning), making a triangle, with other hidden and unnamed units surrounding them. These units are connected through an architectural neural network, continually connecting and firing together, encoding internal representations and outputs. This model is also involved in learning. During the procedure, there can be a slow build-up of connections, increasing in accuracy and strength, leading to skilled performance.

A description of the practical act of reading is summarized in the following passage. Most of the reading act occurs within the thinking brain, but the eye perceives the symbols on the page. According to Crowder and Wagner (1992: 10), when reading, our eyes sweep across the page in movements called saccades. In between each saccade, our eye fixes on the print and can take in approximately two words per fixation and about ten letters to the right beyond the immediate eye span. Seidenberg (2017: 66–68) explains that only seven or eight letters are seen clearly in each fixation, and thereafter our perception of the other letters becomes hazier. It is the fovea in the eye that has the most cones and therefore has the acutest perception in identifying letters. As we see each word, we recognize and decode the phonemes, access meaning and comprehend the context (Mayer 2003: 33). This happens many times across the page in a jumpy manner. Sometimes the eyes move backwards briefly (*regressions*) if we have not comprehended, or to re-read. The size of our saccades and the time sent in pausing with our fixations and the number of them determine the amount of time we take to read (Seidenberg 2017: 63). To make constructions of meaning as we go along, we have to remember the beginning of the sentence and hold that within our short-term memory until we have collected all the information within the whole sentence (Underwood & Batt 1996: 3). As we read, we use the *phonological loop* to convert the words into an immediate internal subvocal representation so that the information is not forgotten and can be transferred from short-term memory into working memory before being put, if required, into long-term memory (Baddeley 2007: 16). Baddeley's hypothesis on working memory and the *phonological loop* is commonly alluded to in the literature on dyslexia (McDougall & Donohoe 2002; Mortimore 2008; Reid 2009).

2 For an informative study about dyslexia and self-concept in university students identified as dyslexic, see Pollak (2005).

References

Baddeley, A. (2007). *Working Memory, Thought, and Action*. Oxford, UK: Oxford University Press.

Barton, J. (1984). *Playing Shakespeare*. London: Methuen.

Beaton, A. (2004). *Dyslexia, Reading and the Brain*. Hove, UK: Psychology Press.

Berry, C. (1993). *The Actor and the Text*. London: Virgin Books.

Block, G. (2013). *Speaking the Speech: An Actor's Guide to Shakespeare*. London: Nick Hern.

Callow, S. (1984). *Being an Actor*. London: Penguin Books.

Carey, D. & Clark Carey, R. (2010). *The Verbal Arts Workbook*. London: Methuen Drama.

Carey, D. & Clark Carey, R. (2015). *The Shakespeare Workbook and Video: A Practical Course for Actors*. London: Bloomsbury.

Coltheart, M. (2005). Modelling reading: the dual-route approach. *In*: Snowling, M.J. & Hulme, C. (eds.) *The Science of Reading: A Handbook*. Oxford, UK: Blackwell, pp. 6–23.

Cooke, R. (2009). Breath, theatrical authenticity and the healing arts. *In*: Boston, J. & Cooke, R. (eds.) *Breath in Action*. London: Jessica Kingsley, pp. 173–182.

Crowder, R, G. & Wagner, R.K. (1992). *The Psychology of Reading*. Oxford, UK: Oxford University Press.

Damasio, A. (2000). *The Feeling of What Happens*. London: Vintage.

Davis, P. (2008). Syntax and pathways. *Interdisciplinary Science Reviews*, 33:4, 265–277.

Dehaene, S. (2009). *Reading in the Brain*. New York: Viking.

Hall, P. (2000). *Exposed by the Mask*. London: Oberon Books.

Hall, P. (2003). *Shakespeare's Advice to the Players*. London: Oberon Books.

Harrop, J. (1992). *Acting*. London: Routledge.

Hood, B. (2012). *The Self Illusion*. London: Constable.

Keidel, J.L., Davis, P.M., Gonzalez-Diaz, V., Martin, C.D., & Thierry, G. (2013). How Shakespeare tempests the brain: neuroimaging insights. *Cortex*, 49, 913–919.

Linklater, K. (1992). *Freeing Shakespeare's Voice*. New York: Theatre Communications Group.

Martin, J. (1991). *Voice in Modern Theatre*. London: Routledge.

Mayer, R.E. (2003). *Learning and Instruction*. Upper Saddle River, NJ: Merrill Prentice Hall.

McDougall, S. & Donohoe, R. (2002). Reading ability and memory span: long-term memory contributions to span for good and poor readers. *Reading and Writing: An Interdisciplinary Journal*, 15, 359–387.

McLoughlin, D. & Leather, C. (2013). *The Dyslexic Adult*, 2nd ed. Chichester, UK: Whurr Publications.

Mortimore, T. (2008). *Dyslexia and Learning Style*, 2nd ed. Chichester, UK: John Wiley and Sons.

Noble, A. (2010). *How to Do Shakespeare*. London: Routledge.

Palfrey, S. (2005). *Doing Shakespeare*. London: Arden Shakespeare.

Plaut, D. (2005). Connectionist approaches to reading. *In*: Snowling, M.J. & Hulme, C. (eds.) *The Science of Reading: A Handbook*. Oxford, UK: Blackwell, pp. 24–38.

Pollak, D. (2005). *Dyslexia, the Self and Higher Education*. Stoke on Trent, UK: Trentham Books.

Poulet, G. (1980). Criticism and the experience of interiority. *In*: Tompkins, J. (ed.) *Reader-response Criticism*. London: John Hopkins University Press.

Reid, G. (2003). *Dyslexia: A Practitioner's Handbook*, 3rd ed. Chichester, UK: John Wiley.

Reid, G. (2009). *The Routledge Companion to Dyslexia*. Oxford, UK: Routledge.

Rodenburg, P. (2002). *Speaking Shakespeare*. London: Methuen Drama.

Rokison, A. (2009). *Shakespearean Verse-speaking*. Cambridge, UK: Cambridge University Press.

Seidenberg, M. (2017). *Language at the Speed of Sight*. New York: Basic Books.

Spurgeon, C. (1935). *Shakespeare's Imagery*. Cambridge, UK: Cambridge University Press.

Underwood, G. & Batt, V. (1996). *Reading and Understanding*. Oxford, UK: Blackwell.

Vannini, P. & Franzese, A. (2008). The authenticity of self: conceptualization, personal experience, and practice. *Sociology Compass*, 2:5, 1621–1637.

Wolf. M. (2008). *Proust and the Squid: The Story and Science of the Reading Brain*. Cambridge, UK: Icon Books.

Worthen, W.B. (1996). Staging 'Shakespeare'. *In*: Bulman, J.C. (ed.) *Shakespeare, Theory, and Performance*. London: Routledge, pp. 12–28.

Worthen, W.B. (1997). *Shakespeare and the Authority of Performance*. Cambridge, UK: Cambridge University Press.

PART II

The Investigatory Practice and Teaching Strategies One to Six

6

THE THEORETICAL PERSPECTIVES AND METHODOLOGY

Attaining a *Verstehen* through Action Research Underpinned by Case Study

Introduction to My Study

Part II of this book includes descriptions of a selection of individual acting students with dyslexia, their processing and performance of the text, and the practical research and teaching work I embarked on with them as part of my study. It presents six teaching strategies that I have developed out of my practical trials, aiming at supporting neurodiversity and dyslexia. It explains how, when, and why these strategies were arrived at and includes accounts of the trials to test their effectiveness in supporting dyslexia with the participants, and in some cases, within the general cohort of dyslexic and non-dyslexic students. Finally, my findings from the study are outlined and recommendations given.

The work explores the questions:

- Does the use of visual and kinesthetic constructs facilitate acting students with dyslexia in the reading, comprehension, and acting of Shakespeare? If so, how, why, and when might such tools and strategies be utilized?
- Can the imprecise articulation of some acting students with dyslexia be assisted by drawing, artwork, or the physicalization of concept symbols associated with the written text?
- How might pedagogical practices be adapted to support the learning strengths of some acting students with dyslexia?

The overall aims of the study were:

- To remove the barriers entrenched within some teaching practices for those with dyslexia when engaging with complex texts such as Shakespeare

- To acquire a deep knowledge about dyslexia in order to inform pedagogical support for students with dyslexia
- To familiarize myself with the range of weaknesses and strengths of some individuals with dyslexia, and how these might be utilized or by-passed
- To promote autonomy in engaging with Shakespeare's text for those with dyslexia
- To encourage individuals with dyslexia to construct personal strategies to enable their reading, acting, and accessing of information from the text
- To support the development of an artistic language of performance – in particular, creative expression originating from the presence of dyslexia and neurodiversity

Matters of Ethics

First, it is important to highlight that all the dyslexic participants have given their permission for examples of their work, their images, and use of first names to be included in this book. In doing this, they stated that they take pride in having ownership of their work, and wish to contribute to helping others with dyslexia. One participant emphasized:

> I don't feel it's something I need to hide, or feel ashamed of. I went through sixteen years of schooling without my dyslexia being picked up on, and that was hard because I felt stupid a lot of the time. But after being diagnosed, I realised that it wasn't stupidity, it was just that I had a different way of way of learning and responded better to a less conventional way of teaching. This made me more confident as a person as well as in my work. So I'd like to help anyone else who may have gone through a similar situation.
>
> *(personal communication, 2016)*

The Setting, Participants, and Material

The focus is primarily on a selection of acting students who were research participants during my six-year doctorate study that concentrated especially on dyslexic acting students and their work with Shakespeare and text. (However, it also includes work that has developed beyond the doctorate study, with a broader range of students.) The accompanying strategies offered for teaching approaches originate out of those studies and my continuing teaching practice. The research participants were all second-year acting students on the Acting (Hons) degree course at the Arts University Bournemouth, and all had been assessed as dyslexic by an educational psychologist. The practical studies were mostly carried out during the nine-week Shakespeare unit annually, with changes of student participants assessed as dyslexic.

The Shakespeare unit explores methods of acting Shakespeare's text through class exercises, monologues, scene study, and a final assessed performance of a scene to an audience. Alongside the Shakespeare acting classes, there is an accompanying Voice unit. Continuing to work on vocal quality and speech, this Voice unit also aims to develop knowledge of Shakespeare's written form and the technical and expressive requirements of the speaking of classical text, and includes an assessed performance of a Shakespeare sonnet. For both units, a wide variety of Shakespeare texts are used as working material.

The Theoretical Perspective

My theoretical perspective is situated within a constructivist paradigm. This is when meaning and knowledge is not discovered in an objective sense, or received passively by the learner, but is actively constructed by the teacher and the student (Waring & Evans 2015: 36). My approach is one of *verstehen* (to understand), and that of *sich miteinander verstehen*, which the philosopher Hans-Georg Gadamer explains as 'to come to an understanding with each other' (1997: 180). Patton describes *verstehen* as a 'placing of emphasis on the human capacity to know and understand others through empathetic introspection and reflection based on direct observation of and interaction with people' (2002: 52).

Methodology

My research methodology is that of action research integrated with case study. The nature of action research, wherein a problem is identified, possible solutions imagined, and action taken with an evaluation of outcomes (McNiff 2013), provided an opportunity to explore practical changes in my teaching. Adoption of a case study approach enabled me to capture the lived experience of individuals with dyslexia, recording their words and actions. As there is little documented knowledge capturing the experiences of acting students with dyslexia in their accessing of classical or linguistically complex texts, nor many teachers' testimonies about facilitating their predicaments, I think it imperative that I (and the reader) *listen/attend* to what my participants say, *notice* how they are behaving, and that their words and actions are captured in a thick description (Geertz 1973). Clifford Geertz's label of a 'thick description' is about situating them in their context, so that constructions of meaning are gained through 'seeing the full picture' – an understanding depending on the situation in which they are happening (ibid.: 9).

In consideration of the methodology of action research, many teachers possess a tacit knowing in their practice, built through experience and skill, an implicit 'knowing more than they can tell' (Polanyi 1966; Prior 2012: 193). Nevertheless, if aiming to improve their teaching, they can reflect more deeply on their actions-in-practice, asking themselves: What am I doing? Why am I doing it? What is the effect of my actions? What did I learn through my actions? What action could I take to lead to a different outcome? This type of knowing-in-action, reflection-on-action, and reflection-in-action (Schön 1987) is characteristic of acting and teaching practices, and is close to the methods inherent in action research. In order to find some answers to my research questions, I had to ask questions such as: What is happening here? How are the participants affected by the experience? Why are they affected? What might be done to improve the situation? To assist in making sense of my own interpretations, I have drawn from the findings of others when they appeared to bear a relationship with my own. Working from the context-specific experience of my participants, I have lifted these theories from the situation in which they were originally presented, stripped them down to their basic components, examined them for their accounts, and through associative links, made connections with my own work.

Matters of Validation

To engender a credibility about knowledge claims, Lincoln and Guba underline the need for a prolonged engagement in the field to understand the phenomenon within the context in which it is embedded, so that it might be 'thoroughly appreciated and understood' (1985: 310). They include the necessity for a 'persistent observation', so that one might identify those elements within the situation that are most relevant to the problem being pursued (ibid.: 304). To assess the knowledge claims resulting from action research, McNiff (2017: 122) includes the role of the critical friend as valuable for peer-validation in observing the work, considering the evidence and data gathered and to offer advice. A teaching colleague who was a professional actor and member of the Royal Shakespeare Company for several years, with an expertise in teaching both Shakespeare and Stanislavski's methods, served in this role for my study and provided critical feedback. Throughout my research workshops and performances, my critical friend observed and commented on almost all of the work of the participants. His contribution fulfilled the requirement for a 'prolonged engagement' and 'persistent observation' as he had obtained a knowledge of the participants and their work throughout my research trials over the years of my study.

Crucially, an essential source of validation was gathered from the dyslexic participants, as the voices of those concerned and affected in the research. Carr and Kemmis and Simons allude to the participants in the research as providing a judicious perspective about the work, 'ensuring accurate and adequate multiple validation of events and experiences' (Simons 2009: 131) and 'the stringent test of participant confirmation' (Carr & Kemmis 1986: 91). As the research participants are at the very center of my research from which I have drawn my suppositions, organized my activities, and assembled my findings, I have continually returned to them for their evaluations, and the formation of my actions and conclusions, through interview, practical work, and discussion.

Conclusion

Narratives are an important device in action research as they help to construct a 'knowing' and 'telling', a making sense of personal experiences, and translating that sense-making to others in a recounting of reflective practice. The telling of the experience is framed within a specific context and situation in relating 'how the participants acted, learned, hoped or despaired, and, most importantly changed' (Toledano & Anderson 2017). By conveying the participants' views, difficulties, and successes, and my own pedagogical journey throughout my narrative descriptions, I believe I fulfill the four conditions that the teaching and learning educationalist Renuka Vithal has declared essential within the use of 'vignettes of crucial descriptions' (Vithal, in Cotton & Griffiths 2007: 459). As set out by Vithal, the four conditions which should be present are that of: *transparency*, which enables the reader to see through the language of description into the context to stimulate critique, *transformacy*, which has the capacity to provoke transformation in the reader by stimulating thought and action, *generativity*, where the descriptions engender theory which can influence practice, and finally *exemplarity*, where the description connects the complexity of the content with the complexity of theory.

Next Chapter

The following chapters introduce the practical investigations of the study, preceded by chapters discussing the underlying theory. The next chapter examines the proposition that for some acting students identified as dyslexic, a visual construct approach may assist them in accessing the content of Shakespeare's text and enable their assured reading of the words. It explores the use of drawing in informing actors' characterizations and their grasp of the text. The ideas of actors and artists who have declared themselves dyslexic and their visual methods to assuage it are discussed.

References

Carr, W. & Kemmis, S. (1986). *Becoming Critical*. London: RoutledgeFarmer.

Cotton, T. & Griffiths, M. (2007). Action research, stories and practical philosophy. *Educational Action Research*, 15:4, 545–560.

Gadamer, H.G. (1997). *Truth and Method*. New York: Continuum.

Geertz, C. (1973). *The Interpretation of Cultures*. New York: Basic Books.

Lincoln, S. & Guba, E. (1985). *Naturalistic Inquiry*. London: SAGE Publications.

McNiff, J. (2013). *Action Research*, 3rd ed. London: Routledge.

McNiff, J. (2017). *Action Research for Professional Development*, 2nd ed. Church Stretton, UK: September Books.

Patton, M. (2002). *Qualitative Research and Evaluation Methods*, 3rd ed. London: SAGE Publications.

Polanyi, M. (1966). *The Tacit Dimension*. Chicago, IL: University of Chicago Press.

Prior, R. (2012). *Teaching Actors*. Bristol, UK: Intellect Books.
Schön, D. (1987). *Educating the Reflective Practitioner*. San Francisco, CA: Jossey-Bass.
Simons, H. (2009). *Case Study Research in Practice*. London: SAGE Publications.
Toledano, N. & Anderson, A.R. (2017). Theoretical reflections on narrative in action research. *Action Research*, 22 December. Available from: https://openair.rgu.ac.uk/handle/10059/2644. Accessed 7 May 2019.
Waring, M. & Evans, C. (2015). *Understanding Pedagogy*. London: Routledge.

7

FINDING THE WAY IN

Picture Thinking

Introduction

My own ideas for those with dyslexia in using drawing and storyboarding for
Shakespeare's text had been independently devised through a close study of my
students with dyslexia long before my discovery of West's, Essley's, and Everitt's
comparable drawing storyboard initiatives discussed in this chapter. My methods had been conceived directly from my observations of my dyslexic students'
personal working practices in classes, and as described by my dyslexic students
in focus group discussions when sharing their methods to engage with written
words. In interview, all my research participants have indicated a visual preference (underpinned by a kinesthetic learning style[1]) as their chosen way into
grasping the text. To broaden my understanding about why many of my dyslexic
students and research participants utilize forms of drawing, graphical symbol-
making and color-coding as an aid to their perception of the content of the
written text, I have searched the literature for similar processes used by others in
the world of acting or teaching.

In his book the *Year of the King*, actor Anthony Sher (1985) gives an account
of his building of the character of Richard III, a role he played at the Royal
Shakespeare Company in 1984. A fundamental element of Sher's process in coming to create his characters involves the use of his considerable skills in drawing
and painting. Through a visually dominant medium, Sher sets about capturing
aspects of his imaginative conception of the character, inspired by things he notes
in the environment (Sher 1989). Sher's research for his creation of Richard III
included his sketching of geographical land structures, the muscular anatomy of
the bull, the contortions of the physically disabled, and individual facial characteristics that might encapsulate elements of Richard III's personality and appearance.

Sher's working drawings are realized in the moment of seeing, or built up at a later point (during rehearsals or after performance) through association and imagination. These drawings are Sher's research data towards acquiring a deeply layered realization of the man he is to inhabit, to be transmuted through the channels of his body. Possessing accomplished artistic skills, Sher's paintings and drawings are as finely executed as his acted characters. His drawings, dispersed through his diary records in the *Year of the King*, reveal his fantasies on the page. However, the image-making process does more than that. There is a kind of interplay between the drawer and the drawn: as the personification comes into being through the emerging sketches on the page, it speaks back to its creator, influencing its formation. Sher's visual concept of the role is apparent in his meta-phorical painting of Richard III, featured on the front cover of the book. The depicted creature, with a black spider-like body, sporting a bull's muscular shoul-ders, topped with the crowned head of a king, scuttling across the floor on thin spider legs, exhibits Sher's visually led 'melting pot' (1989: 38). Sher (1985: 118) explains that Shakespeare's word paintings distributed through the text, wherein he compares Richard to a variety of 'hell bound' animals, are the inspiration for his depictions. However, other than describing his own processes for using art in creation of his characters (Sher 1989), he does not elaborate on any other benefits for the actor in using visual modalities to expand theatrical communication, nor advantages which might be found by entering the text through another medium, such as drawing or painting. This cross-disciplinary approach to acting is idiosyn-cratic to Sher's multiplicities of artistic talents and the power of the visual image in the evolving materiality of his acting work.

In considering the value of art as research, Ross Prior has referred to the crucial role of the reflective sketchbook for some performers, recording and illuminating ideas, and analyzing blocks. Through the use of a 'non-verbal, picto-rial, idiomatic, symbolic and metaphoric' living document created throughout a performer's devising journey, the performer can refer back to this pre-verbal man-uscript, enabling re-examination and future creation (Prior 2013: 61). Although these practices of drawing, visual recording, and referencing utilized by Sher and alluded to by Prior bear a relationship with my research participants' employ-ment of a visual language, there are also major differences which underlie their primary purpose. See endnote 2 for some other examples of drawing or image-led exercises utilized by voice teachers Berry (1993, 2001, 2008) and Carey & Clark Carey (2010).[2]

The Views of Some of Those with Dyslexia, and Visual Approaches

It has frequently been postulated that many of those with dyslexia develop a domi-nant visual modality of processing, and there are strong examples of this presented in some of the literature about dyslexia (West 1997; Davis 1997; Morgan and

Klein 2000; West 2007; Essley 2008; Mortimore 2008; Bacon & Handley 2010; Grant 2010; Alexander-Passe 2010; Schneps et al. 2011; McLoughlin & Leather 2013; Leveroy 2013, 2015). Educational psychologist David Grant (2010: 91) emphasizes that it is important to avoid making generalized statements about those with specific learning differences. Nevertheless, when undertaking psychological assessments of students with dyslexia, Grant has measured their experience of visualization when reading. Through his trialed observations, Grant relates that 'both dyslexic and ADHD students reported a more vibrant visual experience when reading, and a greater number experienced imagery when reading (with only 18% of dyslexics [. . .] reporting no visualisation when reading)' (ibid.: 91). Grant asserts that 'it appears reasonable to conclude that in general visualisation is more common in dyslexics and those with ADHD than in dyspraxics or those who have no specific learning difference' (ibid.: 93).

To ascertain an accurate perception of a visual modality as the preferred medium for some dyslexics, the evidence I am engaging with below is drawn directly from some individuals in the literature who state they are dyslexic. Each of them accentuate a visual dominance in cognitive style. The actor Susan Hampshire has documented her 'life-long battle with words', focusing on her struggle with dyslexia, in her autobiography (1990). When reading a script, she emphasizes that she needs 'hours and hours of preparation' and the use of a devised 'visual code' (ibid.: 118). In personal correspondence in 2011, she emphasized that she 'always uses pictures and colours when working on a script (including Shakespeare) to jog my memory' (her underlining). Hampshire stresses that 'At first sight the average play baffles me' (1990: 118), explaining that she has to process each word individually, and therefore cannot interpret the whole piece as she reads. Using pictures and color-coding, Hampshire states she can immediately 'read' the meaning of the words. Hampshire avers that if she sees a blue color, she knows that bit of the text has a 'spiritual tone', or if red, it would be 'joyous'. In an example given in her book showing her 'visual code' that she has drawn on her television script so she might quickly access it, the symbols are subtle but none the less play an important role in assisting her ability to 'read' the text (ibid.: 121). Hampshire emphasizes that the symbols and colors must be personally developed, because if imposed by another, they would 'seem like mere words' (personal communication).

Oliver West and Roger Essley are both authors, teachers, and artists who state that they are dyslexic and who share adverse school learning experiences. They both argue for change in teaching approaches. Although hailing from different continents (Essley is from America and West from England), they have independently devised and advocated analogous visual strategies to supersede the written text. In West's book *In Search of Words* (2007), he recounts his distressing experiences at school, and criticizes the teaching methods that exclude the 'non-linear thinkers' such as himself. West describes pictures as his first language and English as his second, saying: 'the jump for a dyslexic from thoughts to words is enormous but from thoughts to pictures is natural' (ibid.: 28). In common with dyslexic teacher Ronald Davis (1997: 13), West says that if a word does not have a picture attached to it, he cannot understand it. Essley describes himself as 'an expert on school failure'. His book *Visual Tools* recounts that at school, he 'read slowly, wrote painfully, and spent a lot of time drawing' (2008: 14). When describing his limitations in engaging with written words, he employs the physically jarring metaphor 'banging into text' (ibid.: 21).

Both authors' books are born from a conviction that their methods of drawing and storyboarding can circumvent the text block. Their method of storyboarding involves drawing simplistic pictographs, using stick figures, to represent the content of the written word, almost like comic book drawings (for recording university lectures, encapsulating essay content, writing stories, and so on). Essley asserts that struggling students 'need these tools urgently' (2008: 6). West maintains that 'to accommodate visual learners [and those with dyslexia], in our educational systems we must first properly understand how they think and how they can be encouraged to release their true potential' (2007: 3). He considers that storyboarding allows those with dyslexia to use 'pictures to say what you want to say, and then translate them later into a linear form' (ibid.: 29).

Recently, dyslexic actor Lloyd Everitt, when explaining how he learns his lines for the television role he is currently playing, reported in the British Dyslexia Association publication *Dyslexia Contact* that he 'draws pictures to learn his scripts' (British Dyslexia Association 2017: 18–19). He explains that this technique is a self-taught device, and that trying to learn lines when at drama school had 'affected me greatly as I was unable to get the lines in my head and therefore was unable to express myself' (ibid.). He describes discovering the drawing technique when having to learn lines for an audition, saying: 'I had a 'spiritual' experience, when I started to draw my lines in pictures.' Everitt labels his drawing pictures of the words as a 'true blessing', and consequently, at his audition 'I knew every single word from the pictures in my mind that were ingrained there from the drawings I created' (ibid.: 18). It is striking that Everitt's drawing techniques powerfully resemble the intuitive methods used by my dyslexic participants, as depicted in the following chapters.

Furthermore, teacher Ronald Davis (who states that he is dyslexic) explains in *The Gift of Dyslexia* (1997) that in order for those with dyslexia to process a word, it must have a visual and auditory association attached to it. Davis made a personal discovery about his own learning modalities when he was a child. At school, he found that he could not remember many of the alphabetical letters. When playing with clay, he made some models of letters and discovered that the kinesthetic, haptic, and visual process enabled him to identify and memorize them (ibid.: 70). Consequently, this molding activity now plays a major role in his teaching methods for those with dyslexia. Davis recommends that a three-dimensional illustrative sculptured representation of the meaning of a word be built from clay, along with another sculpted model of the letters. As the builder constructs the word and it comes into a material existence, Davis states that it must be spoken aloud, so that an auditory, haptic, and visual image is simultaneously generated.

How Might References to 'Images' Be Understood?

The definitions of the words 'imagery' or 'image' can be ambiguous. In discussing the formation of mental images through the reading of literature, when bringing together 'the multiple references invoked by the textual signals', Iser (1978: 140) describes the reader as producing an imaginary object for which there is no outside empirical object to relate to it. He deliberates that readers become absorbed into what they have produced in their imagination: the images built are given a presence, a reality, a conception for that which is actually absent in an objective, realist sense. Readers become affected by their production of images and their entering into them. Thereby, by building a schema of images through existing knowledge, readers produce the 'truth' and the 'facts' in the text (ibid.: 136–141). For the philosopher Mark Johnson, image schemas relate to our making sense of the world through spatial sensorimotor experiences, deeply embedded in our unconscious and filtering into our language. This can be evidenced though metaphorical image schema descriptions related to movement, gravity, or a container (Johnson 2007: 136). For example, phrases such as, 'I fell in love', 'I am traveling along the journey of life', 'Onwards and upwards', and 'I dropped out of favor' all describe images of embodied movement, or a sense of being in or out of a container. The images are physical, but also evoke strong visual representations. Johnson also highlights that meaning can be transmitted visually through lines on a page that are understood without language, through embodied experience, such as jagged or curved line patterns. We can grasp the meaning of the patterns through our experience of such movements in our bodies in space and our connected feelings (Johnson 2007: 225). I can recognize that all of these aspects of body, sensory experience, thought, and image are conjured up in the research participants' drawings.

For the actor engaging with Shakespeare's text, Cicely Berry refers to two types of images: an image that 'paints an external picture' and those images that emanate from the 'inner landscape' (Berry: 1993:111). To be clear about the use of the word 'image' in this study, I am guided by Shepherd's (1978: 160–161) terminology, who distinguishes between types which support Berry's classifications.

i)   A *perceptual image* is an internal image created by the view of an external object. Shepherd maintains that these types of images, although reflecting the external, remain subjective, as they are 'internally generated'. For example, we might 'see' a table, but it is in the brain that we actually perceive it. Thus, everyone's conception of that table will be individually represented (this correlates with Berry's 'external picture').

ii)   An *entencephalic image* originates spontaneously within the brain. Phenomenally experienced, complex, and diverse in nature, such images arise from memory, imagination, and dreams. These types of images play a significant role in creative thinking (this is Berry's 'inner landscape').

In my initial interviews with my participants about their working processes and dyslexia, both types of Shepherd's visual images as a primary component of process for them became apparent.

Introduction to the First Four Participants and Their References to Their Image-led Strategies

I now introduce the first four research participants in the study. They are Participants One (Jimmy), Two (Richard), Three (Ashley), and Four (Rose). They have referred to their reliance on images in interviews, and I quote some of their comments below.

In a prior interview, Jimmy explained that when he is acting:

> It's purely images I have, always images, it's never words – it's just thoughts, feelings, and images. The image acts for an anchor for the word – the more detailed and specific to myself the image created, the more I am able to discover things about that word and then use my voice to put in what I have discovered about that word [. . .] just seeing something apart from the dreaded format of what I have been afraid of for years – just simply letters – it helps. I would rather do an image than a word.

Ashley coined an unusual term to describe what he experiences. In an interview, he stated: 'I know I'm looking at lines of text, but, as I say words, I'm kind of *non-vacant* on what I'm reading.' When I queried what he meant by the term 'non-vacant', he elucidated:

> to understand what I am reading I explain it to myself through whatever image I'm going to imagine, so in Shakespeare – I think that's why Shakespeare can be grasped by some dyslexic people because of this – it gives you so much imagery that you can imagine it. I can pick out the images that matter.

Rose described her method of scribbling her responses to the text as 'my subconscious coming out of my finger tips'. She explained that color 'kick starts my brain juices' and that 'everything in my mind is a color and everything I say is a color'. For Rose, 'the picture comes first, and then the movement'.

Richard continued with this visual reliance, saying: 'I think that nearly every word I know, I remember as a picture, not as a word.' He described having no phonological record of a word, 'I just have a picture of the word with no sound', and 'until I've got a picture of what the word looks like in my head, ways of spelling just don't make sense to me'.

The Next Chapter

In the next chapter, I describe and analyze Jimmy, Richard, and Rose's personally devised methods of accessing Shakespeare's text through image towards their acting of it. Responding to their methods in Action Research (Cycle One), I introduce Teaching Strategy One, with an account of the practical trial of the strategy and outcome.

KEY POINTS OF CHAPTER 7

- A consideration of some visual ways of interacting with the written text alluded to by some dyslexics in the literature
- Examples of various definitions of 'image'
- Introduction to four research participants identified as dyslexic.

Notes

1   *Cognitive style* is seen as the spontaneous way in which an individual processes incoming stimuli, and *learning style* is seen more in terms of the strategies a student adopts to cope with learning tasks (Mortimore 2008: 6).
2   Berry, Carey, and Clark Carey are three vocal practitioners who include the act of drawing as an exercise for working on text (Berry 1993: 190, 197, Berry 2001: 227, Berry 2008: 120; Carey & Clark Carey 2010: 35, 37, 46).
      Berry (2008: 105) has labeled her drawing exercise as a 'displacement strategy', a means to distract actors from their preconceived assumptions. In this exercise, Berry asks the actor to speak a monologue and cognitively dual task by simultaneously drawing something which is unrelated to what they are saying, such as a view from the window or the pattern on a carpet (ibid.: 120–122, 2001: 227). Suggesting that the exercise encourages actors to discover their thoughts as they speak, Berry instructs them *not* to illustrate the content of the text in their drawings. She stresses that the drawing must be an antithesis to the images in the speech (ibid.: 121). Berry (2001: 27) acknowledges that she does not understand 'why it works', but suggests that the act of drawing works as a distraction because the speaker has to search further into their mind to focus more specifically on what they are saying.
      This example demonstrates the dual-tasking requirements demanded by some of Berry's exercises that can impede those with dyslexia. Many of those with dyslexia find it hard to multi-task, especially when an assignment involves reading written text, speaking words, doing a physical task, and the use of short-term and working memory. It is common for those with dyslexia to have attention difficulties, 'springing from an inability to integrate [...] information from different sensory channels' (Broomfield & Combley 2003: 6) due to a possible lack of automaticity (Nicolson & Fawcett 2010: 68), and many have problems in any situation that involves a number of sub-skills (Mortimore 2008 111).

Carey and Clark Carey devote a whole chapter of their *Verbal Arts Workbook* to 'image', underlining that 'language creates pictures in the mind's eye that we respond to as if real' (2010: 33). They emphasize that the actor needs to activate a vivid inner landscape of images related to the text in order to transfer them to the listener (ibid.: xi). In their collection of exercises, Carey and Clark Carey have included some drawing exercises to engage with the text (ibid.: 35). The exercises utilize a balance of visual, auditory, and kinesthetic modalities. They are often paired or solitary pursuits, experiential in nature, thereby removing the pressure of a 'correct' performance of a finished product. These exercises might well be beneficial to those with dyslexia.

References

Alexander-Passe, N. (2010). *Dyslexia and Creativity: Investigations from Differing Perspectives.* New York: Nova Science.

Bacon, A. & Handley, S. (2010). Dyslexia, reasoning and the importance of visual-spatial processes. *In:* Alexander-Passe, N., ed. *Dyslexia and Creativity: Investigations from Differing Perspectives.* New York: Nova Science, pp. 25–49.

Berry, C. (1993). *The Actor and the Text.* London: Virgin Books.

Berry, C. (2001). *Text in Action.* London: Virgin Books.

Berry, C. (2008). *From Word to Play.* London: Oberon Books.

British Dyslexia Association (2017). BBC Casualty star Lloyd Everitt draws pictures to learn his scripts. *Dyslexia Contact. The Official Magazine of the British Dyslexia Association.* Bracknell, UK: British Dyslexia Association.

Broomfield, H. & Combley, M. (2003). *Overcoming Dyslexia,* 2nd edition. London: Whurr.

Carey, D. & Clark Carey, R. (2010). *The Verbal Arts Workbook.* London: Methuen Drama.

Davis, R. (1997). *The Gift of Dyslexia.* London: Souvenir Press.

Essley, R. (2008). *Visual Tools for Differentiating Reading and Writing Instruction.* New York: Scholastic Press.

Grant, D. (2010). *That's the Way I Think.* London: Routledge.

Hampshire, S. (1990). *Susan's Story.* London: Corgi Books.

Iser, W. (1978). *The Act of Reading.* London: John Hopkins University Press.

Johnson, M. (2007). *The Meaning of the Body.* Chicago, IL: University of Chicago Press.

Leveroy, D. (2013). Locating dyslexic performance: text, identity and creativity. *Research in Drama Education. The Journal of Applied Theatre and Performance,* 18:4, 374–387.

Leveroy, D. (2015). A date with the script: exploring the learning strategies of actors who are dyslexic. *Theatre, Dance and Performance Training,* 6:3, 307–322.

McLoughlin, D. & Leather, C. (2013). *The Dyslexic Adult,* 2nd edition. Chichester, UK: Whurr Publications.

Morgan, E. & Klein, C. (2000). *The Dyslexic Adult.* London: Whurr.

Mortimore, T. (2008) *Dyslexia and Learning Style,* 2nd edition. Chichester, UK: John Wiley & Sons.

Nicolson, R. & Fawcett, A. (2010). *Dyslexia, Learning and the Brain.* London: MIT Press.

Prior, R. (2013). Knowing what is known: accessing craft-based meanings in research by artists. *In:* McNiff, S. (ed.) *Art as Research.* Bristol, UK: Intellect Books, pp. 57–65.

Schneps, M., Brockmole, J.R., Rose, L.T., Pomplun, M., Sonnert, G., & Greenhill, L.J. (2011). Dyslexia linked to visual strengths useful in astronomy. *Bulletin of the American Astronomical Society,* 43.

Shepherd, R.N. (1978). Externalization of mental images and the act of creation. *In:* Rhandhawa, B.S. & Coffman, W.E. (eds.) *Visual Learning, Thinking, and Communication.* London: Academic Press, pp. 133–189.

Sher, A. (1985). *Year of the King.* London: Nick Hern.

Sher, A. (1989). *Characters.* London: Nick Hern.

West, O. (2007). *In Search of Words.* England: Oliver West.

West, T. (1997). *In the Mind's Eye: Visual Thinkers, Gifted People with Dyslexia and Other Learning Difficulties, Computer Images and the Ironies of Creativity.* New York: Prometheus Books.

8

IMAGES AS VISIBLE THOUGHT, ACTING STIMULUS, AND MNEMONIC PEGS

Action Research (Cycle One) and Teaching Strategy One

Introduction

Before I could decide on any remedial action in my teaching methods, I needed to gain some insight into how the participants approached a text and what pathways might be more accessible to them than the written word. It was therefore imperative that I listened to what my participants said and recorded their words and actions in depth. I initially narrowed my focus down to examining the function of their drawing and visual representations, and how these processes were enabling their reading and embodiment of Shakespeare's text. I asked the participants what personal methods they had devised for themselves, recorded their answers, and examined examples of their working activities in detail.

The Participants' Methods of Trans-mediation – Working between the Language of Pictures and the Language of Words

The participants' descriptions of their experience of language-as-image supports Shepherd's (1978: 160) theory of perceptual and entencephalic image-making as a phenomenological experience. It is important to recognize that the participants' use of drawing is not about achieving a high level of skill in art. The drawing is a process of exploration towards a knowing and embodiment of language and character. The visual journey functions as a cipher, capturing the words and their connotations, engendering layers of thought and feelings, eventually expressed through their spoken acting performance. To gain some understanding about how the participants are using pictures and symbols as conveyers of textual meaning, I have analyzed the relationships between the written language and the manner of visual representation they have employed. Their pictures sometimes convey the object or message literally, or it is communicated through metaphors, colors, or spatial configurations, where the shapes and journey of movement (on the page, or made physically in the space) symbolize and activate meaning. It is of interest to note how their individual language sometimes correlates or differs, in their denotation (describing something directly) and connotations (implying ideas, feelings, associations) shaping their thinking about the text, and their subsequent reading and performance.

Case Studies – Participants Jimmy, Richard, and Rose

Method

Present: myself, the participant, the critical friend as observer, and an additional student to film the sequence. The participants' comments are taken from the transcribed filmed workshops. The participants chose their Shakespeare text as their working material, and the manner in which they wanted to demonstrate their techniques. The case study observations lasted approximately sixty minutes.

Participant One – Jimmy: His Approach Used on Aaron's Monologue (Titus Andronicus, Act V, Scene i)

Jimmy had brought an example of his work on one of Aaron's monologues with him, which he went through in detailed explanation. The whole monologue had been broken down into short phrases or sentences, colors, and drawn pictures, covering three pages. First, Jimmy stated he divided the text up into thoughts, to which he allotted different colors. Like Hampshire (personal communication, 2011), associating colors with feelings, he elaborated, 'anger filled chunks of text would be red' or 'I'll get a sort of blue in my head, it's a change of thought for the character, so from yellow to blue'. Jimmy explained:

> When I think of text, it is hard for me to remember words and visualize letters. I need to grab hold of the text and transform it into something I can understand by breaking it down into colors. I remember almost like a film in my head of what's happening and the color, and that film's awash with the color I have learnt it in.

Secondly, Jimmy drew small pictures he associated with the text:

> a strong symbolist picture, and to help me remember that picture, I will always base it around something red – a lot of the time it is the eyes [. . .] so I just build the picture around the red part. The use of red throughout helps me to pinpoint the main points.

He reflected that 'the benefit from spending time with the pictures is you spend longer thinking about the lines you are going to associate with that picture. I couldn't imagine any other way of working – only through pictures.

The Passage of Text from Titus Andronicus (Shakespeare 1995) from Jimmy's Storyboard of Aaron's Monologue

> Aaron:
> Ay that I had not done a thousand more.
> Even now I curse the day, and yet, I think,
> Few come within the compass of my curse,
> Wherein I did not some notorious ill:
> As kill a man, or else devise his death;
> Ravish a maid, or plot the way to do it.

Comment on the Function of the Symbols

Jimmy's drawings are deliberately naïve (see Figure 8.1). He emphasized: 'the rougher and simpler you can make it the better'. In trying to understand how Jimmy uses his drawings to access the words of the text, and to encourage a deeper self-analysis of his personalized learning processes, I drew Jimmy's attention to the fact that he used a mix of types of images in his interpretation of Aaron's speech. The symbols seem to work concurrently as first-person inner enactments of experience, and third-person external narratives. Jimmy replied that he does not think about what kinds of image he uses, saying: 'it just comes, so that is the image I will use, and then I start to add the text – it just runs like a film in my head'.

i)   For the line 'Ay that I had not done a thousand more', Jimmy's drawing is of a man trapped within a box, with only his eyes revealed. This is a metaphorical drawing, which could be an external description of the character, although it might stimulate internal feelings and an inner monologue if arising from Aaron's experience of isolation.

ii) His second drawing, for the line 'As kill a man, or else devise his death', is depicted through metonymy: signifying a knife dripping with blood, as a murder weapon. This could be Aaron's perception of his own knife or an external descriptive representation.

iii) The third picture, for the line 'Ravish a maid, or plot the way to do it', is of an injured female and is external, descriptive, and literal. (Note that Jimmy has written the word 'devise' here in his drawing example, rather than 'plot', thereby demonstrating lack of accuracy with the actual words of the text.)

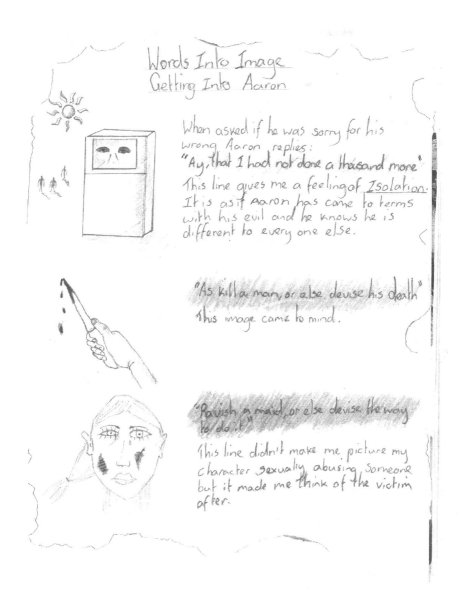

FIGURE 8.1 Clip from Jimmy's visual storyboard for Aaron's speech

Participant Two – Richard: His Approach Used on Shakespeare's Sonnet 147

The Extract from the Text Taken from Sonnet 147 (Shakespeare 1997), Focused on Here

> My love is as a fever, longing still
> For that which longer nurseth the disease . . .

First, Richard said he color-coded the different themes within the sonnet. All the words that are to do with love, he highlighted in a red color, blue for medical, and green for diseases. He explained that the color is important to him because:

> the words are pictures in my head and if I give them this color, that means the picture in my head will be in that color and helps me to real-ize what that word and meaning is, through the color. I will remember the whole sonnet as a picture. I'll know exactly where each word is on the page and what each word looks like and what font it is written in. This color-coding process infuses it a lot more.

Richard then moved on, 'to try to excite my imagination a bit more' with the use of pictures. As he spoke, Richard drew his examples on the white board on the wall, breaking down the sonnet into symbolic images, saying, 'the first thing that comes into my head is usually the best – if I think about it too much it becomes over-complicated'. He drew a heart for the word *love*, and *fever* was represented by a thermometer in someone's mouth, saying, 'My drawing's atrocious, but it doesn't really matter how it looks as long as I know what it means and for *longing* – I have drawn a clock that is melting, I thought of time melting.'

Next, when speaking Shakespeare's word 'nurseth', Richard reversed the sequence of the letters in the syllables in his formation of the word. Instead of 'nurseth', he said: '*Nurthes* is really simple, just a woman with a stereotype nurse's bonnet on.' Richard then sketched the figure of a man, explaining:

> it is someone who is quite strong with broad shoulders, but he is get-ting smaller and smaller to almost nothing, as the love is draining him and because he is so ill and is on his knees because his love – this fever has bought him to his knees and this woman has taken everything from him – he is becoming nothing and he is going down and down.

On the white board, Richard drew two kneeling figures. One had a chain around his ankles and wrists and knelt on a melting clock (the clock representing the word *longing*) (see Figures 8.2 and 8.3).

FIGURE 8.2 Clip from Richard's storyboard for *Sonnet 147*: 'My love is as a fever longing still for that which longer nurseth the disease'

Comment on the Function of the Symbols

i) Richard's symbols are literal, acting as direct prompts for the words. 'Longing still' is an ideograph of embodied experience – represented by the metaphor of a melting clock, as time is passing, with the chained man upon it being controlled by the commanding huge pointed finger of the subject of the sonnet.

ii) Note that when writing the word 'still', Richard has written *sitl*, muddling the letter sequence, as he did when speaking the words nurseth (*nurthes*) .

iii) Richard explained that his drawings of the kneeling man became his physical actions when he performed the sonnet. Having observed his physical performance of the sonnet, I recognized his drawn figures as resembling how Richard had acted the sonnet. I realized that Richard, through his drawing, was employing a version of Michael Chekhov's *Psychological Gesture*.

In explaining his *Psychological Gesture*, Michael Chekhov (1985: 107) used the example of the phrase 'to draw a conclusion', illustrating how the human

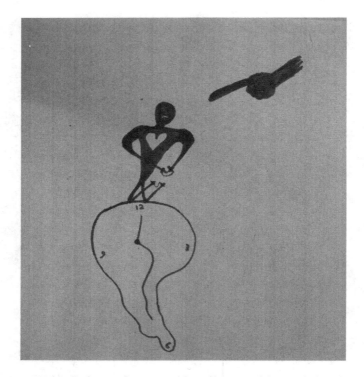

FIGURE 8.3 Richard's figures show examples of his use of the *Psychological Gesture* (Chekhov 1985)

action is revealed within the words in language. Chekhov said: 'the hidden gesture slipped into the word, is the true driving force of the spoken word' (1991: 74). Chekhov explored how the doing of a physical gesture which is embedded within the language of the text can activate the psychology and emotion, experienced internally (Figure 8.4).

Despite Richard's care taken in his drawing (see Figure 8.4), note the assimilation of the words *is, as*, and *a* in the line 'my love is as a fever'. The word *as* is possibly represented backwards, thereby dual-tasking as the letter *a* and *as* backwards; the omission of the letter 'e' in the word Sonnet (*Sonnt*) and the incorrect spelling of the word 'razor' as *razer*. Richard also muddled the sequence of letters in the syllables of words when speaking.

Speech and language therapist Maria Farry specializes in working with dyslexic actors on their speech difficulties (see Farry, in Whitfield 2009). She advises that articulation exercises for clarity and muscularity are not helpful for the dyslexic. Farry describes her work with dyslexic adults on phonological awareness as breaking up the syllables into segments, taking each segment alone and then blending them together, or removing a syllable and asking the reader to identify what is there. She explains:

FIGURE 8.4 Clip from Richard's storyboard for his sonnet presentation, showing the *Psychological Gesture* positions he assumed in his performance

adults with dyslexia have a weak internal representation of the speech sound system and a problem with the brain's ability to decode the sound system for smooth and easy retrieval. New words continue to present difficulties in the 'mapping' of alphabetical symbols to speech sounds.

(personal communication, 2009)

According to Farry (and as frequently stated, e.g. in Thomson 2009; Grant 2010), the condition of dyspraxia is often associated with dyslexia, due to 'shared brain mechanisms involved in both disorders'. Farry points out that dyspraxia is a problem with organization of movement which involves motor planning, sequencing of speech sounds, and slower processing, therefore the articulators and the brain work more slowly or more clumsily. This can mean that speech can become 'faltering, hesitant with omission of sounds'.

Participant Three – Rose

Rose described the approach she uses on any Shakespeare text in words and actions rather than bringing an example of prepared work to show me.

Rose said that first, she will re-type the text and print it out onto colored paper. She does not change the black print, only the color of the page it is printed on. For example, she said:

> If it was a Lady Macbeth speech, the paper would be red or dark green. The colors send a spark in my brain which help me relate to the text because usually by the next line that I've read, I'll have forgotten the line before. If I've got a color I can remember the theme of the piece I'm reading.

Rose then customizes the page of text as she works through it, activating the visual, tactile, and kinesthetic. She explained:

> I'll take my piece of paper and doodle some dots, or some clouds or whatever it made me feel, maybe cut a wiggly line here or cut a circle out, next to something that I'd have a hole in and ripped. I'd have a rubbishy piece of paper to most other people, but to me that's everything that I felt as I went through it. If it's not directly related to the psychology of the piece, it's related to my connection with it.

Rose said she will then draw or stick pictures onto the text, or use physical gestures to feel her way through it. Making gestures with her arms as she spoke, Rose said:

> I'd do all this, and what I felt with my hands would be the same idea [as drawing], but physically rather than on paper, they might be a sharp line [she made a staccato movement with her arms in the space] or something might be more flouncy because that's what I felt when I was reading the line [she made elaborate arm gestures].

Rose emphasized that her physical gestures demonstrate the *feeling* she received from the words rather than the *meaning*, because 'the word is what I find so hard to comprehend – if I just have the word, it is empty'.

It is interesting to note that the three participants (and actress Susan Hampshire) all mention an initial foundation of color-coding to capture aspects of feelings emanating from the text and as a short cut to reading and emotionally expressing the text when they re-visit it.

Action Research Workshop (Cycle One) and Teaching Strategy One

Present: myself, the participants, the critical friend as observer, and a student to film. The workshops were filmed, and lasted sixty to ninety minutes.

Before beginning my planned sequence on Shakespeare's *Sonnet 57* (which I had checked in advance none of the participants were familiar with), I handed each participant a book of Shakespeare sonnets and asked them to randomly open it and sight-read whatever sonnet was on the page. When doing so, as they read, they tripped over the words, displaying various degrees of difficulty with a fluency in reading. I then asked them if they had understood the sonnet and to relate what they had read. They all reported that they were not able to take in the meaning of the sonnet, nor be sure if they knew what actual words they had read. This test was carried out in advance so I could compare the difference in their ability to access the text before and after my action research trial of the teaching strategy.

Rationale: I chose *Sonnet 57* as a working tool for trial because the language is not overly obscure. It does not contain difficult words that are out of modern use, rely on clever puns and double meanings of words, nor the necessity of a dictionary before one begins to read. The thoughts and feelings in the sonnet, although passionate, are simply expressed and easily identified with. Having studied my participants' visually led procedures, I planned to trial an imagistic/aural approach rather than the traditional method of the actor reading the text.

Aim: Through this sequence of work, my aim is that the participant will achieve a phonological, visual, kinesthetic, and semantic deep coding of the text. According to Baddeley (2007: 51), an auditory presentation ensures an access to the phonological store. Drawing from Baddeley's model of memory, my goal is to activate the phonological loop through the hearing and vocalized repetition of the words, to activate the visuospatial sketchpad through the drawing, and embed the phonological–grapheme relationship in long-term memory through the writing of the words (see endnote 3 in Chapter 4 for information regarding the role of the phonological loop and the visuospatial sketchpad in Baddeley's model of memory). Baddeley (2007: 148) states that integrated information from the phonological loop and visuospatial sketchpad is bound within the episodic buffer (a component of working memory), and then the information is moved into long-term memory.

Trial of Teaching Strategy One

The Text: Sonnet 57 *(Shakespeare 1997: 225)*

> Being your slave, what should I do but tend
> Upon the hours and times of your desire?
> I have no precious time at all to spend,
> Nor services to do, till you require;
> Nor dare I chide the world-without-end hour
> Whilst I, my sovereign, watch the clock for you,
> Nor think the bitterness of absence sour

When you have bid your servant once adieu;
Nor dare I question with my jealous thought
Where you may be, or your affairs suppose,
But like a sad slave stay and think of naught,
Save, where you are, how happy you make those.
So true a fool is love, that in your will,
Though you do anything, he thinks no ill.

Method

Materials: each individual has a large pad of paper (the larger the better, such as a flipchart pad) and a mix of lead pencils, oil pastels, felt tips, crayons, and board pens.

Stage One: Warm-up. This exercise can take some time to establish, and should not to be rushed. The participant begins by working on the pad of paper on the floor with a grey-colored lead pencil. I instruct them to let the breath release outwards as they make pencil marks freely on the page, working with the movement and quality of the breath. I guide the participant to let the whole body and breath flow together (without self-censoring) with the sketching of pencil strokes on the page. Take a little time to let this work establish itself and the body and breath to warm up, working as one together with the pencil marks as a spontaneous instrument of expression. The breath causes the body to move and the pencil sketches onto the paper simultaneously. Let this work develop in conjunction with any arising feelings. Then get a fresh sheet of paper and introduce the use of colors. The participant can choose various types of colored markers according to their different materiality and the participant's growing mood and inclination. Along with the noting of colors and textures of the marker, I now introduce voice. I instruct the participant to let the vibrations and expressive sounds of their voices and breath be released, responding to the warmth and associations arising from the colors, substance, rhythms, sounds, and shapes of the colored pencil/pastel/felt-tip strokes made on the page. Let their whole body, imagination, breath, and voice become fully activated and responsive to whatever shapes, colors, and expressions emerge onto the page. Take some time to let the mark-making images develop in tandem with the voice, breath, and physical movement.

Stage Two: Get a fresh sheet of paper. Now, working through the sonnet's text line by line, I speak aloud key words from the sonnet, in their sequence of the line. Receiving the word aurally, the participant repeats the word aloud in their own voice, exploring the sounds and meaning of the word in their mouth and the acoustic space, and at the same time drawing a response to the word on the paper. Consideration should be given as to what colors and type of utensil are used in the expressive quality related to the word. There must be no sense of performance pressure or of getting it 'right' or being hurried: this is an experiential process. When the drawing is completed, I direct them to write the word alphabetically underneath the drawing, as they speak it aloud, cementing meaning with the drawing, spoken word, and colors.

Stage Three: Get a fresh sheet of paper. I then introduce short key phrases from the sonnet, building up the sequence in the sonnet. The participant, while repeating and speaking the phrase aloud, draws symbols representing the phrases, and then they write the phrase next to the picture (correct spelling is not crucial, but if they ask how to spell words, they can be prompted).

Stage Four: I speak the same short phrases from the sonnet, and I direct the participant to physicalize the phrases in the space while repeating the words aloud, creating a kinesthetic motor image of their concept, connected to their voiced sounds. These physical actions can be replicas of their drawings, or they may find another way to express the phrases using a somatic sense.

Stage Five: The participant is then given the written text of the sonnet and is instructed to read aloud the first four of the lines of the sonnet. They are then asked to paraphrase the lines into contemporary language, and discuss the meaning with me, as teacher.

Stage Six: The participant continues to work through the whole sonnet in sequence using the same process, reading four lines and then paraphrasing them and discussing them, chunk by chunk.

Stage Seven: The participant then reads the whole sonnet aloud.

Stage Eight: The participant returns to their drawings and re-tells the sonnet through their pictures, explaining the narrative of the sonnet and meaning of their drawn storyboard to the observer. This post-reading story-telling act assists in their re-connection with their interpretation, assimilation, and comprehension of the words and their consideration of meaning. At this stage, they can correct, develop, or change their pictures if they want as the narrative of the sonnet becomes more defined, forming a strong link from the pictures to the words.

Stage Nine: The participant gives a performed reading of the sonnet from the printed text, using their expressive faculties of body and voice in communicating it to an audience.

Outcome of the Teaching Strategy Trial and Workshop

Although each individual differed in their acting style and drawing/image methods, their combined enthusiasm for my approach was evident in observation of their behavior, the energy with which they tackled their drawings, and in what they said. When the participants finally gave a performed reading of the sonnet from the printed text, after working through the whole sequence, they had much-improved fluency, comprehension, and confidence in their spoken interpretation. As the sequence included deconstruction and repetition before re-building the sonnet, this fluency is not surprising, but their expressed pleasure in their immersion in the drawing exercise method and animated application in the task revealed a deeper cause for their enjoyment.

The Critical Friend's Observation

The critical friend commented that the participants expressed a sense of vindication after finishing the exercise. He noted that when talking about their participation in the drawing, they all spoke of a feeling of tremendous relief and pleasure that their method of learning was being recognized, given credence, and encouraged. Moreover, he observed that when reading the phrases of the sonnet to the participants, I spoke the text with little attempt to contribute my personal interpretation through vocal expression; however, my speech was carefully articulated. This was an intentional strategy. I was aware that any vocal presentation might have some influence on their own interpretive choices, and as I needed to impart the text to them aurally, this approach aimed to minimize an imposed style.

Having already gained a perspective on the participants' reading prowess from prior observations, the critical friend deliberated that if they had sight-read the text without this process, they would have misread and misunderstood many of the words and overall meanings. He commented that he thought my defined articulation of the spoken word was beneficial to them in gaining a precise auditory image of the text to hold in working memory as they drew their interpretations and repeated the words aloud, imbued with their own vocal explorations. He proposed that this method engendered an expressive freedom in their speaking of the text hitherto not experienced or observed when they read the words themselves without this process.

Examination of Some of the Participants' Drawings of the Text

Example of the Piece of Text Shown, from Sonnet 57

> Being your slave, what should I do but tend
> Upon the hours and times of your desire?
> I have no precious time at all to spend
> Nor services to do till you require;

Jimmy

Comments on the Function of the Symbols

Jimmy's ideas for his images (Figure 8.5) came to him immediately he heard the words, demonstrating a fluency in drawing linked to thought.

i) All the images (except the clock, which is literally denoted) represent the enactment of the speaker of the sonnet, in first-person perspective and their physical actions.

ii) 'I have': Depicting a bodily action, Jimmy has made a concrete embodiment of the abstract idea of 'I have' by drawing a person holding the word *have* as an object on his hand while pointing to himself.

iii) Similarly, the phrase 'at all' has been made into a concrete physical action through placing the hand into the spatial capacity within a box – the space being *all* (this is an example of Mark Johnson's idea of a container metaphor in linguistic understanding; Johnson 2007: 137).

iv) 'Time': Jimmy has created a physical metaphor for the word *time*, depicting a man bent backwards over the clock. This uncomfortable effortful physical position reveals the emotional state of the speaker within the sonnet. This could a *Psychological Gesture* for the sonnet.

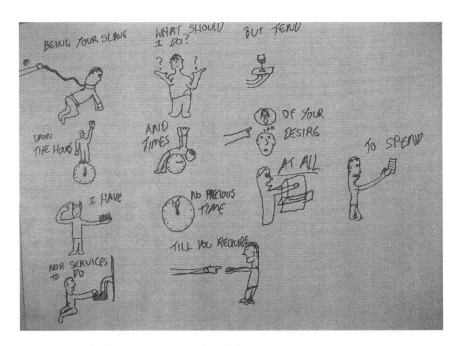

FIGURE 8.5 Clip from Jimmy's storyboard for *Sonnet 57*

v) 'Upon the hours' is a literal translation of the words – a man standing upon a clock.

vi) The color red is mostly centrally placed within every the picture, to 'set' the image in Jimmy's memory.

Richard

Comments on the Function of the Symbols

Richard was quick in the translation from hearing the word to devising the picture, his idea translating into drawing almost instantaneously (Figure 8.6).

i) Some images are from an embodied first-person perspective, and some represent descriptive ideas from an exterior perspective.

ii) 'At all' is a metaphorical concept represented by an empty circle (note Richard's incorrect spelling again, *nothness*, missing a syllable, for the word *nothingness*). The empty circle represents the idea of 'I have no precious time at all to spend' through an empty container (this is again an example of Johnson's container metaphor).

iii) 'Have' is comparable to Jimmy's idea, being made concrete by being something held physically in the hands as an object.

FIGURE 8.6 Clip from Richard's storyboard for *Sonnet 57*

iv) It is interesting to note that Richard's representation for 'upon the hours' replicates Jimmy's conception of a figure on top of a clock, although independently conceived.

v) 'no precious time' is made into a concrete graphic representation. It is neatly summed up by a Rolex watch face with a cross through it, which captures the words *precious/time/no* in one image.

vi) 'and times' is an interesting spatial configuration of two circular shapes intertwined into a figure of eight, or could be a singular twisted circle, thereby representing the idea of the plurality of the word *times*.

Rose

Example of the Piece of Text Shown, from Sonnet 57

> Nor dare I chide the world-without-end hour
> Whilst I (my sovereign) watch the clock for you,
> Nor think the bitterness of absence sour
> When you have bid your servant once adieu

Comments on the Function of the Symbols

Rose set about her drawing (Figure 8.7) with an energetic zeal, calling this process her way of 'making friends with the text'. Rose sometimes uses non-literal language of symbols, shapes, and color, which represent her inner visuospatial concepts or feelings.

i) Using literal symbols, the image of a mask with one open eye next to a clock denotes the phrase 'watch the clock for you', while the picture of the crown denotes the word 'sovereign'.

ii) Rose's auditory image of a word, its intonation, and pitch movement is depicted by the shapes and colors of the drawn lines. Her internal conception, along with the auditory memory of the sound shape, can be observed as spatially configured in her signs for the words 'chide' and 'servant'. The drawn line for 'servant' dips downwards in the center, as though 'below' in status.

iii) Her onomatopoeic perceptions are demonstrated by her red explosive star shape for the word 'dare' (contained within the shape) and the textured dots enclosed within a jagged circle of orange and black, denoting the physical experience of 'bitterness' and the yellow star for 'sour'. 'Absence' is made clear by two yellow lines with an empty center (the container is empty).

Analysis

In this work, I am exploring ways that enable the participants to enter the text through open channels, rather than persisting with a mode which invites a

FIGURE 8.7 Clip from Rose's storyboard for *Sonnet 57*

'banging into', being 'stalled', or 'blocked' by the text (Essley 2008: 21, 29). Psychologists Alison Bacon and Simon Handley (2010) have investigated the primary use of visual strategies in dyslexics. In their tests, they presented several reasoning tasks to a group of dyslexics and non-dyslexics. They found that those without dyslexia could analyze abstractedly in their heads, communicating their reasoning verbally. However, most of those with dyslexia adopted visuospatial drawing strategies to work out their answers, making:

> [v]ivid pictorial representations of the specific properties described by the problems. Even the less imagable properties [. . .] presented little problem, being creatively illustrated by depictions such as pound signs, halos/horns, smiley/sad/angry faces or stars and dunce hats [. . .] the majority of dyslexic participants (75%) used this type of visual-spatial strategy. The association between strategy choice and dyslexic status was highly significant.
>
> *(ibid.: 33)*

Bacon and Handley's description of the use of illustrative symbols as a system for thinking through problems in those with dyslexia exactly replicates the work of my participants' delineations of Shakespeare's text. When engaging with the spoken and written word, my participants display a preference for visuospatial processing, sometimes described as right brain activities. Reporting on brain imaging findings, Wolf states that 'the dyslexic brain consistently employs more right brain structures then left brain structures, beginning with visual association areas' (2008: 186). There is research that verifies this, and one example of a scientific trial with dyslexic readers showing right brain dominance is given in endnote 1.[1]

Conclusion

Unlike actor Anthony Sher's artwork, which serves to illuminate the physical appearance and psychological 'feel' of his characters (Sher 1985, 1989), my participants' drawings function as purveyor, decoder, and memory buttress for the meanings and phonological sounds of the words within the text. In my spoken delivery of the text in Teaching Strategy One, the words are received aurally, and then anchored into memory through the creation of personal images. These word denotations act as referential prompts, setting in motion a chain of connotations. Unlike the written word, wherein information is imparted progressively and through orthographic rules, the pictorial form can allow a holistic rendition of several meanings caught within one illustration. Dyslexia specialists Eide and Eide claim that many individuals with dyslexia 'reason in largely nonverbal ways and often find it difficult to translate their thoughts into words'. However, they accentuate that the use of imagery is only helpful for dyslexics if directly useful for solving a problem, as 'irrelevant imagery is distracting and worsens performance' (Eide & Eide 2011: 65–66). In this case, the images are produced by the dyslexic individuals themselves, thereby having direct relevance to them in solving the problem of accessing the written text. The images are not artificially imposed upon them through an external source.

One of the prevailing aspects of dyslexia (and highlighted by the majority of my participants in interview) is a weakness in verbal working memory (Gathercole & Packiam Alloway 2008; Nicolson & Fawcett 2010). Functioning as cognitive tools, the symbols assist in off-loading working memory by externalizing the information onto the page in a stable format. This concept mapping facilitates the building of a mental model of the whole text. This enables participants with dyslexic difficulties to freely interpret the words in expressive action, switching back and forth from the pictorial symbols held in their minds or on the page to the written form and then into physical performance.

In this chapter, I have focused closely on three participants' individual methods and my development of their individual methods into Teaching Strategy One. Through my trials of this visual, physical and aurally led method, it has been shown to have efficacy as a pedagogical solution which can assist in removing the blocks to reading the text while promoting artistic accomplishment. Furthermore, I have taught this sequence with Shakespeare sonnets in voice classes and with Shakespeare monologues in acting classes involving the whole cohort of students (dyslexic and non-dyslexic). It is effective in producing striking performances through an acute attention to the words as ignitors of imagination and anchors of meaning and spoken articulation. My teaching sequence described here is offered as a template, and each teacher and set of students can replicate or develop it to suit their own cognitive styles, needs, research, and strengths.

The Next Chapter

In her study of Shakespeare's images, Caroline Spurgeon (1935: 57) describes Shakespeare's visual sense as 'all embracing' and a gateway through which Shakespeare receives life. She also emphasizes that Shakespeare's ideas are frequently expressed through verbs of movement (ibid.: 51). Stanislavski compared the actor's 'inner stream of images' to a painter's, stressing that the 'inner moving picture film' works as a lure to galvanize the feelings attached to the words. He promoted the stimulation of image, saying: 'Let what you say convey the images and not just the words' (Stanislavski 1968: 125–126). He amalgamated the use of imaging with his method of *Physical Actions*, calling the visual image 'the secret of the Psycho-technique' (ibid.: 126). Michael Chekhov was Stanislavski's pupil, and there is an evident relationship between Stanislavski's method of *Physical Actions* and Chekhov's *Psychological Gesture*. In my observations, I had noted a link with the participants' figurative drawings, interconnected with their physical actions in performance.

This subject of physical action leads me on to the next chapter's focus. In the next chapter, I explore the historical background of Stanislavski's work with Shakespeare, and the origins behind Cicely Berry's vocal and physical approach to the text. It questions the effectiveness of using Stanislavski's method of actions (which are led by character, objective, and context), when working on Shakespeare's text for acting students with dyslexia. This method is compared with Cicely Berry's approach, which has an emphasis on 'being on the word', 'hearing the different textures' of the thoughts and language, and physicalizing 'the spaces in the mind' (Berry 2001: 122, 221, 223). There is an introduction to two new participants. A case study of two individuals' with dyslexia and their creation of a physical storyboard in representing the words of the text is presented. There is further exploration of their physical actions/gestures in the space, wherein the internal representation of the text is made tangible through the body.

KEY POINTS OF CHAPTER 8

- Case study observations of the personally devised methods of three participants when working with Shakespeare's text
- Introduction of Teaching Strategy One, based on the participants' ways of working with a text

- The trial of the teaching strategy and outcome (Action Research Cycle One)
- Analysis of the effectiveness of the teaching strategy
- Presentation of theories about the systems of the brain activated when reading for those with dyslexia (see the note at the end of the chapter)
- Evaluation of the teaching strategy's function and value for dyslexic students and as a viable teaching approach for all students.

Note

1 In consideration of the brain hemispheres and their involvement in language, Bear et al. (2016: 717) emphasize that brain imaging has shown that both hemispheres of the brain are involved in language, which can vary from person to person. This is because language involves several elements, such as sound, meaning, grammar, and articulation of speech (ibid.: 703). However it is of note that the left hemisphere of the brain holds *Wernicke's Area*, which is involved in the recognition and comprehension of spoken and written language, and *Broca's Area*, which is responsible for the motor organization of speech and breaking words into segments (ibid.: 695). Baddeley (personal correspondence) refers to the phonological loop (the part of our working memory system that handles auditory and verbal information) as dependent on the left hemisphere. The right hemisphere recognizes faces, visual patterns, spatial orientation, pictures, rhythm, intonation of poetic structure, emotional expression, intuition, and the bigger picture, without the detail (Perkins & Kent 1991: 441; Eide & Eide 2011: 35; Seidenberg 2017: 204). The visuospatial sketchpad (the component of working memory responsible for handling visual and spatial information) relies mostly on the right side of the brain (Baddeley 2007: 8).

There are some apparent differences in the hemispheric use in those with dyslexia, indicating right hemisphere reliance. In a whole brain connectivity study of dyslexia using fMRI scanning, Finn et al. (2014) compared dyslexic readers' brains with non-dyslexic readers' brains. In a scientific analysis of the brain's differing areas activated when reading for those with non-impaired readers and those with dyslexia, their findings showed that in dyslexic readers, the right hemisphere of the brain is more active, with dyslexic readers having an 'increased overall connectivity in the right hemisphere'. This indicates that the right hemisphere is more active in those with dyslexia and more strongly connected to the rest of the brain (ibid.: 402). Finn et al. found that, as young readers get older, they can attain more of a left-dominant hemisphere language connectivity, but to 'a lesser degree than non-impaired readers (ibid.). Neuro-learning and dyslexia specialists Eide and Eide point out that even when dyslexic readers have been trained to make the right to left hemisphere shift in their reading circuit like 'normal' readers, they do not become the same as 'normal' readers. They claim that dyslexic readers, even when skilled, generally read more slowly than non-dyslexics and show 'highly interconnected, gist and context-dependent, imagery-based, big pictures reading comprehension style shown by most other individuals with dyslexia' (Eide & Eide 2011: 37).

Reference List

Bacon, A. & Handley, S. (2010). Dyslexia, reasoning and the importance of visual-spatial processes. *In*: Alexander-Passe, N. (ed.) *Dyslexia and Creativity*. New York: Nova Science, pp. 25–49.

Baddeley, A. (2007). *Working Memory, Thought, and Action.* Oxford, UK: Oxford University Press.

Bear, M., Connors, B.W., & Paradiso, M.A. (2016). *Neuroscience: Exploring the Brain,* 4th ed. Philadelphia, PA: Wolters Kluwer.

Berry, C. (2001). *Text in Action.* London: Virgin Books.

Chekhov, M. (1985). *Lessons for the Professional Actor.* New York: Performing Arts Journal Publications.

Chekhov, M. (1991). *On the Technique of Acting.* New York: HarperCollins.

Eide, B. & Eide, F. (2011). *The Dyslexia Advantage.* London: Hay House.

Essley, R. (2008). *Visual Tools for Differentiating Reading and Writing Instruction.* New York: Scholastic Press.

Finn, E.S., Shen, X., Holahan, J.M., Papademetris, X., Scheinost, D., Lacadie, C., Shaywitz, S.E., Shaywitz, B.A., & Constable, R.T. (2014). Disruption of functional networks in dyslexia: a whole-brain, data-driven approach to fMRI connectivity analysis. *Biological Psychiatry,* 76:5, 397–404

Gathercole, S. & Packiam Alloway, T. (2008). *Working Memory and Learning.* London: SAGE Publications.

Grant, D. (2010). *That's the Way I Think.* London: Routledge.

Johnson, M. (2007). *The Meaning of the Body.* Chicago, IL: University of Chicago Press.

Nicolson, R. & Fawcett, A. (2010). *Dyslexia, Learning and the Brain.* London: MIT Press.

Perkins, W.H. & Kent, D.R. (1991). *Functional Anatomy of Speech, Language and Hearing.* Boston, MA: Allyn & Bacon.

Seidenberg, M. (2017). *Language at the Speed of Sight.* New York: Basic Books.

Shakespeare, W. (1995). *Titus Andronicus.* Ed. Bate, J. London: Arden Shakespeare.

Shakespeare, W. (1997). *Shakespeare Sonnets.* Ed. Duncan-Jones, K. London: Arden Shakespeare.

Shepherd, R.N. (1978). Externalization of mental images and the act of creation. *In*: Rhandhawa, B.S., & Coffman, W.E. (eds.) *Visual Learning, Thinking, and Communication.* London: Academic Press, pp. 133–189.

Sher, A. (1985). *Year of the King.* London: Nick Hern.

Sher, A. (1989). *Characters.* London: Nick Hern.

Spurgeon, C. (1935). *Shakespeare's Imagery and What It Tells Us.* Cambridge, UK: Cambridge University Press.

Stanislavski, C. (1968). *Building a Character.* London: Methuen Drama.

Thomson, M. (2009). *The Psychology of Dyslexia,* 2nd ed. Chichester, UK: Wiley-Blackwell.

Whitfield, P. (2009). Shakespeare, pedagogy and dyslexia. *In*: Cooke, R. (ed.) *The Moving Voice: The Integration of Voice and Movement. The Voice and Speech Trainers Review,* 6, pp. 254–262. Published online in *The Voice and Speech Review,* 2013. Available from: https://doi.org/10.1080/23268263.2009.10767576. Accessed 7 May 2019.

Wolf, M. (2008). *Proust and the Squid: The Story of Science and the Reading Brain.* London: Icon Books.

9

THE PHYSICAL PATH AND STANISLAVSKI'S ACTIONS

Action in Pursuit of the Objective or as an Anchor of Verbal Meaning?

Introduction

Stanislavski's Methods and Shakespeare, in Comparison with Cicely Berry's Foregrounding of the Word

Before the outset of my research investigations, I agreed with theatre director and actor trainer Ben Naylor's view that a classical training for actors benefits from an inclusion of Stanislavski rehearsal techniques in tandem with a study of the speaking of the verse (Naylor 2009: 1; Naylor 2018). My own training as an actor was heavily influenced by Stanislavski's methods. In particular, we studied Stanislavski's Circles of Attention, the need for Justification, defining the Given Circumstances, and the unearthing of the Motivation prompting the actor to speak or move. Naylor (2018) and Barton (1984), in considering approaches to Shakespeare, have stated that Stanislavski's methods are now ingrained through-out Western actor approaches. Naylor (2018) comments: 'It could be said that the whole history of modern Western actor training is a series of footnotes to Stanislavsky [. . .] almost all contemporary actors are consciously or uncon-sciously deploying Stanislavskian approaches.' Throughout my acting career, I drew from the Stanislavskian approach and found that his methods provided a fundamental key to believable acting choices. As Stanislavski delineates, 'truth on the stage is whatever we can believe in with sincerity [. . .] everything that happens must be convincing to the actor himself, to his associates and to the spectators' (1980a: 129).

However, for those with dyslexia, the exploratory practice carried out within the research in this chapter (and in Chapters 10 and 11) has revealed an incompat-ibility in some aspects with the use of Stanislavski's system of actions in enabling an amalgamation of character needs, objectives and physical actions, while being consciously 'present' within the words of Shakespeare's text. This is despite some practitioners' endorsements declaring the advantages of utilizing Stanislavski's actions on a Shakespeare text (for example, Gillet 2007; Alfreds 2007; Merlin 2007; Gillett & Gutekunst 2014). A contradiction can emerge between the support Stanislavski's system of units and actions offers to those with dyslexia, the complexity in marrying Shakespeare's language with Stanislavski's methods, and the prominence he gives to subtext. There is an enduring debate in the literature on the applicability of using Stanislavski's system of objectives and actions, with an aim of psychological realism, when working on Shakespeare. Voice practitioner Kristin Linklater, theatre directors Peter Brook and William Gaskill, and Shakespearean actor Oliver Ford Davis (who are all immensely skilled practitioners experienced in working with Shakespeare) point out some of the challenges.

Linklater refers to the problem of fitting Shakespeare into Stanislavski's methods of playing actions and intentions, remarking: 'the trouble with Shakespeare is that you can't put everything under the impetus of playing an objective, because quite often the character is letting off steam, or exploring a philosophical idea' (Linklater, in Saklad 2011: 200). In agreement, theatre director Peter Brook adds that 'a psychological approach is inadequate [. . .]. Our way into the character must be through recognising that the words that he uses show us who he is' (1998: 45). This assertion is further backed up by theatre practitioners William Gaskill and Oliver Ford Davis. When considering how Stanislavski's physical methods might be utilized by the contemporary actor 'as an antidote to the tyranny of the text', actor Oliver Ford Davis cautions that Stanislavski's actions cannot substitute for Shakespeare's verbal dexterity or emotional variety. He argues that 'there are heightened passages of verse that defy naturalistic delivery' (Ford Davis 2007: 109, 173). Theatre director William Gaskill specifies that although the system of actioning can be valuable for contemporary texts, on Shakespeare's text the method of actions can ruin the intellectual meditation, the 'fluid shift between the character's relationship with the outside world and his communication with himself in response to that world', and an actor's intuitive awareness of the sound of Shakespeare's language and verse (Gaskill 2010: 56). Likening the planned actions sequence to a mechanical process rather like pictures that are revealed by joining up the dots, Gaskill relates that his observance of several attempts to action Hamlet's soliloquies 'destroyed the flow of the speech and the poetry had gone' (ibid.).

Advocating a Stanislavski approach to the acting of Shakespeare, acting teacher John Gillett and voice teacher Christina Gutekunst (2014) have detailed the background preparation they deem to be necessary for the actor when interacting with Shakespeare's text. In their comprehensive manual for acting practitioners and students, they include the established components of Stanislavski's method, such as reflection on the Given Circumstances, deciphering the Super Objective, pinpointing the lesser Objectives, the Inner Motives, the Previous Circumstances, and analysis of the text through action. In consideration of approaching a scene from *Othello*, and to guide the actions chosen by the actor, Gillett and Gutekunst propose that the following questions be answered (ibid.: 312):

- I am in these circumstances, saying these words, what do I want?
- What might my range of actions be?
- What is at stake for me in pursuing my objective?
- What obstacles are in my way?

Such questions are fundamental for character realization, and are pertinent for deep immersion into a character's situation in the world of the play. However, in regard to those with dyslexia who struggle with perceiving and retaining the words and their meaning from the written text, the focus of these questions does not involve scrutiny of the semantics, syntax, and literary devices of the language, nor of the very word itself.

Many individuals without reading difficulties can be challenged in capturing the intricacy of these multi-dimensional phrases and narrowing them down into an objective, verb, and action, and such ambiguities can intensify the confusion in the shifting word-meanings for those with dyslexia. Although many of Stanislavski's methods have been absorbed into Western acting culture as powerful implements of process and discovery, in my research workshops with my students, I have found that there can be obstacles when attempting to apply them to acting Shakespeare. In the following chapters, entailing both theory and practical trials of physical work, I am supporting aspects of Stanislavski's approaches, but also pointing out some parts of his work that are not so helpful for those with dyslexia. (Some of Stanislavski's methods can cause dyslexic students considerable difficulties beyond working on Shakespeare. Please see the note at the end of this chapter for comments written by a dyslexic and dyspraxic MA Actor Training student/director about trying to engage with Stanislavski's work and its effect on her sense of self, in her actor training; Cubberley Lobb 2017.[1])

Since encountering this quandary in my teaching approach, and noting some dyslexic students' confusion when I had taken a Stanislavski-inspired actions approach to the acting of the text (as described in Chapter 10), I endeavored to gain some insight into this apparent contradiction from which I might unravel a way forward in my working practice. I have therefore examined the historical background and methodological issues underlying the disputes arising from the amalgamation of elements of Stanislavski's system with Shakespeare's text.

An Historical Overview of Stanislavski and Shakespeare, Hall, and Barton

According to Weingust (2006: 142–146), in Shakespeare's era there was little time in the actors' preparation for any psychological approach to the building of a character, nor any idea of 'character' as actors define it today. The actors were given a script that contained only their lines in the play and a few cue words from the other characters' lines. They would have a very short rehearsal period, mostly involving individual study (Tucker 2002: 37; Weingust 2006: 142–143). John Barton, while admitting that 'we would all like to know [. . .] how Shakespeare's actors rehearsed a part and how their minds worked', suggests that the Elizabethan actor 'must have instinctively gleaned from the text', and that 'you have to look for and follow the clues that he [Shakespeare] offers. If an actor does that then he'll find that Shakespeare himself starts to direct him' (Barton 1984: 30, 168).

Stanislavski's views on acting were formed during the early twentieth century in an environment of emerging psychological ideas, focusing on the emotion and the subconscious. In her monograph on the history of Stanislavski's praxis, Rose Whyman reports that Stanislavski's study of 'truthful' acting emerged in the early twentieth century, and was pre-Freudian. In Russia, the ideas of the German philosopher Edouard von Hartmann, published in his book *The Philosophy of the Unconscious* in 1869, had a pervading influence, informing several of Stanislavski's theories on the unconscious, subconscious, and super-conscious (Whyman 2008: 4–5, 89). Freud's writing was translated into Russian in 1910, expanding the concept of the analysis of the inner motives and the desires of the unconscious (ibid.: 66). Preceding Freud, Stanislavski was enlightened by Charles Darwin's theories of evolution and emotion, Pavlov and his study of animal behavior, and the psychologist Theodule Ribot's experiments on memory and associations. These ideas encouraged an exploration of the relationship between mind, physiology, reflex, and interactions with the environment. Merlin relates that Stanislavski had read about the idea of 'affective memory' in Ribot's books *Les Maladies de la Vonte* and *Les Maladies de la Memoire*, published in Russian in 1900. Ribot's investigations involved a stimulation of the five senses to re-awaken seemingly forgotten memories recorded in the nervous system. These ideas led to Stanislavski's fascination with finding 'lures' to unlock emotional memories placed in the subconscious (Merlin 2007: 143; Benedetti 1982: 31).

Stanislavski underlined that actors should search for an emotional memory of feeling, based on a real experience of the senses, 'and resurrect within themselves memories of visual and aural images' (Stanislavski, cited in Whyman 2008: 54). As Stanislavski argues:

> preserved in the affective memory of the artist himself/herself, from knowledge acquired by learning preserved in the intellectual memory, from experience s/he has gained in life [. . .] these memories must be absolutely analogous with the feelings of the play and the role.
>
> *(Stanislavski, cited in ibid.: 55)*

In order to find a convincing truth in performance, Stanislavski urged actors to uncover the goals and objectives of their characters through an excavation of what might be derived from the text. In Stanislavski's teaching, actors' empathetic recognition of the emotional needs of their character's inner subconscious (within the given circumstances of the play) can be released through physical actions. Through the doing of the physical action, the associative feelings will be ignited. However, the action must have a particular psychological purpose, or there is no foundation behind the action (Stanislavski 1980a: 43). It was imperative to Stanislavski that actors work from their own responses to the given circumstances of their roles, and he underlines that it would be the initial implementation of the defined actions that would release the feelings (Stanislavski 1981: 201).

When investigating the text, Stanislavski tells us:

> In art it is the feeling that creates, not the mind [. . .] the role of the mind is purely auxiliary, subordinate. The analysis made by an artist is quite different from one made by a scholar [. . .]. If the result of a scholarly analysis is thought, the result of an artistic one is feeling. An actor's analysis is first of all an analysis of feeling, and it is carried out by feeling.
>
> *(1981: 8)*

In apparent conflict with an observance of the clues provided by Shakespeare within his text, Stanislavski instructs the actor to 'approach the role in your own person, from life and not from the author's directions [. . .] you would be staking everything on him, you would parrot his lines, ape his actions that were not akin to yours' (ibid.: 218). In his process of active discovery, Stanislavski tells actors not to speak the playwright's text, but to improvise, using a few words and physical actions, to grasp the general gist of their characters' intentions and resulting feelings (ibid.: 216). Stanislavski stresses the importance of the physical life of the part, accentuating that the physical actions must have an inner justification: 'in every physical action unless it is purely mechanical, there is concealed some inner action, some feelings' (ibid.: 228). He puts an emphasis on emotion first, saying:

> Inside each and every word there is an emotion, a thought that produced the word and justifies it being there. Empty words are [. . .] concepts without content [. . .] they are harmful [. . .]. Until the actor is able to fill out each word of the text with live emotions, the text of his role will remain dead.
>
> *(ibid.: 94)*

Stanislavski's attention on initially uncovering a psycho/emotional response, rather than examining in detail playwrights' choices in their use of language, exposes a polemic when applying his methods to Shakespeare.

According to Robert Gordon, Stanislavski did not have full success with Shakespeare, as his psychologically truthful 'living out' of the character did not always fit with Shakespeare's sometimes abstruse, evocative use of language

(Gordon 2006: 56). Indeed, Stanislavski writes about his struggle with performing Shakespeare in his autobiography, lamenting:

> there are roles and plays in Shakespeare that I cannot read without a shudder. Yet why can I express my perceptions of Chekhov but cannot express my perceptions of Shakespeare? [. . .] Apparently it is not the inner feeling itself, but the technique of its expression that prevents us from doing that in the plays of Shakespeare which we are able to do to a certain degree in the plays of Chekhov [. . .] we have created a technique and method for the artistic interpretation of Chekhov, but we do not possess a technique for the saying of artistic truth in the plays of Shakespeare.
>
> *(Stanislavski 1980b: 350)*

Stanislavski was hampered by poor translations and a lack of awareness of differences in word syntax between English and Russian (1980b: 512). Nonetheless, when working on Shakespeare, he appears to have diverted his attention away from the text and onto the unwritten subtext created in his imagination, the given circumstances, the off stage scenarios and a creation of naturalistic stage settings (Stanislavski 1981: 194–201).

In his writings, Stanislavski returns to Shakespeare frequently as prime working material for the actor. He did make it clear that he placed great value on the author's words, remarking: 'the verbal text of a play, especially one by a genius, is the manifestation of the clarity, the subtlety, the concrete power to express visible thoughts and feelings of the author himself' (ibid.: 94). However, he does not seem to relate his own assumptions about the characters' psychological and emotional states directly to the intricacies and content of Shakespeare's words, verse, and form (for example, Stanislavski 1981: 165–193, 256–271; Stanislavski 1980b: 277–283). When speaking the text, he also ignores the iambic pentameter and whole thought phrases, thereby disrupting the flow of meaning, by inserting psychological pauses into the verse line, as in his instructions on distributing numerous pauses throughout Othello's speech: 'Like to the pontic sea [. . .]' (Stanislavski 1968: 129). Benedetti states that Stanislavski aimed to refrain from a false, declamatory manner of acting Shakespeare, but was not proficient with verse. Stanislavski grabbled with his deficiencies, remarking: 'I understood that knowing how to speak verse simply and elegantly was itself a science, with its own laws. But I did not know them' (in Benedetti 1982: 46–47).

Peter Hall (founder of the Royal Shakespeare Theatre Company) acknowledged that his attitude towards Shakespeare had been influenced by his time at Cambridge University. As a member of the Marlowe Society, the Shakespearean director William Poel taught Hall to value 'quick and witty' speaking of the verse, while his Cambridge university teachers, George Rylands and F.R Leavis, embedded a scholarly scrutiny of the verse (Hall 2000: 66–67, 88–89; Hall 2003: 191–193). Hall cautions that Stanislavski's methods of asking what the character *wants (or feels)* is *not* what is paramount in acting Shakespeare. He argues that instead, one must ask *what* the characters *say* and *how* they say it through an examination of the structured form and analysis of language that Shakespeare has provided (Hall 2003: 18). 'As in music, you must learn the notes correctly before you start to express the emotion', but once the rules are learnt, 'the actor can make them his and apply them in his own way' (Hall 2000: 89). Thus, Hall advocates a literary approach in the first instance, advising that the concomitant emotions, enmeshed within the written form, will naturally emerge at a later stage of the work.

The potential complication of merging Shakespeare's imagist and metaphoric verse structures with an actor's improvised words and actions derived from a character's psychological and emotional objectives is recognized by Stanislavski. He has alluded to this dilemma in a fictional actor's notes when working on *Othello* (Stanislavski 1981: 262). The fictional actor remarks:

> it is one thing to use your own words and thoughts and quite another to adopt those of someone else, which are permanently fixed, cast as it were in bronze, in strong clear shapes. They are unalterable [. . .] for the first time we were being faced with the process of assimilating the words of another person. And our amateurish babbling of inanimate sounds which is what Paul and I were doing with the magnificent words of *Othello* did not count [. . .]. I felt incapable of coping with the problem put to me.

In this account, the actor asks for time to study the text in order to 'enliven the lines which up to now had been so many inert words', but he curiously proceeds to concentrate on a supposed subtext and 'what Shakespeare had left unsaid' (ibid.: 263), rather than examining what Shakespeare had said.

John Barton, along with Hall, began directing Shakespeare as a member of the Marlowe Society at Cambridge University, and was also influenced by William Poel (Gordon 2006: 170; Hall 2003: 195). Poel wanted his audience to *hear* rather than *see* a Shakespeare play, with an emphasis on the speaking of the verse, poetic structure, and the meaning of the words (Gordon 2006: 144). In regard to speaking Shakespeare, Poel asserted: 'the hunting for the key words gives you the eyes of a lynx in searching all the corners of a sentence, and compels you to study closely the thought of an author and weigh all his words' (Speaight 1954: 64). Barton acknowledges the influence of Stanislavski's methods, which he recognizes inevitably percolate, subconsciously, through contemporary actors' minds. Within the first few pages of his proposed principles in acting Shakespeare, Barton introduces the idea of dual pathways into the text (1984: 8). He believes that a fusion of Stanislavski's ideas interlinked with a literary examination of Shakespeare's language is essential. However, in antithesis to Hall, Barton advocates that the actor commences the work from a Stanislavskian perspective by initially asking: 'What is my intention?' Then, unifying with Hall's foregrounding of the text, he recommends that actors should pursue their intentions through a careful observance of the written form, utilizing the heightened, poetic language to produce the words as 'freshly minted' and 'needed' by the actor and character (ibid.: 12–18). Theatre director Adrian Noble underscores the wisdom of this union. He describes Stanislavski's focus on experienced feeling as working from 'inside out', and that an 'outside in' approach is gained by a scrutiny of the 'how' within the text. Noble claims that a coupling of both traditions leads to something 'exciting [. . .] original, truthful and [. . .] realistic' (2010: 3–4).

An Historical Overview of the Origins of Cicely Berry's Language and Action Work

Cicely Berry has reflected on the variances of the two techniques, comparing American Method acting (which fosters an enhanced awareness of the senses and the inner subconscious life, derived from Stanislavski's ideas) with the English tradition of using verbal skills focused on language (Berry 1993: 42). She concludes by proposing that an interaction between the two approaches of *argument* (English tradition) and *emotion* (Method) is efficacious (Berry 2001: 61). Notably, diverging from Stanislavski, Berry cautions that an overly emotional approach can suffocate Shakespeare's language. Berry is convinced that searching for the *physical action inside the words themselves* releases the thoughts behind the language (ibid.: 63).

Gordon traces Berry's foregrounding of the words directly back to the actor, theatre teacher, and director Michel Saint-Denis (1897–1971), nephew to French theatre practitioner Jacques Copeau (1879–1949) (Gordon 2006: 174). Michel Saint-Denis also directed at the Royal Shakespeare Company with Peter Hall and Peter Brook, and Hall describes his contribution to the RSC as 'incalculable' (Hall 2000: 168–170). In 1922, Saint-Denis saw Stanislavski and his Moscow Art Theatre actors' performances of Chekhov and other Russian plays in Paris. He admired Stanislavski's work, describing Stanislavski as 'a giant', and wrote that his ability to make the characters come to life was an 'amazing experience' to witness (Saint-Denis 1964: 77–78). Nevertheless, Saint-Denis criticized Stanislavski for his naturalistic motivations and obsession with psychologically driven acting in Shakespeare. Saint-Denis proposed that we should use Stanislavski's methods as a basic foundation, but underlined that it is the text that should be studied for technical and poetic evidence. He opined that playing the enormity of Shakespeare's roles cannot be reduced to a lived naturalism, as the text itself is not natural. He emphasized that acting Shakespeare demands a flexible ability to merge naturalism with poetic response, and frequently a heightened style, and that the text is a 'precious foundation' in which actors should root their acting, linking technique with imagination. This, Saint-Denis is convinced, is the most efficacious route to fulfill the exigencies of performing Shakespeare (ibid.: 81–83).

Berry's methods cast a connecting line between herself, Saint-Denis, and Stanislavski. Saint-Denis taught 'l'expression parlée', in which he merged voice work with movement and text. Berry asserts that her exercises which involve a physical expression of voiced sounds are originally inspired by *Eurythmy*, a movement art created by the Austrian philosopher Rudolf Steiner (Berry 1993: 147; Berry 2001: 167). Steiner's *Eurythmy* 'begins [. . .] with the [. . .] task of interpreting speech in movement', believing 'every sound of speech is an invisible gesture'. Working with poetry and movement, Steiner wanted to see 'the dance living within the words themselves' (Raffe et al. 1974: 14–15). Stanislavski knew Rudolf Steiner and introduced him to Michael Chekhov, who extended Steiner's work into his *Psychological Gesture* at a later stage (Whyman 2008: 86).

Not to be confused with Steiner's *Eurythmy*, the music composer and teacher Jacque Emile Dalcroze (1865–1950) originated a system called *Eurhythmics*. Dalcroze's *Eurhythmics* aimed to develop an understanding of music and its rhythms by translating musical sounds into physical movement. Dalcroze said that the 'aim of *Eurhythmics* is to enable pupils [. . .] to say, not that "I know", but "I have experienced"' (1921: 63). Dalcroze was popular in the early twentieth century in Russia. Whyman reports that Stanislavski's brother, V.S. Alekseev, taught Dalcroze's methods in his studios in the 1920s and 1930s, wanting to develop expressiveness in the actors' bodies (Whyman 2008: 129). Stanislavski's studies of an individual's inner and outer emotional rhythms, examined within his tempo rhythm exercises, also originated from Dalcroze's ideas (ibid.: 152). There is a consonance in Dalcroze, Steiner's, Stanislavski's, and Berry's teaching within the premise that 'the activity of the limbs [. . .] wakes up and vitalizes the experience of the head' (Raffe et al. 1974: 26).

Berry's Physical Embodiment of the Language

With echoes of Dalcroze and Steiner's convictions, Berry (in her writing and practical exercises) regularly imparts the benefit of physicalizing the images Shakespeare has invoked in his writing, while speaking the verbal images aloud. In accordance with Dalcroze's ideas of the need to experience both visually and spatially to deeply understand, and Steiner's premise of the sounds of speech being latent gestures (Raffe et al. 1974: 15), Berry wants actors to extend their intellectual engagement with the word, to 'embrace' and activate the conjured images, so they permeate through their body. Having investigated the word/image and its source, intellectually and somatically, the actor finds something of the center of the character and their state of being. Berry asks the actor to mime the speech, as though translating the text for those who might be deaf, or who cannot understand the language. She explains that she does not want the actor to always describe the image literally, but to encapsulate and experience 'the essence of the images' arising from the words themselves in the body and voice. She emphasizes that her rationale for this is to find delight in the freedom of the movement, but also to investigate and 'find the cost of the image' in the expression of it.

Through this search for the genetic code of the word/image, whilst shaping and sounding the word through the articulatory musculature, Berry aims for accuracy, apprehension of the word's inner life, and discovery of its implicit energy. Seemingly simple in description, Berry cautions that this can be challenging, as Shakespeare's textual images can be dense (Berry 1993: 168). It is relevant to this study that in practice, Berry's physical language differs in intention and effect from Stanislavski's actions – as explored in my practice further on.

Embodied Cognition and Memory – the Use of the Physical Storyboard, Providing the Gateway into Stanislavski-inspired Physical Actions

Two Case Studies – Participants Callum and Amelia

Background

At the beginning of the second-year autumn term, Callum came to speak to me, expressing anxiety about his inability to remember a text. He explained that he had to learn a speech from the play *Medea* (Euripides) for the study of Greek tragedy in his movement class. As he often has difficulty memorizing words, several years ago Callum had devised his own memory system, which he commonly utilizes as a survival strategy. This strategy involves his creation of a sequence of physical movements, with each action tallying in some way with the words of the text. His worry had arisen because he found it hard to speak the speech without applying his devised actions. Callum explained that he finds learning text incredibly hard and uses his physical actions as a device to hold the words in his memory. In particular, its sequence assists with the retention of the order, without jumbling it up, missing large chunks out, or forgetting the words altogether. Following his first reading through of a text, he tries to learn it. He said: 'I always get tripped up by certain words, so that's when I start putting the physical actions to it, trying to give it some sort of position – so I can root back to it.' He likens his physicalization sequence – or, as he labeled it, 'the visual thing' – to a dance: 'I can remember the way my hands moved or I know where I placed them on my body – like a timeline kind of thing with my hands.'

Callum states that when doing a monologue, 'there are no cues, it's all yourself'. So, to counter this lack of directions, he will:

> physically walk through it, to try to understand at this point I raise my hand and at this point I bend down to pick this up, because it gives me cues. If I've got a physical cue I can work out that during this line I walk there, and on that line, because I pick that thing up, so it's like giving me a physical map almost, it becomes almost like a scrap book where I'm taking photos of myself.

It is noteworthy that Callum describes the act of remembering as 'taking photos' of himself, 'looking *at pictures*' (my italics) of himself doing the movements, fixed into the 'scrap book'. By working through the movement sequence, the visuospatial-motor-sensory associations trigger his stored mental images of the words of the text:

> I try to give everything a movement so I can link the two together – the words help the movement and the movement helps the words, so if I forget one I've got the other one to back it up.' I asked Callum whether his movement process was similar to Cicely Berry's method of physically inhabiting the words of the text: 'Yes, it is like the Berry stuff – there's a word 'fiend' and I just pretend that I've got a big nose and pull a big nose away from my face, and I realized I was doing the whole emotion with my face as well, so [. . .] it's sort of illustrative and it's not exactly emotionally true, but through doing the movements a sort of emotion will come through, but it is literally word by word.

The Jason monologue in *Medea* was challenging to him as he could not see how each line was connected to the other. He explained:

> I put basic, almost sign language, kind of mimes to it. If the next word was walking, I might literally put the fingers on my palm and literally walk my fingers along so that a muscle memory emerged. Each of the physical movements that I did merged into the next one. If the word was bird I could merge my hands into a bird shape so I could remember the order and the words and the structure of the piece in particular. Rather than it being an emotional thing, it's much more a visual, literal meaning of the word bird, rather than thinking about the bird that soars and is free. I literally think, 'What does a bird look like?' and then I do my hands placed together flapping up and down.

I pointed out that, although he mentions his motor memory (the connection of his brain with the muscles of his body) as an initiator for the words, as he was speaking to me, his demonstrative gestures created the shape, movement, and animated picture of a bird. I noticed that he coupled the word 'visual' with 'literal meaning' in his explanation. I asked him whether the visual aspect was important for him, as well as the physical. He replied: 'Yes, very much so. I'm looking at my hands as clues, everything is prompting itself.' Having learned the *Medea* text in this manner, the problem Callum faced was that he could not remember the piece if he didn't carry out his planned physical actions to it. The movement class performance of the piece demanded a different set of actions from those Callum had personally created and fixed to the text.

Similarly to Callum, Amelia relayed that she had devised physical movements to enable her memorization of the *Medea* text. Amelia's approach seemed akin to

Callum's, although both denied having any knowledge of each other's process. Amelia reported that she finds it a struggle to learn lines quickly, so she relied on her muscle memory if she had to learn a big speech. Callum had labeled his process 'a kind of dance', and Amelia also used dance vocabulary, saying: 'because of the nature of the text and it being full of imagery, it was easy to build a choreography which meant the lines would come with the choreography – it sped my learning process up'. Amelia expanded:

> I think my strongest modality is definitely physical. If you showed me twenty movements and I went over them with you once, I could remember them straight away, my body has got an amazing memory. Like that Medea speech we did for movement, I did a movement sequence for it so that I could remember.

To explain what she meant, Amelia demonstrated a literal movement of drawing a bow and arrow, depicting a strong image in space as she spoke the phrase 'bright arrow of the sun' (Euripides *Medea*). She might use the physical actions on simply a couple of lines or choreograph a whole monologue if she couldn't remember the lines. She reported:

> The lines come with the choreography, which really makes the learning process much quicker with Shakespeare when the language can be such a barrier, when you have to work so hard to get to the truth and real meanings, I need to learn it first, so then I can put my script down and start to act and feel those feelings. I can't do that straight away, I need to break down that language barrier, and I take all the beautiful imagery – similes and nice words that he gives you – and I remember those. I can't learn it straight away, it just won't go in like a contemporary piece of text because the language is so different.

Although she uses the physicalized actions as a memory aid, Amelia also recognizes that the process of devising the actions assists her in finding underlying meanings in the text. Agreeing with Callum, Amelia likens the work to Cicely Berry's exercises of physically connecting to the text, describing her own method as:

> almost illustrative. I find big strong bold shapes, moving from one to another helps my memory more than if I did small emotional-like movements. I want to use the images. It is images – if you give me any text I make pictures, but for me making those pictures physically is a good learning tool.

As Callum had already discovered, the embedding of the physical movements attached to the words can prove problematic to future work on the text.

Amelia explained that through performing the movements in tandem with the speaking of the text, an entrenched rhythm emerges. This rhythm is repeated every time she works through it: 'I sometimes have a rhythm of how I say those words, and sometimes this can be a problem – to break out of that rhythm.'

I asked to see their use of their actions with the *Medea* text, as I wanted to see an example of their personal strategies in accessing a text without any interventions from me. Although not Shakespeare, the *Medea* speeches are classical language, encompassing large dramatic content. I was interested in the fact that they were employing (and appeared dependant on) a method of creating physical spatial shapes (for example, mental models of images) as a way of not only remembering the text, but of taking ownership of the text.

Example of Callum's Movement Storyboard: Jason from Medea by Euripides

Present: myself, my critical friend as observer, and the participant Callum. The session was filmed, and lasted approximately sixty minutes.

Callum's actions were performed vigorously, with a precise denotation of the words, spoken with an energized vocal projection. However, halfway through the monologue he suddenly stopped, as he had forgotten his sequence of movements and therefore could not remember the words or carry on with the rest of the speech.

Text: Jason from Medea – a Short Example of Some of Callum's Actions

You ~ (Callum points forwards)

Abomination ~ (he draws a circular movement with both arms, coming up his body and then downwards to the floor; see Figure 9.1)

Most detested ~ (he points his finger downwards to the right – pointing to the floor; see Figure 9.2)

Of all women ~ (he draws the curves of a woman's shape)

By every god ~ (his hands take up a praying position)

By me ~ (he points to his chest)

By the whole human race ~ (he draws a big circle like a globe)

Example of Amelia's Movement Storyboard: The Chorus from Medea by Euripides

Amelia worked through this sequence with concentration and expressive feeling, both in her formation of the movements and in her vocal intonation.

FIGURE 9.1 'Abomination'

FIGURE 9.2 'Most detested'

Although not performed as an acting piece, she gave an artistic interpretation with changes in rhythm, stress, tempo, and imaginative choreography.

Text: Chorus from Medea – a Short Example of Some of Amelia's Actions

Earth ~ (she creates a four dimensional globe with her hands)

Awake ~ (she lifts her arms up and then opens them outwards)

Bright arrow of the sun ~ (she pulls her body and arms back as though drawing a bow and arrow; see Figure 9.3)

Look down on the accursed woman ~ (she uses both her arms alternately to draw an arc shape going down to the floor as she looks downwards)

Before she lifts up her murderous hand ~ (she lifts her arm and hand as though she was holding a knife; see Figure 9.4)

To pollute it with her children's blood ~ (she brings down her arms and hand as though stabbing a body)

For they are of your own golden race ~ (she lifts her arms up to the ceiling)

FIGURE 9.3   'Bright arrow of the sun'

FIGURE 9.4 'she lifts up her murderous hand'

Analysis of Their Use of the Movement Storyboard – 'How Can I Know What My Phrase Is until I See What I do?' (Kirsh 2010)

Observing Callum's choice of gestures and words in action, it appears that his spoken movement sequence is an emotionally detached, factual process. The sequence is run through mechanically, like steps in a dance routine. The line structure of the poetic form of the text is not adhered to, but broken up into single words or short phrases of no more than four words together, with a gesture/image attached to each piece. This disruption to the line means that the overall meaning of the speech, or the 'ladder of thoughts' of constructed sense (Berry 2001: 149) within the speech, is not represented through Callum's series of significations. His gestures vary in their semantic route, sometimes being literal denotations, or acting as connotative metaphors, with few emotionally driven gestures. It is likely that Callum is using his movements to create hooks on which to hang his perceptions derived from the text, as in Sadoski and Paivio's *Conceptual Peg Hypothesis* (2013: 65). By breaking up the text into physical images/ideographs on which to hook/anchor the words in his mind, his gesture formation turns the words into images that are noun-led, or verbs that are demonstrated in a representational image, rather than being experienced in an inner action.

Interestingly, Stanislavski warns his actors against using nouns to name the objective, stating that a noun intellectualizes a concept, which becomes 'presented by an image'. This will become representational, rather than 'full, integrated, true action' (Stanislavski 1981: 123–124). Whyman (2008) writes that Stanislavski was skeptical of relying on only a representational use of gesture, which would create what he called 'stencils', an external display of the creative process, in crude, unfelt exaggerations. He warned that the external stencil becomes unchangeable, and 'like the painter he realises every feature and fixes the likeness not on canvas but on himself' (cited in ibid.: 48). Callum could not remember his monologue without galvanizing his imprinted model of representational actions. Was this because, in fixing his actions to single words and short phrases (becoming noun-like), he had not interpreted/experienced the full meaning of the line and the thought progression throughout the piece? He had created 'stencils' – representations, as Stanislavski had warned against. Callum mentioned in his interviews that his working memory is weak, so he has to break the text into small chunks, with an anchored image to place into his episodic long-term memory.

Amelia's route is analogous with Callum's, but has variances. She too sometimes breaks up the lines, but unlike Callum, she frequently actions a whole sense phrase of up to eleven words, or a complete line as one piece, thereby achieving more idea of the complete thoughts behind it. In her interview, it is significant that, although working through the body, she stressed that the visual picture is important. She stated: 'I want to use the images. It is images – pictures. For me making those pictures physically is a good learning tool.' In parallel with Callum's sequence, it appears that some of Amelia's process is about rooting the words to an image, rather than grasping the gestalt behind the whole speech. In contrast to Callum, Amelia could remember her whole speech, and her enactment was aesthetically inventive. Although pleasing to watch in performance, Amelia's physical translation of the words did obscure the global meaning of the text, her sign references being confused in function. This mixed use of gesture signification could interfere with her higher concept comprehension as the precise meanings of the lines are confused through her actions. In her commentator's role of Chorus, her actions have unclear functions. They are sometimes utilized as literal illustrators, and at other times she inhabits the action of the phrase from a subjective, first-person perspective. For example, when Amelia says, 'she lifts up her murderous hand', she is speaking from the spectator's role of the Chorus, describing Medea's action in killing her children; however, Amelia's physical action is to lift her arm as though her hand contains a knife. At other times, the choice of action is ambiguous within the context. On the words 'hold her', meaning the Chorus's instruction to capture Medea, Amelia places her arms around herself, which could be interpreted as an embrace rather than an imprisoning action.

This tendency to take the words alone, or in small chunks of meaning, mirrors the reading action of some people with dyslexia. They often report that when they read the text, they see each word individually, or take in small bits of text, therefore struggling with grasping the meaning of the whole piece: 'It [dyslexia], stops me from understanding the meaning of the text because I'm just concentrating on trying to say one word in a sentence correctly' (Amelia, in explanation of her work). There are empirical studies that throw light on the participants' dependence on these movement sequences, especially for individuals with dyslexia and memory weaknesses. The cognitive scientist David Kirsh, in a study of dancers' physical 'marking' of their dance routines, argues that the body works as a representational vehicle providing a scaffold to mentally project more detail than could be held in the mind, augmenting cognition. Working as a semiotic code, Kirsh suggests the dancers utilize their bodies to 'drive thought deeper' than through mental stimulation alone. Their physical actions generate an external product in which to think through (2010: 2864–2866). Lending early support to the embodied cognition perspective, and useful in exploring Callum's and Amelia's reliance on the physical storyboard, in his book *Memory for Actions*, Engelkamp (1998) presents his *multimodal enactment theory* investigations. These investigations have shown that short verbal phrases that are accompanied by physical actions are better remembered than if they are simply read or listened to. Engelkamp postulates that this is because the cognitive planning and creation of the physical action compels the mind to focus strongly on the reason for the action, so there is an item-specific encoding in the brain (ibid.: 41). Engelkamp writes that there are three distinct phases in the encoding of information: the sensory, conceptual, and motor phases. The sensory encoding processes are divided into two areas. They can be verbal representations, which they designate as *word nodes*, and visual representations, referred to as *picture nodes*. With a correlation to Sadoski and Paivio's (2013) *Dual Code Theory* (where cognition in reading involves activity in the verbal and non-verbal systems through types of imagery), these two separate pathways connect together to form conceptual meaning. If there is a thought or an instruction given to carry out an action, an activation of the two nodes, word and picture, combine to make a concept of the idea. This is followed by motor encoding, which activates the motor movement. In Engelkamp's view, the motor encoding and movement create the enactment effect on memory, rather than the imagination alone (1998: 35–49).

Through the observation of both Callum's and Amelia's choreography, it is apparent that their bodily movements encapsulate a body/mind/world space pattern derived from their imaginative associations of the word. The marriage of the picture nodes with the word nodes forms an idea concept that is transferred into discrete motor movements. The spatial directions of the body have a specificity, creating a conceptual peg, similar to the strokes of the pen on the page. However, Engelkamp specifies that the enactment of an action enforces concentration on the information relevant to that action alone, and suppresses other information that is not relevant to that action. The actions are coded independently of each other in an item-specificity. This means it is difficult to create associations and connections with the other actions. This is what happens with Callum and his embedded single actions, and his inability to shift away from his actions when speaking the text. Conversely, according to Engelkamp, visual-imaginal encoding is freer and is adept at making connections with other items. The visual-imaginal encoding restricts information processing less than performing the actions (Engelkamp 1998: 77–78). This might be why the drawing and use of visual symbols is an effective and freer tool for those with dyslexia.

The Next Chapter

In the next chapter, Action Research (Cycle Two) and Teaching Strategy Two is embarked upon with a set of four research participants (including Amelia and Callum). The effectiveness of using a Stanislavski-inspired Active Analysis and Units and Action Five stage sequence is trialed. This is explored in comparison with Cicely Berry's approach to the text, specifically as a teaching method in assisting dyslexic students' access to meaning, character intention, and retention of language in their speaking and acting of Shakespeare's text. Specific difficulties are revealed through the participants' responses, and an extra sixth stage of drawing is added to the five stages of physical action sequence.

KEY POINTS OF CHAPTER 9

- The debate surrounding the effectiveness of using Stanislavski's actions on a Shakespeare text, especially for those with dyslexia
- An overview of the history of Stanislavski and Shakespeare, Peter Hall, and John Barton
- An overview of the historical roots of some practitioners' disciplines informing Cicely Berry's use of voice and action in experiencing the images in the words
- Case study observation of two dyslexic participants and their choreographing of a physical storyboard to support their memory of text

---

Note

1 In the quote below, actor and theatre director Kirsty Cubberley Lobb (who is identified as both dyslexic and dyspraxic) attempts to capture in words the negative effect that training in Stanislavski's methods had on her sense of self when at drama school, as written in her MA dissertation in Actor Training (Cubberley Lobb 2017). Her words are backed up by the experience of my dyslexic students with Stanislavski methods, as evidenced in the trials described in this book.

Stanislavski wrote in *An Actor Prepares* his aim was to 'find a way to truly live on stage' [. . .]. He catalogued a system of acting by breaking down the experience of theatre into elements, attentions, tasks, communications, and suggested that if the actor was trained in each of these elements, when rolled together the actor would be in a 'creative state' and able to achieve genuine life on stage. From the experience of my own actor training, being dyslexic and dyspraxic, this idea of breaking things down, chunking the whole into bitesize manageable pieces, should provide a clearer understanding but in practice, it did not. My reality was disconnected, unrelated to me [. . .]. Compartmentalizing acting does not make the experience of training more profound and bring deeper understanding, rather it dislocates you from the experience, leaves you less assured and feeling the skills learned are light weight and superficial [. . .]. If we remove the structure that we have to recognise: [. . .] remove labels and definitions that create so many boxes that we must climb up over the sides to escape, only to fall into another box – the journey is so full of seesaws that it is no wonder [dyslexic] students are fed up, tired, disillusioned, disenchanted, lacking in confidence and any idea of self within Actor Training.

(ibid.)

References

Alfreds, M. (2007). *Different Every Night*. London: Nick Hern Books.

Barton, J. (1984). *Playing Shakespeare*. London: Methuen.

Benedetti, J. (1982). *Stanislavski: An Introduction*. London: Methuen Drama.

Berry, C. (1993). *The Actor and the Text*. London: Virgin Books

Berry, C. (2001). *Text in Action*. London: Virgin Books.

Brook, P. (1998). *Evoking Shakespeare*. London: Nick Hern.

Cubberley Lobb, K. (2017) *Recognising a Seesaw Self and Building a SpLD Inclusive Actor Training*. Special Independent Project (MA), Royal Central School of Speech and Drama, London.

Dalcroze, E. (1921). *Rhythm, Music and Education*. Kennford, UK: The Dalcroze Society.

Engelkamp, J. (1998). *Memory for Actions*. Hove, UK: Psychology Press.

Ford Davis, O. (2007). *Performing Shakespeare*. London: Nick Hern.

Gaskill, W. (2010). *Words into Action*. London: Nick Hern.

Gillet, J. (2007). *Acting on Impulse*. London: Methuen Drama.

Gillett, J. & Gutekunst, K. (2014). *Voice into Acting*. London: Bloomsbury.

Gordon, R. (2006). *The Purpose of Playing: Modern Acting Theories in Perspective*. Ann Arbor, MI: University of Michigan Press.

Hall, P. (2000). *Making an Exhibition of Myself*. London: Oberon Books.

Hall, P. (2003). *Shakespeare's Advice to the Players*. London: Oberon Books.

Harrison, C. (2004). *Understanding Reading Development*. London: SAGE Publications.

Kirsh, D. (2010). Thinking with the body. In: Ohlsson, S. & Catrambone, R. (eds.) *Proceedings of the 32nd Annual Conference of the Cognitive Science Society*. Austin, TX: Cognitive Science Society, pp. 2864–2869.

Merlin, B. (2007). *The Complete Stanislavsky Toolkit*. London: Nick Hern.

Naylor, B. (2009). Here let us breathe, and haply institute. A course of learning and ingenious study. Academia, actor training and Shakespeare. Paper given at *'Local/Global Shakespeares': The Fourth British Shakespeare Association Conference*, Kings College/Globe Theatre, 11–13 September.

Naylor, B. (2018). Advice to the players. Paper given at *Barton, Hall and Shakespeare Conference*, Rose Theatre, Kingston University, 8 September.

Noble, A. (2010). *How to Do Shakespeare*. London: Routledge.

Raffe, M., Harwood, C., & Lundgren, M. (1974). *Eurythmy and the Impulse of Dance*. London: Rudolf Steiner Press.

Sadoski, M. & Paivio, A. (2013). *Imagery and Text*. New York: Routledge.

Saint-Denis, M. (1964). Stanislavski and Shakespeare. *The Tulane Drama Review*, 9:1, pp. 77–84

Saklad, N. (2011). *Voice and Speech Training in the New Millennium: Conversations with Master Teachers*. Milwaukee, WI: Applause Theatre and Cinema Books.

Speaight, R. (1954). *William Poel and the Elizabethan Revival*. London: William Heinemann.

Stanislavski, C. (1968). *Building a Character*. London: Methuen Drama.

Stanislavski, C. (1980a). *An Actor Prepares*. London: Methuen Drama.

Stanislavski, C. (1980b). *My Life in Art*. London: Methuen.

Stanislavski, C. (1981). *Creating a Role*. London: Methuen Drama.

Tucker, P. (2002). *Secrets of Acting Shakespeare*. London: Routledge.

Weingust, D. (2006). *Acting from Shakespeare's First Folio Theory, Text and Performance*. London: Routledge.

Whyman, R. (2008). *The Stanislavski System of Acting*. Cambridge, UK: Cambridge University Press.

10

A TRIAL OF THE PHYSICAL ACTIONS METHOD INSPIRED BY STANISLAVSKI

Action Research (Cycle Two) and Teaching Strategy Two

Introduction

In the early stages of my teaching of the Shakespeare unit, we explore diverse methods in approaching the reading and acting of Shakespeare. This includes paraphrasing the text into contemporary language, looking for stage directions, character actions, and motivations written into the text, Linklater's auto-suggestive 'dropping in' of the words (Linklater 1992: 36–39, 105–108), Houseman's use of objects and spaces to clarify thoughts and actions (2008: 125–126), observance of Shakespeare's verse form (Hall 2003; Rodenburg 2002), and Berry's corporeal way into the text (1993: 168; 2001: 223; 2008: 95).

As part of this procedure, I include Stanislavski-inspired methods of breaking down a scene into Units and Actions and his Active Analysis score. The particular process I use was initially taught to me when I attended a director's training course (*How To Rehearse*, 2006) at the Royal Academy of Dramatic Art, taught by the theatre, television director, and actor trainer Sue Dunderdale (formerly head of the MA Text and Performance and the MA Director's courses at the Royal Academy of Dramatic Art). There are a variety of interpretations of the methods of Units and Actions on text extrapolated from Stanislavski's writings. Dunderdale relates that she first learnt this method of Uniting and Actioning when she was working with theatre director Howard Lloyd Lewis at the Theatre Royal, Lincoln in 1972, which she has since solidified into her own method. She says: 'the full method I use is something I've developed over the years, and most importantly, I have found a way of making it active rather than a spoken or written exercise. It is the basis of how I work.' Dunderdale sees this method as 'a release for the actor, especially with Shakespeare, to get the language inside them' (personal communication). My critical friend in this study also learnt this particular style of Actioning when working as an actor with the directors Clare Venables and Howard Lloyd Lewis at the Theatre Royal, Lincoln in 1973.

Active Analysis: The Stages of Physical Actions

This sequence is clearly adapted from many of Stanislavski's ideas for rehearsal methods on text as variously described in his books. Dunderdale's method involves several more stages, but in this case, I use a basic version.

There are three beginning steps:

- First, the actors (and director/teacher) read the scene aloud together and discuss the meaning, character journey, and any particular aspects to note or difficulty in comprehending the narrative or language.
- Secondly, the actors, usually through discussion with others in the scene, break the scene down into units (sections) of what is happening within the text, and then each unit is given an overall title.
- Thirdly, the actors examine what their character is doing as they speak the lines. They analyze what they are saying and why they are saying it, what they want to achieve, or possibly do to the other actor in the scene. Having made a decision on those questions, the actor gives each want/intention/objective an action, labeling it with an active verb. So the line 'I love you' could have a psychological objective such as 'I press you for an answer', depending on the character's intentions or their Given Circumstances within the scene (*press* as the active verb and getting an answer as the objective). Alternatively, the action can be descriptive, such as 'I embrace you'. (Merlin asserts that there are no formal rules in the process of actions in Stanislavski's system. She explains that there are also two types of actions: those driven by imaginary needs, or actions that simply describe the physical life of the role; 2003: 134–135.)
- The action might be for one line, or it can involve a chunk of text.

Having broken the scene up into Units and Actions, the *Active Analysis* begins. There are four parts to this active stage, each building on the other:

- When first working on their feet, the actors put down their texts. The director will read aloud the chosen title of each unit and then read out the individual actions, using the actors' chosen verbs (for example, 'Isabella hits Claudio'). The verbs can include metaphorical actions (such as 'Isabella squeezes Claudio' if she is pressurizing him at that moment). The actors remain silent, and as the director reads the verb action aloud, they physicalize their actions, using exaggerated movements which encapsulate the psychological want/drive behind the verb. This is related to what Stanislavski called the *Silent Etude* (Merlin 2003: 30). Although the movements are encouraged to be large, they are carried out with a vivid inner monologue of conviction. The actors work through the whole unit using movement only, and then return to the beginning for the unit for the next stage of the sequence.

- The director reads out the actions again. The actor now introduces improvised voiced sound (no words yet) in tandem with the physical actions. The sound must be as bold and psychologically truthful as the physical actions. This is to get an idea of the emotional wants behind the actions, is related to Stanislavski's work on expression of feelings through nonsense syllables, and is not intellectualized (Stanislavski 1981: 254; Whyman 2008: 152, 268).
- They repeat the whole sequence and unit again, retaining the physical actions, but using brief improvised words of their own which capture the gist of what the character is saying or feeling. (In the process of living truthfully as the character, Stanislavski tells the actor to improvise the text 'in your own words' to achieve the 'live feelings of himself'; Stanislavski 1981: 216.)
- Finally, they repeat the whole unit again, but now the actors read/speak the actual lines of the author's text, keeping the actions and feeling, but reducing them down to a more naturalistic level in size and expression.

According to Dunderdale, the rationale for this gradual extension is 'to get an intuitive response, rather than a thought out response'. Dunderdale maintains that for her as director, 'the physicalization and free vocalization are the most important part because it is very releasing for the actors to find out what is going on in the scene, beneath their ability to talk about things, so you have to be *doing* things to work out what is happening' (personal communication).

Rejecting an intellectual study of the text, Stanislavski believed that:

> Generally the lines of the play become indispensable to the actor only in the last phase of his creative preparations, when all the inner material he has accumulated is crystallized in a series of definite moments, and the physical embodiment of his role is working out methods of expressing characteristic emotions.
>
> *(1981: 95)*

Before I began this dyslexia enquiry, my experience was that this exercise allows the actor to work out the character's needs and intentions, utilizing physical and vocal communication through a spontaneous, intuitive process, rather than an intellectual analysis. The vocal sounds made without forming words, intertwined with the actions, release the basic feelings, rooting and stimulating the emotions and thoughts aroused through embodying the content of the text. There can be a danger that sometimes chosen actions can become fixed, or restrict any fresh responses from being investigated, but this will not happen if there is a flexible attitude towards the *Active Analysis*.

Action Research (Cycle Two) and Teaching Strategy Two

Case Studies – Callum, Amelia, Verity, and Abigail

For the practice of Units and Actions, I had chosen a scene to work on from Shakespeare's *Measure for Measure* (Act III, Scene i) where Isabella comes to tell her imprisoned brother Claudio that he must die unless she sleeps with Angelo. In this scene, the language, graphic imagery, use of metaphor, semantics, and need for a precise articulation of the words related to the underlying psychology are complex. In addition, the emotional stakes for the characters are extremely heightened. The scene offers an excellent exercise piece to engage with acting Shakespeare.

The Class Work

Method

This action research trial with my dyslexic participants initially had to be included as part of my overall teaching of the whole cohort in the Shakespeare unit syllabus. At the start, it included all twenty-five second-year students I was teaching and the dyslexic participants.

We began by reading the scene aloud in class, with various individuals taking the roles of Isabella and Claudio, followed by a discussion on the meaning of the words and what was happening within the scene. Before the class, I had already divided the scene up into small units, and I titled each unit separately from A to F. This was to form the individual sections for the students to work on. As a demonstration piece, I had previously prepared Unit A in advance with my own action and verb choices, to model the exercise with the students in the class.

At this point, I deviated from the practice usually proposed when utilizing Stanislavski's actions. Rather than begin with asking what is the character's *objective* (Caldarone & Lloyd-Williams 2004: xviii), I suggested they ask themselves what their character is *doing through the words* when they speak. My reason for this is twofold:

1) In Shakespeare, language is *doing*, the character is doing something with the words. The words are the event. In this exercise, I want the student to get inside each word, to become conversant with the meaning of it, why they are saying it, and in the utterance, to match word with meaning and action in a symbiotic relationship. This is a necessity for any actor speaking Shakespeare's words, but particularly for those with dyslexia.

Much that is said within this scene between Isabella and Claudio is multi-layered and convoluted in the language. Therefore searching for the objective of the character could become muddling, especially for those with difficulties with reading, words, and syntax. It also places the language as secondary in focus. By putting the attention outside of the words, it would be easy for the individual to miss what is actually within the detail of the language, to articulate the words without conscious thought as mere empty sounds, and to become lost within the layers.

2) I did not guide them to use a transitive verb to describe their action, rather than an intransitive verb (as is often advised, for example by Gillet 2007: 210; Alfreds 2007: 73). Adding more word rules to an already intricate reading and language analysis task could exacerbate stress levels for those with dyslexia. This could obscure the goal, rather than offering a pathway into the scene.

In the whole cohort class, we worked through Unit A in the prescribed sequence. As a demonstration exercise, I took the role of the director and read the verb actions out while student volunteers acted the parts of Isabella and Claudio proceeding through the four stages: (1) actions, (2) actions and sounds, (3) actions and improvised words, (4) actions and reading the text – delivered in a more naturalistic style. This class demonstration established the sequence. We also paraphrased the unit into everyday language and the students acted out the paraphrased Unit A using contemporary language, to anchor their understanding. Finally, for homework, I divided my cohort of twenty-five students into groups of three. I gave each group a small unit of the scene to action together, in order to perform their devised sequence in the next class. One student was to be the director, while the other students would play the roles of Isabella or Claudio. I put three of my research participants together in one group: Callum as director, Abigail as Claudio, and Amelia as Isabella. Verity had to be placed with two non-dyslexic students, and she played Isabella. I gave them a preparation time of two days before giving a class performance of their Units and Actions sequence. They needed adequate time for the shared task of discussing and absorbing the text, deciding on their verbs and actions, creating their movement, sounds, and improvised words, and rehearsal of the text, ready to perform.

The Class Performance

In the class performances of their unit amongst the whole cohort, I noticed that Amelia, Abigail, and Verity were strikingly impactful in their physical actions. Their choreography included inventive physical shapes symbolizing interesting interpretations. Their physical actions, vocal sounds, and improvised words were energetically committed to, with an apparent ease. As their Active Analysis appeared to be deeply embedded, my expectation was that their final stage of the sequence (playing the scene with the actual text) would be equally assured. I was therefore surprised when, in both groups, Amelia and Verity (who had the most to say in their units) still stumbled on the reading of certain bits of the text. They read some of the text as though they were unfamiliar with the words, giving an impression of insecurity, lack of comprehension, and poor communication despite their rehearsed preparation. Their reading of Shakespeare's words lacked the liberated confidence they had just given to their movements, vocal sounds, and improvised words. This insecurity with the text was notable in comparison with their fellow students of similar acting ability without dyslexia and the accurate assurance with which they read the lines. The actions sequence had also helped the less fluent readers without dyslexia to gain autonomy in their acting and speaking of the lines in their unit. I was puzzled that Amelia and Verity's hard work on each stage of their unit had not provided an effective stepping-stone into the reading and speaking of the text, promoting a familiarity with Shakespeare's actual words. I therefore decided to work further with them, repeating the same units in a separate workshop outside of the general cohort class. I wanted to investigate why this discrepancy might be happening.

Peer Advice from My Critical Friend

I reported my participants' problem of tripping over some of the words in the fourth stage of the process when reading the text to my critical friend (he is familiar with the sequence, having learnt it when he was professional actor). He advised me that in his practice, before finally giving the actors the text, he reads the lines of the text aloud to them. The actors carry out their actions as he reads and they listen, but they still do not speak the actual words of the text. He suggested that I might insert this stage into my own practice.

In examining Stanislavski's methods, I discovered that in order to try to bridge the gap between the improvised words and the speaking of the text, Stanislavski (1981: 207) mentions feeding his actors the words of the text aurally, before they finally speak them from the script. He writes:

> You scarcely had to work on your lines because for some time in advance I had been suggesting to you Shakespeare's own words when you had to have them, when you were reaching out for them for the verbal accomplishment of this or that objective.
>
> *(ibid.)*

I therefore decided to follow my critical friend's advice and to include his recommended stage in the workshops. I would read out the text, and ask the participants to physicalize what they heard. For clarity, this additional stage would now be called Stage Five in the sequence. This was an expedient decision. The inclusion of Stage Five made their difficulties, and the causes of them, transparent.

Examples of Verity's Process as Isabella: The Filming of Unit C of Act III, Scene i, Measure for Measure

It is important to note that the participants had already done considerable work on their unit before engaging with me in this workshop. Their unit was taken from the scene we had previously read and discussed in detail in the general acting class. We had discussed the characters' situations and views, the meaning of the text, what they were saying, and the language shifts Shakespeare has made with metaphors and double meanings. We had paraphrased it into contemporary language to ensure all was understood. They had already rehearsed their unit with their fellow actor and director for their homework and performed it in the class. They had also had a few extra days to work on it before beginning the workshops with me. They were conscientious students who applied themselves to their work with focus, showing strong abilities in many areas of their training.

Present: my critical friend as observer, and to assist with filming their work. Research participant Verity is playing Isabella, and another non-participant student is playing Claudio. Another non-participant student, as the director of their Unit C, is reading out the actions for the actors. The time spent was three hours approximately.

In this short description, I am focusing particularly on Verity's insecurity on the text. She had been imprecise when reading much of the text in the class presentation, but in this workshop, Verity's lack of fluency was on Isabella's first speech. Verity and her fellow actor ran through their sequence as they had rehearsed it for the earlier class performance. Below is a very short section of Unit C and Isabella's text (see Table 10.1). On the right side of the table, Verity's action title, movement, sound, and improvised words are included, with my comments.

What Happened in Verity's Performance of Stages One, Two, Three, and Four in Her Active Analysis

As in Verity's earlier class presentation, Stages One, Two, and Three of the Active Analysis were performed with a lively, assured commitment. Also replicating her class presentation (despite having ample rehearsal time), when reading the text in Stage Four, Verity made many noticeable mistakes over several phrases by missing out, tripping over, and supplanting small words. For example, in her spoken inaccuracies, she said:

- ' i'head' rather than 'i' th' head'
- 'as falcon as the fowl' rather than 'as falcon doth the fowl'
- 'he would appear as deep as a pond', rather than 'he would appear a pond as deep as hell'
- She also tripped over the articulation of many other words throughout the speech, displaying an insecurity with the language. As so much prior rehearsal had been done previously on this text, these mistakes were striking.

TABLE 10.1 Unit C: Isabella unburdens herself/Claudio tests and protects her

Isabella: . . . *This outward sainted deputy,*	***Action 1. Isabella unveils the devil***
Whose settled visage and deliberate word	Movement: Verity's action is as though she is pulling a cloth away from what it was concealing.
Nips youth i' th' head and follies doth anew	Sound: 'Aha!'
As falcon doth the fowl, is yet a devil:	Improvised words: 'Look at him'
His filth within being cast, he would appear	*(My comment: this is a very brief verb action to capture the whole speech and skims over the multiplicity of*
A pond as deep as hell.	*meanings of the words within it.)*
Claudio: *The prenzie Angelo!*	***Action 2. Claudio is shocked***
	Movement: Josh steps back and opens his arms
	Sound: Intake of breath – 'ah!'
	Improvised words: 'I don't believe it'
Isabella: *O, 'tis the cunning livery of hell,*	***Action 3. Isabella parades the beast***
The damned'st body to invest and cover	Movement: Verity walks about holding her arms out as though presenting something in front of her
In prenzie guards.	Sound: 'ooofff!'
	Improvised words: 'Yes, this is what he wants me to do'
	(My comment: these improvised words demonstrate that Isabella's specific word meaning of this section of the speech is not being directly addressed, or connected with.)

Inserting Stage Five: Feeding the Lines to Verity

Taking the advice of my critical friend, in an attempt to secure the words in Verity's mind, I now added Stanislavski's Fifth Stage; his method of feeding the words aurally to the actor. I read Isabella's lines aloud, directing Verity to action the words as she heard them.

Stage Five: What Happened with Verity

During this aurally received process of the text, Verity became lost. As I read Isabella's speech aloud in short, easily assimilated sense phrases, Verity's gestures remained energized, but transformed into vague, poking movements, indicating a scant correlation with the words in the text. In addition, there was an obvious mismatch between Verity's attempts to find a physical relationship with the words being read to her and her pre-planned verb actions that she had already entrenched in the previous stages of the work. As Isabella's speeches have obscure words linked with images in Shakespeare's multi-layered metaphors, it was clearly hard for Verity to hold all the words in her working memory, make sense of them, and translate them into actions. When carrying out Stanislavski's sequence in the class situation, Verity's actions, sounds, and few improvised words had appeared extremely effective in the first showing. To an observer, it was not evident that she had not fully comprehended the elements within the words. However, when I introduced Stanislavski's method of aurally feeding the words to the actor, as she attempted to action them, Verity's lack of the grasp of the details within the text was revealed.

Verity's Action One is entitled: 'Isabella unveils the devil'. This simple statement is meant to summarize Isabella's six-line speech:

> This outward sainted deputy
> Whose settled visage and deliberate word
> Nips youth i' th' head and follies doth anew
> As falcon doth the fowl, is yet a devil:
> His filth within being cast, he would appear
> A pond as deep as hell.

Here Isabella describes Angelo's actions and her strong feelings about his character. The speech involves vivid imagery, with homonymic, multi-layered meanings entrenched within the word/images. Verity's single action to encapsulate all the six lines was too generalized to capture what Isabella is actually saying. Verity's improvised words were simply: 'look at him'. This is a skimpy translation of what Shakespeare has included. In a subsequent discussion, Verity admitted that, although we had done so much work on the meanings in the class and she had prepared it for class presentation, she did not understand the meaning of some of the words in this speech, nor did she have a precise grasp of the intricacies of what she was saying. She had thought that if she had a general gist of what the speech was about, it might be enough to get by without her puzzlement being revealed.

Her dyslexia meant that the spelling of words did not offer a key to meaning. Verity had misread the word 'fowl' thinking it meant 'foul'. She knew Isabella meant something about Angelo being horrible, but she had forgotten our class discussion explaining the reference to the falcon preying on the small bird and swooping down to bite off its head, thereby missing the metaphor illustrating Angelo's destructive power over her and her brother Claudio. (In the editor's notes for *Measure for Measure*, Lever reports that a bird of prey kills by nipping in the head; in Shakespeare 1965: 72.) Isabella's description of Angelo nipping youth in the head captures the triple meaning of his condemning Claudio to death (by beheading him), wanting to take away Isabella's maidenhead, plus killing in the manner of a bird of prey. Shakespeare's polysemic metaphor was completely forgotten and missed by Verity. This is a prime example of the layers within Shakespeare's words that need to be perceived by the actor to enhance performance and to serve Shakespeare's intentions.

Verity also disclosed to me that she had not understood the speech about Angelo's body being dressed in 'prenzie guards and the livery of hell', for the lines:

> O, tis the cunning livery of hell,
> The damned'st body to invest and cover
> In prenzie guards [. . .].

In the initial reading of the scene in class, I had previously explained to all of the students that there is a question about the meaning of the word 'prenzie', and advised them to retain the use of the word, but to understand the meaning of 'prenzie' as 'precise'; Angelo is hyper-correct and precise in his behavior, views, and, no doubt, his clothes (guards). (It is acknowledged here that the word 'prenzie' comes from the First Folio. Editors Bate and Rasmussen in the RSC edition of the play's text state that the meaning of the word 'prenzie' is unclear, and could mean precise, puritanical, priestly, or princely; Shakespeare 2010: 60.) Some editors, such as J.W. Lever in the Arden edition of the play (Shakespeare 1965) have amended 'prenzie' to 'precise' in the play script.

Verity's improvised words for this bit of the text were 'Yes, this is what he wants me to do.' Isabella's exposure of Angelo's double-crossing hypocrisy, hidden underneath his robes of authority, is overlooked by Verity. Verity is speaking words wherein the meaning for her is a blur. Through an inability to engage with all of the words and their meaning, or make an actor's informed decision about what she wanted to play within the lines (despite her hard work on the unit and actions), Verity struggled to give a fluent reading or speaking of the content of her scene.

Examples of Amelia as Isabella and Abigail as Claudio in Units A and B in Act III, Scene i, Measure for Measure (with Callum in the Role of Director)

Present: my critical friend as observer and assisting with filming. Participant Amelia is playing Isabella, Abigail is playing Claudio, and Callum is the director of their Units A and B.

What Happened in Amelia and Abigail's Stages One, Two, Three, and Four

In the class presentation, Amelia had used imaginative and confident actions and voiced sounds in her unit. Nevertheless, like Verity, during the reading of the text in Stage Four, she had stumbled over many of the words when reading. As I had already done with Verity in the previous workshop, I now decided to add Stage Five – Stanislavski's idea of feeding the actors with the words whilst asking them to physicalize what they hear. Abigail as Claudio had less to say than Amelia, so her management of the text was less exposed in these units.

Inserting Stage Five: The Feeding of the Lines and What Happened with Amelia and Abigail

At the beginning of this stage of the exercise, both Amelia's and Abigail's actions were illustrative, using a literal translation from individual words and phrases into movements, demonstrating an evident comprehension of some of the text. However, as they continued further, it became obvious that important words were not being engaged with.

Some examples of Amelia's indistinct apprehension of the text, revealed through her physical actions, were as follows:

- For the words, 'an everlasting leiger', in her action, Amelia made a vague jab forward with the arms, without any defined signification. (This is discussed later after my insertion of Stage Six.)
- Amelia's semantic mis-conceptions were obviously transparent in Isabella's lines:

  None, but such a remedy as, to save a head,
  To cleave a heart in twain [. . .]

(This is also discussed later, after insertion of Stage Six.)

- For the word 'save', Amelia rubbed her fingers together using a gesture commonly understood to symbolize saving money or being miserly, rather than saving a life, or maidenhood, as in this case.
- She represented 'cleave' using an action as though winding something around some object, rather than cutting something.
- 'in twain' was physically represented by an action reminiscent of pulling string between her fingers ('in twain' meaning 'in two pieces').
- Only the word 'heart' (denoted by Amelia's clenched fist forming the image of a heart) was discernibly related to meaning.
- In other doubtful action choices, Amelia mimed a dog's barking mouth for Isabella's lines: 'Would bark your honour from that trunk you bear, And leave you naked.' Barking like a dog is a literal action, not related to Shakespeare's references to a tree. Here Shakespeare is using the noun 'bark' (the outer layer that grows on a tree) in a verb-like manner, denoting the verb action 'to strip'. Isabella is intimating through metaphor that Claudio's body is like a trunk of a tree, and his honor is like the bark of the tree that could be stripped off – 'barked'. It could be argued that Shakespeare also meant that Claudio's loss of honor would become known (as though 'barked' to the world), but Amelia's improvised words showed this was not what she meant.

- For Isabella's words about the 'corporal sufferance' of a beetle being stepped on and killed, Amelia made a soldier's gesture for saluting. The word 'corporal', in Isabella's description, means the body of the beetle; Amelia's saluting gesture as though a military reference of a soldier reveals her muddled grasp of the meaning of what Isabella is saying.
- Abigail, as Claudio, had less to say than Amelia as Isabella in this unit. However, when physicalizing Claudio's question 'Perpetual durance?', Abigail wildly swung her arms vaguely, giving an indefinite signification of Claudio's meaning.

Insertion of Stage Six: The Physicalization of the Word

Perceiving that some of their actions related to the words were ambiguous or appeared empty of meaning, and building on the exploratory work in Stage Five with Verity, I now decided to add yet another step with Amelia and Abigail, comprising a Stage Six. My aim was to further investigate their comprehension of the text, to more precisely embed the language meaning in their minds, in conjunction with their movements of the body and accuracy of speech.

Leaving aside their Stanislavski-type actions that they had already worked on, I asked them to read the text aloud while acting the scene, but to particularly explore the words themselves through physical movement as they actually spoke them, as with some Cicely Berry exercises. As Berry recommends: 'first speak it and then mime it [. . .] filling out the spirit of the picture – and you will begin to realise how detailed each image is, and how filled with three dimensional pictures, and even whole actions'; 'The actor has to be accurate to his own understanding of that image, we must take on the images, fill them with our imagination, for it is only this way we will get into the skin of the character' (Berry 1993: 112–113). I directed them to investigate the sense of what they were saying as they read it by illustrating the meaning through their action. As they were already extremely familiar with the text through prior rehearsals and preparation, I believed that this dual coding process would not overload them.

Stage Six: What Happened with Amelia and Abigail

- When reading the text, Amelia (although sometimes adding succinct actions to some of the words) gives no action to the words: 'Where you shall be an everlasting leiger'.
- In Isabella's hint of the possibility of her being able to save Claudio's life by having sex with Angelo, 'None, but such a remedy as, to save a head, To cleave a heart in twain', Amelia gives no action for the crucial word 'save' as she speaks it.
- She wraps her hands around her head for the word 'cleave'.
- She says 'twine' rather than 'twain', with a mimed action of string passing through her fingers.

- When reading Isabella's phrase 'There is a devilish mercy in the judge', Amelia graphically illustrates the adjective 'devilish' by placing two fingers on the front of her head like horns, giving it tremendous emphasis, but gives no action for the pivotal word 'mercy', and speaks it very quickly as though unimportant. The word 'mercy' is immediately related to the news Isabella had for Claudio to save his life, so should not be ignored.

Significantly, Abigail (playing Claudio) now interrupted the work and asked me what Claudio's words 'perpetual durance' meant before she had to action it, halting the exercise. As Abigail's question had broken the playing of the scene, and as I had observed several apparent misapprehensions, I decided to abandon the playing of the rest of the scene and question them about their choices and experience.

Lack of Realization of the Content of the Text

I asked Amelia why, in Stage Six, she gave no action to the words 'where you will be an everlasting leiger'. When actioning in Stage Five, as I had read out the text, I had noted that she had jabbed the air in a vague manner on these words. Amelia confessed that she had forgotten what a leiger was.

The extent of Isabella's determination that she will not have sex with Claudio is portrayed by her promoting a positive perspective for Claudio to accept his death. Her elevation of Claudio to an ambassador status (leiger) to meet God is not realized by Amelia, despite thorough explanations in class and Amelia's rehearsals.

In the speech 'to save a head, to cleave a heart in twain', Amelia divulged that she had misread the word 'twain' and had thought it meant twine, like string. She did not know what 'cleave' meant. The lack of comprehension of the whole speech was shown in several of her actions, as I have already described in 'Inserting Stage Five: The Feeding of the Lines and What Happened with Amelia and Abigail'.

In Isabella's lines 'In such a one as, you consenting to't, would bark your honour from that trunk you bear and leave you naked', Amelia's improvised words for this were: 'fine, take it, but it will hurt me' (her action in Stage Five had been a barking dog). This is not what Isabella is saying here.

When Isabella talks about the 'poor beetle that we tread upon in corporal sufferance', Amelia had saluted as though talking about an army soldier. In her prepared improvised words, Amelia had said 'dying is just like sleeping', which, although containing the psychological *feel* of what she is saying, is a rough approximation of the overall meaning.

I was not surprised that Abigail had asked me in Stage Six for the meaning of Claudio's question 'Perpetual durance?' I had already noted that her action of swinging her arms about in Stage Five had been undefinable. In her *Active Analysis* sequence, Abigail had copied the actions, sounds, and improvised words Amelia had used at this point. It was therefore not apparent that Abigail had not understood the meaning of the words (as she was imitating Amelia) until she was asked to action it individually as she heard it in Stage Five. Abigail divulged that she had never understood or had forgotten what 'Perpetual durance?' meant, despite the class discussion and her rehearsal of the unit.

The process of working through Stages One to Six in this action research workshop had tested Abigail and Amelia. As they had worked hard on their preparation of the units, the revealing of their misconceptions was uncomfortable for them. It had become clear to all of us through the additional stages that there was still much within the language that was evading them. The mixing of the aims and types of actions from Berry to Stanislavski which I had introduced in Stages Five and Six were also becoming bewildering for us all. Amelia said that she would like to now *draw* the text rather than *action* it, so as to un-muddle all the meanings. We stopped work to discuss our findings. Through this exploration, we had much to grapple with.

Reflection and Analysis of the Work

The Structure of This Section of the Chapter

In the following section, I first review the facility of Stanislavski's units and actions as an aid for those with dyslexia, and arrive at some conclusions about this work. Secondly, I continue with my Action Research Cycle Two for the next step in my research investigation; linking the exercise of drawing with Stanislavski's Active Analysis stages as part of Teaching Strategy Two, and thirdly, I present my conclusions.

A Consideration of the Possible Advantages and Disadvantages in Using Stanislavski's Method of Units and Actions for Those with Dyslexia on Shakespeare's Text

The dyslexia specialist Gavin Reid has pinpointed key principles to support those with dyslexia. One of the components is the necessity for *overlearning* in order to achieve automaticity of procedure (Reid 2003: 151–152, 206). The task of acting in Shakespeare and working through Stanislavski's *Active Analysis* demands substantial automaticity of procedure on several levels, with a high use of episodic and semantic memory. The notion of the storing of information in long-term memory is crucial for understanding and comprehension of text (Harrison 2004: 53). Functioning underneath the playing of the role, the actor is working through planned and practiced patterns, following directions, signaling, receiving, and observing. Adequate time must be provided for overlearning to take place, with repetition as an important ingredient. Rehearsal, planning of structure, sequencing, use of prior knowledge, self-originated ideas and questions, and utilization of multisensory modalities all enhance deep learning and retention, especially for those with dyslexia (Reid 2003: 201, 206).

In theory, Stanislavski's system of Units and Actions would appear to fulfill Reid's recommendations, although this has been demonstrated as not completely effective. The breaking down of the overall text into smaller segments of units, which are then further broken down into consideration of the motivation/objective for actions, would seem to offer a perspicuous route into the text, the repeated stages providing the critical overlearning process Reid recommends while presenting an opportunity for individual construction of meaning and shared invention with scene partners. When applying Stanislavski's Units and Actions as an exercise, I assumed that the task of reflective analysis of the text would ensure that the participants gained a solid connection with the meaning of the written words, which would then trigger their actions and underpin their speaking of the words with confidence. Nonetheless, as observed in the practice, an apprehension of the language itself (and therefore the character's thoughts) was not fully gained. See the note at the end of this chapter for the participants' views of the advantages and disadvantages of a Stanislavski actions approach.[1]

My Conclusions about the Efficacy of Stanislavski's Unit and Action Method on Shakespeare's Text

The clash of aims between carrying out Stanislavski's actions and retaining a focus on Shakespeare's words became evident as soon as I added Stages Five and Six to the sequence. Amelia, Verity, and Abigail were all insecure on reading and speaking various parts of the text despite their conscientious application of verb-action identification and improvised sounds, devised actions, and words. When observing them trying to action the words in Stages Five and Six, I realized that use of Stanislavski's actions method can camouflage the fact that the actor has not fully understood all of the word content. Summarizing a chunk of the text under a single heading with a verb action can truncate and skim the details. Contextual information or emotional feeling alone can produce a generalized action that evades the details, avoiding a precise decoding of individual words. If the actions and feelings are delivered with a committed creative expression, the observer can be misled into believing that all is understood.

In examining the experience of those with dyslexia, phenomenologist researcher Mathew Philpott has labeled dyslexics' interaction with the text and their bodies as a 'dys-location'. The dyslexic learner having an overpowering freedom over the objects in the text can fail to recognize or settle on the fixed meaning of the word (Philpott 2000: 132). Philpott (who is himself dyslexic) suggests that a disequilibrium occurs between the meshing of the text with the body of the reader (ibid.: 143). He claims:

> Symptoms such as blurring or moving words, the inability to recognise words and the passing over of single words and sometimes whole lines can be interpreted as a peculiar slackening of the tensional arc or fold that brings an object and body together in the form of co-existence and presence.

(ibid.)

Throwing light on the mistakes Verity, Abigail, and Amelia made in skimming over significant details in the words (and Callum's difficulty in remembering his *Medea* speech), Philpott argues: 'the dyslexic can be susceptible to an insufficiency of involvement with the text which results in diminishing of meaning. The objects of the text (letters, words and syntax) become undifferentiated so that all objects are equally important' (ibid.: 132–133). In exploring Stanislavski's actions on Shakespeare, it appears that those with the 'dis-location' effect of dyslexia (Philpott 2000) consistently missed details of import in the text. Despite these difficulties, when paying attention to the participants' appraisal of the Stanislavski action work (see the endnote), it is also apparent that they found value in the foundational base it gave them. I therefore conclude that this Stanislavski-inspired work is a helpful tool for those with dyslexia to a limited degree, in entering and gaining a familiarity with the character's situation and the text. In my experience of teaching the participants, I am convinced that if they had attempted to read and perform the scenes without this Stanislavski work, their reading and understanding would have been even more inconsistent. However, I understand that although Stanislavski's methods are beneficial with a less demanding verbal text, a deeper level of syntactic and semantic attention is necessary for speaking Shakespeare, especially for those with dyslexia.

Action Research (Cycle Two) Teaching Strategy Two Continued: A Bridge into Speaking the Text, Inserting the Drawing of Words-ideas-images-feeling into Stanislavski's Unit and Action Sequence

Reflecting on what might assist in the participants' unearthing of what is secreted within the text, I pondered whether the exercise of drawing and a re-reading of the drawings (if amalgamated into Stanislavski's stages of actions) might provide the means for a word focus and recognition and the grounding of meaning. When Amelia and Abigail's actions in Stage Six came to a halt, they remarked that the drawing of the text should be used as part of the Actioning sequence in place of Step Five (having the words read aloud, and then actioned). Responding to their suggestion, I decided to explore the *Measure for Measure* text with Verity and Abigail in this manner.

Verity's Drawing of Isabella's Speech

Present: Verity and myself. The workshop lasted thirty-five minutes.

Method

Materials: a large pad of paper and selection of felt tips and crayons.

Verity had consistently stumbled over the speaking of the nine lines of Isabella's speech 'This outward sainted deputy' to 'The damneds't body to invest and cover in prenzie guards'. This therefore seemed an appropriate section to work on. Having discovered that Verity had not understood what she was saying, we discussed the word meanings within the speech until I was sure that Verity was clear about the whole text.

I then read out key phrases from the speech in their sequence. She repeated the words aloud while drawing her personal interpretation of what she was saying, feeling, and visualizing. She worked rapidly, committing her images to paper. Her images were evocative and symbolic, rather than literal illustrations. When she completed her drawing, she wrote the phrase underneath it while speaking it aloud.

When we had finished working on the nine lines up to 'prenzie guards', Verity then read the phrases aloud connected to her pictures, taking time to explore the words with a variety of vocal expressions connected to her inner experience. She spoke each phrase several times over, linking the words to her images.

I then asked her to get up on her feet and to read the speech, bringing all that she had discovered about the words through her drawing process into her reading. There was a marked contrast in the quality of her reading from her previous speaking of it when she performed her Units and Actions. She now spoke the words more slowly, giving them weight, and they were laden with intention, meaning, and connection, without any tripping over articulation.

Verity then explained her images to me and what they contained. Figures 10.1–10.3 are examples of some of them, demonstrating the ability to capture the textual detail through her interpretations.

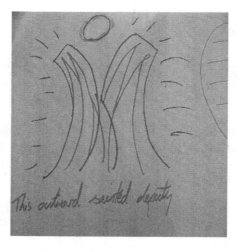

FIGURE 10.1 'This outward sainted deputy'

Verity's explanation: 'There is a halo on top as Angelo is supposed to be a holy man – "deputy" – represented by using the blue color because he is royal in the sense that he has power in his situation – "this outward" – his robes (the sweeping down of the pen) showing his richness and the outward lines say "Surprise! Look at me!" He is seen as a person with power.'

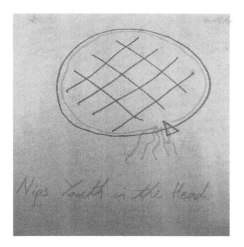

FIGURE 10.2 'Nips youth i' the head'

Verity's explanation: 'This is in two colors. Claudio is represented by green, although he made the mistake by making his girlfriend pregnant, shown in the journey of the circle, he gets found out and it's bad; however, Angelo wants to make the same journey. In the center of the circle is Isabella's virginity. Angelo wants to get inside the circle to Isabella's virginity – this triangle is Angelo piercing Claudio's circle, causing him to fall – Isabella wants to protect her virginity inside the circle, but Angelo can pierce through the circle with the triangle.'

FIGURE 10.3 'As falcon doth the fowl'

Verity's explanation: 'It's a bird shape here – swooping down to kill the fowl at the bottom of the line, and it's circled in green to remind me that the green is Claudio, and Isabella – I see Isabella as green – pure and innocent.'

Verity says that doing the drawings allowed her to gain a deeper understanding of the words. Each individual image for a small chunk of text was important, rather than a single picture conveying a large amount of text. Verity said that she uses this type of imaging in her life all the time. As she forgets words easily, she has developed a way of deliberately fixing a strong image with the word to embed it in her mind as a mnemonic tool. Verity commented that she thought she was able to capture more details in the drawn pictures than in the physical actions. Verity stated that if doing physical actions alone, there was no concrete thing left to refer back to and develop further. Verity thought that the drawing process should precede the actioning of the words.

Abigail's Drawing of Claudio's Monologue (Measure for Measure, Act III, Scene i)

Present: Abigail and myself.

The tools: a large sketchpad and a selection of colored pens and pencils. The workshop lasted sixty minutes.

Abigail went through a comparable process to Verity, working on Claudio's speech. The speech is packed with images and intricate language, and is emotionally demanding. To begin, we worked through the text discussing meaning of words, Claudio's emotional state, his situation, and so on.

The Text

> *Claudio*:
> Ay, but to die, and go we know not where;
> To lie in cold obstruction, and to rot;
> This sensible warm motion to become
> A kneaded clod; and the delighted spirit
> To bath in fiery floods, or to reside
> In thrilling region of thick- ribbed ice;
> To be imprisoned in the viewless winds
> And blown with restless violence round about
> The pendent world: or to be worse than worst
> Of those that lawless and incertain thought
> Imagine howling, – tis too horrible.
> The weariest and most loathed worldly life
> That age, penury and imprisonment
> Can lay on nature, is a paradise
> To what we fear of death.

First, Abigail read Claudio's speech aloud, stumbling over several of the words. I then took her through the drawing process by feeding her crucial phrases from the speech, line by line, which she responded to by drawing and speaking the phrases, then writing them next to her drawing. After 'reading' through and explaining her drawing interpretations to me, she read the speech again. As with Verity, her reading had gained enormously in fluency and connection.

In the Stanislavski physical work, Abigail's actions had been predominantly emotionally and psychologically derived. Here, in her drawing, she used a similar approach, of emotional arousal, delineated in expressive pen use. In comparison with Verity's drawings (which are symbolic), Abigail's pictures (Figures 10.4–10.6) are immediately readable for the observer and do not require much explanation of meaning.

Abigail underlined that at the start of the process, she was skeptical about the rationale for drawing. She explained:

> I found it challenging to draw my first response to the words, as well as letting my lack of drawing skills censor my creativity. But after analyzing my drawings and looking at the emotions I felt when creating them, I realized I was able to deliver the text with a much greater understanding of the psychology and meaning.

FIGURE 10.4 Abigail's storyboard for Claudio's speech: 'Ay, but to die and go we know not where'

FIGURE 10.5 'Death is a fearful thing'

Note: Abigail has used a forceful scribbling for the word 'Death'. She has torn the paper by committing to heavy, frenzied pen strokes, revealing the intensity with which she engaged with the meaning in the word. For both the words 'death' and 'fearful', she has included a layering of colors, signifying the depth of her feeling attached to the words, and the analogous emotions evoked through her perception of the colors red, blue, and brown.

Despite her original doubt, through engaging with the drawing process Abigail stated:

> there are many benefits to this work for a dyslexic student. It really helps to build confidence when approaching Shakespeare's text. The text itself is what's most daunting, so analyzing it using drawings and physical actions helps to build the confidence.

Conclusion

The Stanislavski-inspired action process is proficient for providing a knowledge schema: a holistic overview of the psychology, feelings, wants, and narrative journey of the character within the circumstances of the scene or play. The doing of the actions stirs the feelings within the actor and assists in clarifying some of the aims/objectives of the character. It also offers a comprehensive procedure with which to approach the text. In reading comprehension theory, the gathering of information when processing the text is sometimes labeled a *top-down approach*. This top-down approach is about recognizing, understanding, and remembering the overall story produced within the text, the *macro* narrative (Crystal 1987: 71; Spiro, in Spiro et al. 1980: 265; Harrison 2004: 35).

FIGURE 10.6 'Reside in thrilling region of thick-ribbed ice'

Note: This picture encapsulates the meaning of 'residing' by the idea of an existence within the house. The term 'thick-ribbed ice' is created by the figurative representation of thick chunks of ice in a rib-like enclosure, imprisoning those residing in the house. The 'thrilling region' is delineated by rough strokes in the background. A silver color has been chosen to capture the coldness of the ice and the 'thrillingness' of the region.

The influence of Cicely Berry's work in somatically and intellectually experiencing each word or phrase can be said to answer the crucial question: *What exactly am I saying?* This calls for an examination of each word – to be 'on the word' (Berry 2001: 122). In reading comprehension, Spiro (in Spiro et al. 1980: 265) labels this examination of each word as a *bottom-up approach*, while Crystal (1987: 71) identifies it as a *micro* approach. A bottom-up approach (the *micro*) is an examination of the sounds, grammar and individual words (ibid.). In methods of processing and constructing meaning from the text, Spiro stresses that an over reliance on top-down (*macro*) approaches can be detrimental for those who have difficulty with taking in the words. As demonstrated by Amelia and Verity, relying on top-down processing encourages guessing of unfamiliar words, based on context rather than a decoding of what is actually there. However, too much reliance on bottom-up (*micro*) processing, literally breaking the text up letter by letter and word by word, can detract from comprehension and retention of the whole (Adams 1980: 16–17). Adams recommends that an interplay between top-down and bottom-up process is necessary to obtain fluent reading and comprehension, but stresses that this most successfully occurs when word recognition is over-learned (ibid.: 18). Harrison (2004: 36) reports that the latest findings in reading state that bottom-up processing is vital, as word meaning is obtained in one eye fixation before moving to the next fixation, as we read.

The psychologist David McNeill (1992), whose research focus is the role, meaning, and rationale for human gesture, stresses that physical gesture has an impact on thought. McNeill's gesture-types are the spontaneous paralanguage that occurs as we speak, in concurrence with what we are meaning. He states that language is linear, with ideas presented in segmented, standardized form, but the accompanying gesture is a distinctively personal presentation of the individual's inner imagery twinned with the thought – the gesture revealing the mind. The meaning of the text lives through the mind of the reader, and it is thus important that the gesture is authentically rooted to the word. A gesture that does not belong in any sense with the word distracts the individual away from the meaning.

Through the observation of my participants' reliance on the building of visual constructs through drawing or physicalizing of the text, it has become apparent that their image schema channels and expressions are frequently muddled in their linguistic function, reference, and intentions. It appears that my participants (although relying on visual-spatial imagery) are not alert to organizing their types of signs with the referents they signal to define and extract the meaning of the words.

The Next Chapter

In the next chapter, I introduce a new set of participants. In Action Research (Cycle Three), Teaching Strategy Three, I investigate whether using a more conscious application of the type of gesture, its *representamen, object,* and *interpretant* (Peirce, in Tejera 1988: 11), might assist in more precise identification of the words and perceptions of meaning, offering further tools for an entry into the text.

KEY POINTS OF CHAPTER 10

- Introduction of a system inspired by Stanislavski's *Units and Actions* and *Active Analysis* as a teaching method for acting Shakespeare
- Action Research (Cycle Two) and Teaching Strategy Two, examining the advantages and problems revealed through using a Stanislavski-inspired approach for those with dyslexia in grasping the text
- An Action Research trial in merging the act of drawing with Stanislavski's physical action sequence
- Observation of confusion in the meanings extrapolated from the text and the chosen symbols/gesture signification as representing that meaning, as demonstrated by the research participants with dyslexia in this study

Note

1   What the participants stated they found helpful about the Stanislavski process:

i)   Callum proposed that Stanislavski's units and actions are 'very good for getting the first layer out of the way. When you get confronted with a text, you think "this makes no sense" – so you use the Stanislavski methods, just to get rid of the first layer of confusion.' He thinks the Stanislavski action method is good in an 'initial, possibly quite simplified vague way, because one action can condense large amounts of text or visual descriptions into just one movement, one sound, one sentence'. Callum finds the movement element helps him to learn his lines and that the use of the large actions in the exercise assists him in finding a truth in what he is saying, which gives him more confidence with the words and movements.

My comment: Although it is probable that the actions provide a memory support and expressive tool for Callum, it is notable that he uses the words 'simplified' and 'a vague kind of way' in describing the effectiveness of Stanislavski actions in encapsulating the 'large chunks of the text' into 'one action'.

ii)   Amelia said that she found the process enabled her 'to pick up the lines quicker than if I had to sight-read or just read it'. Finding the verbs, voice and improvised text helped her concentrate on the character's intentions. She said that 'putting a physicalized action to it reminds the body so that when we came to reading the text I had that thought in my head. I had the text but I had that muscle memory in my body, so, yes, this process helped me with that.' She added: 'I might have stumbled over my lines but I felt more truthful in my acting.'

My comment: In consonance with Callum's physical storyboard for *Medea*, it seems that the physical actions can provide a valuable mnemonic device for Amelia (although they do not necessarily provide a recognition and particularization of all of the language). In observation, it would appear likely that Amelia's sense of 'truth' might stem from her energized commitment and imagination in creating physical actions/images related to a generalized feeling and meaning, rather than directly related to the truth of the words.

iii)   Verity pointed out that the Stanislavski method 'is good to familiarize and justify' and that the 'process helped her to learn the language faster by associating the physical movements with the text'. Verity surmised that the use of actions had helped her to understand the meanings and emotions behind the words, whereas before this work, the words would be empty when she read them. Verity prefers to use large stylized movements rather than naturalistic ones. Verity thinks the benefits of the Stanislavski work for those with dyslexia are 'huge', saying: 'It broadened my understanding of what I perceived to be a daunting subject matter, something I have always tried to avoid, as I saw it as an impossible challenge.'

iv)   Abigail felt that Stanislavski's Units and Actions were useful in breaking down the text, to help her understand the meaning. She underlined that she learnt through the workshop experience that the actions must be accurate to the language, and not generalized. The process of having to paraphrase the text first to understand it and then putting movement, sound, and improvised words to it helped to highlight any uncertain words or phrases and to build her confidence in understanding and speaking 'a very daunting piece of text. It is a really good basis – like building a wall.'

My comment: In doing the exercise, Abigail revealed that she had not understood the words 'perpetual durance', although she had repeated them several times throughout the sequence. It is recognized that despite Abigail determining the meanings, it is likely that she could quickly forget them. Abigail's difficulties with sight-reading and absorbing the text were facilitated to a certain extent by this work, forming, as she remarks, 'a basis'.

What the participants stated they did not find helpful about the Stanislavski process:

i) Callum reported that he struggles with 'finding the right words to describe what I want to convey, whether it's a lack of vocabulary or just a block in my brain, but I find that I'm never that articulate when it comes to choosing the words I'm looking for'. He finds it difficult to choose a verb to identify the character's actions. When he has settled on a word, he often finds it no longer seems to fit when he is up on his feet acting.

ii) Amelia stated that it is hard for the physical actions to leave the body once imprinted through practice. Sometimes having to physicalize the words can become confusing and you cannot show everything you imagine through the body. She would prefer to use drawings for this stage.

iii) Verity observed that when using Stanislavski's Units and Actions on a text without heightened language, the process can be done almost 'on the spot', but it is much harder and takes much more time to understand the words and structure of the text in Shakespeare.

iv) Abigail reported that she found it too hard to multi-task when I had asked her to read and physicalize the meaning. She now realizes that she would have been more confident with this if she had 'explored the text in greater depth'. Abigail said she would prefer to have do the drawing instead of the physicalization of the words.

References

Adams, M.J. (1980). Failures to comprehend and levels of processing. *In*: Spiro, R.J., Bruce, B., & Brewer, W.F. (eds.) *Theoretical Issues in Reading Comprehension*. Hillsdale, NJ: Lawrence Erlbaum, pp. 11–28.

Alfreds, M. (2007). *Different Every Night*. London: Nick Hern.

Berry, C. (1993). *The Actor and the Text*. London: Virgin Books.

Berry, C. (2001). *Text in Action*. London: Virgin Books.

Berry, C. (2008). *From Word to Play*. London: Oberon Books.

Caldarone, M. & Lloyd-Williams, M. (2004). *Actions: The Actors' Thesaurus*. London: Nick Hern.

Crystal, D. (1987). *The Cambridge Encyclopaedia of Language*. Cambridge, UK: Cambridge University Press.

Gillet, J. (2007). *Acting on Impulse*. London: Methuen Drama.

Hall, P. (2003). *Shakespeare's Advice to the Players*. London: Oberon Books.

Harrison, C. (2004). *Understanding Reading Development*. London: SAGE Publications.

Houseman, B. (2008). *Tackling Text [and Subtext]*. London: Nick Hern.

Linklater, K. (1992). *Freeing Shakespeare's Voice*. New York: Theatre Communications Group.

McNeill, D. (1992). *Hand and Mind: What Gestures Tell Us about Thought*. Chicago, IL: University of Chicago Press.

Merlin, B. (2003). *Konstantin Stanislavsky*. Oxford, UK: Routledge.

Philpott, M. (2000) *Towards a Phenomenology of Dyslexia*. PhD thesis, University of Warwick, UK.

Reid, G. (2003). *Dyslexia: A Practitioner's Handbook*, 3rd ed. Chichester, UK: John Wiley.

Rodenburg, P. (2002). *Speaking Shakespeare*. London: Methuen Drama.

Shakespeare, W. (1965). *Measure for Measure*. Ed. Lever, J.W. London: Arden Shakespeare.

Shakespeare, W. (2010). *Measure for Measure*. Ed. Bate, J. & Rasmussen, E. Basingstoke, UK: Macmillan.

Spiro, R., Bruce, B., & Brewer, W. (eds.) (1980). *Theoretical Issues in Reading Comprehension*. Hillsdale, NJ: Lawrence Erlbaum.

Stanislavski, C. (1981). *Creating a Role*. London: Methuen Drama.

Tejera, V. (1988). *Semiotics from Peirce to Barthes*. Leiden, The Netherlands: Brill.

Whyman, R. (2008). *The Stanislavski System of Acting*. Cambridge, UK: Cambridge University Press.

11

GRASPING TOWARDS BEING PRESENT IN THE TEXT, ENTANGLING MEANING INTO MEMORY

Action Research (Cycle Three) and Teaching Strategy Three

Introduction

How to Untangle the Text: Ascertaining the Words of Significance

The reader-response theorist Wolfgang Iser employs the term *entanglement* to describe readers' experience when they are wholly involved and present within the presence of the text (Iser 1978: 131–132). Iser's definition of readers being in a state of presentness within the text correlates with actors' performance in their thinking and speaking of the words as 'alive at the moment you speak it' (Barton 1984: 110). Text and reader become entangled together, permeating into each other, and the more present readers become in the text, the more their habitual selves recede into the past (Iser 1978: 131).

As demonstrated in the work in the last chapter, for many acting students with dyslexia, there is a painful contradiction in Iser's depiction of the *entangled* reader. For those with dyslexia, the word 'entangled' commonly encapsulates a more troubled meaning: that of being ensnared or tangled up in their interaction with the text. Individuals are thereby impeded in their awareness of any presence, in themselves, in the author, or of the text. In her instructions on how to speak Shakespeare's words, the voice teacher Patsy Rodenburg advises:

> You must understand what every word means. Know every word and reference. Never enter a rehearsal 'sort of knowing' the meaning of a word [. . .]. Words are easily debased and their sense made flabby, so an exploration of the exact meaning of a word will often hoist acting onto a higher level.
>
> *(2002: 72)*

Theatre director Mike Alfreds lays an emphasis on the 'elaborate and sophisticated thoughts in Shakespeare's text', and the need for the actor to sustain the thoughts behind the numerous clauses embedded within the lines of verse. As many voice teachers will recognize, Alfreds warns that if actors distrust the words, the communication of the words is mumbled, inarticulate, and vocally unreleased (2007: 196). Using an exercise which he calls the *Logic Text* with the actors, he combs through the text's structure, grammar, and word sense. Although he admits that this process can irritate some actors, he stipulates that actors cannot play the situation if they do not recognize connections in the text, or understand it (ibid.: 196–199). When using Stanislavski's Actions in rehearsals, Alfreds underlines that some actors struggle with selecting appropriate verbs for their actions. A lack of facility in grammar can lead to feelings of inferiority within a group where others may have superior literacy skills. To counter this, rather than insisting on coining exact verbs, Alfreds encourages a feeling-led approach. For example, the actor might say, '*I m'mmmm you*', or '*I grrrrr you*', relying on an emotion-led, pre-verbal expression (ibid.: 168). This accords with the sequence I use in the stages of Actions, where, in Stage Two, the actor uses only actions and sounds. Although actors with dyslexia could be freed by not having to select a verb, the lack of definition in '*I ahhhhhh you*' (ibid.: 168) maintains an ambiguity about the precise word and its apprehended meaning. Barton points out that sometimes, in Shakespeare, the language can be more important than the character, and that one should, 'make the language your first concern' (Barton 1984: 59).

Rationale: The Transaction with the Text

First, in order to establish how we make sense when reading (particularly in the reading of Shakespeare), I begin from the premise that there is no external reality presented by the printed marks on the page, which might be assumed to contain Shakespeare's intended meanings. However, through a convoluted process involving the reader's interaction with the written words and the literary form presented by Shakespeare (and his myriad of editors) as 'a shared system of rules [. . .] so understanding will be uniform', the alphabetical symbols and grammatical form are cognitively processed by the reader (Tompkins 1980: xviii). Meanings are constructed through word recognition, mental images, feelings, memory, and selective ideas (Rosenblatt 2005: xxv). Iser maintains that the symbols of literary language do not represent an empirical reality, but have a representative function through the language itself. Although the iconic signs in writing do not directly represent an object, they 'designate instructions' to enable the reader to construct an object through conception and perception, 'intended by the signs' (Iser 1978: 64).

Reminding actors not to take words for granted, Carey and Clark Carey encourage them to stimulate images in the mind to engage with the text (2010: 33). They refer to various types of symbols in language, representing both the image and the idea, and the need for these linguistic symbols and images to be attended to by the reader to enhance a communication of the text (ibid.: 45). Introducing the idea of *literal* and *evocative* images in their physical imaging exercises, Carey and Clark Carey advise the actor not to worry about 'getting it right', nor about making 'complete sense of the speech', when transferring their mental images into physical actions (ibid.: 44–46, 176). However, Carey and Clark Carey's exercises are not aimed particularly at those who may have dyslexic difficulties in grasping or retaining what the written words are pointing towards. Theatre director, performer, and academic Rhonda Blair (2008: 84) recommends a careful 'excavation' of the text, and after finding personal connections with the words, to keep re-reading it through embodiment, enactment, and repetition. She accentuates that clarity of the language in the text is crucial, as a lack of clarity produces unclear images in the imagination, which then translate into unclear actions (as was demonstrated by some of the participants in the previous chapter). Linking directly with the work in my study, Blair reiterates the need for the actor to have strong sensory images directly related to the words, creating personal meanings, which then anchor the referents found in the text, driving the action of the moment. The conscious application of the images diverts the actor away from unconscious, mundane interpretations of the text (ibid.: 91–92). Usefully for the actor, Iser points out that meaning and significance are separate things and are two distinct stages of comprehension. While meaning refers to aspects of reference found in the text, the perception of significance – 'the absorption of the reader's meaning into their own existence' – is constructed in the world of the interpreter's imagination (Iser 1978: 151). It is these strands of meaning and significance that I am searching for in the participants' ability to find a 'presentness' in their absorption of and rendition of the text.

To attempt to build a framework for my participants, I introduced an additional Stage Seven into my six-stage version of the Stanislavski-inspired *Units and Actions* sequence: to identify what *type* of gesture was being used, and what precisely it was signifying in relation to the word. To assist in defining and accessing meaning and significance, I have found Charles Peirce's theory of semiotic signs (Tejera 1988: 11) helpful to gain clarity for myself about the process of attaching a gesture or drawing to the words, in particular the triadic relationship of three basic elements, which are:

- The *representamen*: 'a *representamen* is something which stands to somebody for something in some respect' (Peirce, in ibid.).

    When reading Shakespeare, this could be the word-sign on the page. This sign stands in reference to its object.
- The *object*: 'I have sometimes called the *object* the ground of the *representamen*' (Peirce, in ibid.).

    This is the literal sense of the word.

- The *interpretant*: what has been created inside a person's mind by the *representamen* (Peirce, in ibid.).

    This is the comprehension and interpretation of the *object* relation, leading to the realization of the significance.

Peirce proposes that there are three classes of the *interpretant*. The first is the *emotional*, which is the feeling produced from it; the second is the *energetic*, which involves the effect and the manner in which the *emotional interpretant* is produced; and the third is the *logical*, where the meaning and significance is appropriated (in ibid.: 24).

Peirce's three classes of the *interpretant* are related to my purpose in asking my participants to identify what *type* of gesture they had chosen for each action (*the energetic*), the concomitant feeling (*emotional*), and intended meaning (*logical significance*), mapped to the content of the word (the *representamen* and its *object*). Through the task of clarifying their *interpretant* served through the 'holding form' of their gesture/action, my supposition was that their reflection about their constructed meanings, interpretations, and significance directly related to the word content would become more distinctly clarified in their minds.

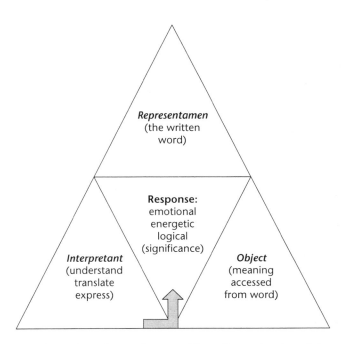

FIGURE 11.1 Relationship of Peirce's signs with reading and acting of the text

Action Research (Cycle Three) and Teaching Strategy Three: Identify the Gesture, Its Referent and Its Significance in Making Meaning from the Text

Case Studies – Sophie, Hollie, Elizabeth, and James

Method

In this third action research cycle, I began the work with the whole cohort of students, including the non-dyslexic students and the four new dyslexic participants, Sophie, Hollie, Elizabeth, and James. I followed the Stanislavski-inspired exercise sequence using the same scene taken from Shakespeare's *Measure for Measure* (Act iii, Scene i) that I had used in the last action research cycle with the previous set of dyslexic participants, as outlined in Chapter 10. I divided the class into groups of three, with each individual in the group working as either Claudio, Isabella, or the director. For homework, leading to a prepared class performance, I asked the students to break their allotted unit of the scene down into actions, each of which must be given a verb capturing what their character is doing and their intention as they speak, through an analysis of the text. Then, building on my work done in Chapter 10 with my previous participants, I introduced an additional Stage Seven. I asked them to identify (through discussion with each other and rehearsal) *what type* of physical action they had chosen to couple with the words/phrase, and to reflect on why they had chosen that type of gesture in relation to the meaning and significance of the words spoken and their characters' needs. As part of their class presentation, following their acting of the sequence they would go back over their unit, present to the class their action labels, and explain their rationale for their choice of type of gesture/action.

Following exploring some practical examples of differing gestures related to the text in the class, for further guidance I gave the class a handout naming and describing the different categories that I had devised for types of actions. The gesture types I categorized were adapted and extended from psychologist David McNeill's description of gestures in *Hand and Mind* (1992). They were:

i) The *literal gesture*: This is an illustrative presentation of the word, with the gesture similar in shape to the object. It makes the mental image explicit, such as drawing a rounded shape with the hands to denote a ball, or a square for a window.

ii) The *metaphorical gesture*: This makes an image of an idea – by one thing representing another – and through the image, makes the idea concrete. For example, 'to be free' could be represented by the arms and body denoting the flying of a bird towards the sky.

iii) The *symbolic or representational gesture*: This is a mimicking of something, like a pantomiming, rather than an expression of something that is felt inwardly – a showing of something through an externally led physical representation.

This could be an acting out of something in a melodramatic style, with little inner psychological truth, or simple practical actions, such as opening a door.

iv)   The *affective or Psychological Realism gesture*: This expresses the emotional or psychological state and has an inner feeling driving it, shown through natural gesture stimulated by feelings and thoughts.

v)   The *evocative gesture.*: This is created through associations, a sensory response fired non- literally from the word meanings; it might be instigated through letter sounds, imagined textures, shapes, colors, atmospheres – auditory, visual, tactile, or kinesthetic images arising through the speaking and hearing of the words.

Recognizing that distinguishing a gesture type might be an intimidating task for some, I gave them an example of Claudio's speech ('Ay, but to die and go we know not where', Act iii, Scene i) in which I had already broken down and actioned the speech from my perspective, giving examples of what type of actions/gestures I might give to it and why. As a model of practice, we worked on some of this in class together, exploring how one might identify the type of gesture and how this can heighten the understanding and connection with meaning and expression of the text. I emphasized that there is no 'correct' type of gesture. If there was an overlap with another, part of the process was their recognition of this, their analysis and artistic creation through the body, related to what they perceived in the language.

What Happened with Participants Elizabeth, Hollie, and Sophie

I put three participants together to work on Unit C: Sophie as director, Elizabeth as Isabella, and Hollie as Claudio (while James was placed with two other members of the group who are not dyslexic). It quickly became evident that the three participants' response to the task differed radically from the non-dyslexic cohort (and participant James). While their non-dyslexic fellows all stated they understood the task, the three participants came to speak to me on two occasions outside of class time, expressing bewilderment and anxiety about what they had to do.

In the class presentation of the unit work, the non-dyslexic students performed the gesture-labeling task on their units of text effectively, identifying their types of action and explanations with confidence and coherence. James (my fourth participant) appeared to do well in this exercise, using interesting actions and appearing assured of their type and rationale. However, as I had placed him with two non-dyslexic students, it might be that their contribution supported him in this. Alternatively, it could be an example of the differences that are found in those with dyslexia. Conversely, when it came to Elizabeth, Hollie, and Sophie's presentation of their unit within the class, they were unable to complete the exercise. Elizabeth (playing Isabella) carried the main responsibility for the actions of the unit, while Hollie (as Claudio) had little to say. Sophie, in the director's role, read out their chosen verbs and actions, but Elizabeth became flustered and began to merge all her actions together in a chaotic sequence. It was unclear what she was actioning, related to which words. Elizabeth stopped early on in the process. She tried a few times to continue, but kept stopping, in confusion. Due to the additional stress caused by the class observation of Elizabeth's difficulties, I decided not to pursue this further, resolving to come back to it later in an action research trial.

Action Research (Cycle Three) Continued – the Workshop

It is important to highlight that Sophie, Hollie, and Elizabeth, at the time of this research, were hardworking students of ability who applied themselves to their work on the acting course with some distinction in spite of their dyslexia. The outcome of this action research trial is an example of how some teaching strategies can lead to a disablement of talented individuals. I include this description of my trialed strategy here as an example of its failure with three of the participants when put into action, along with my reflection on the reasons why it had a negative outcome for those particular dyslexic students.

At the completion of the Shakespeare unit, I arranged a workshop for Sophie, Elizabeth, and Hollie to perform Unit C again. I gave them two weeks' notice, so they might have time to re-think and practice what they had originally planned to do in the class presentation.

Present: participants Hollie, Sophie, Elizabeth, and the critical friend.

On commencing the scene, almost immediately at the beginning of Isabella's lines, Elizabeth came to a standstill and said she could not remember the actions, the sequence of sounds, or the improvised words. She stated that she found the exercise stressful and overpowering. She explained that rather than thinking about the meaning of what she was doing, she was simply trying to remember the planned actions, and they were in chaos in her mind. Elizabeth attempted the sequence three times, sometimes getting a little further on in the unit, but finally she seemed to find it impossible to remember her gestures, sounds, or words, or any of the rehearsed sequence. The other participants appeared unable to assist her through contribution or explanation. I then abandoned this exercise, as it was clearly an anxiety-laden experience, particularly for Elizabeth, but also for Hollie and Sophie.

Report and Analysis of the Three Participants' Difficulties with the Gesture Identification Sequence

To decipher why this exercise had placed my participants in such a disabling situation, I combed through the transcripts of the initial interviews that I had carried out at the start of my research with them. In re-reading their words, it was apparent that all four participants had remarked on their poor memories and challenges with processing.

References to Memory and Processing Weakness in Initial Interviews with Sophie, Elizabeth, and Hollie

In her interview, Elizabeth said: '[At school], I had a lot of help with spelling and my memory, like retaining things short term, I find it hard to remember [. . .] my memory is quite a big problem, my short-term memory.' She also spoke about her tendency not to take things in when people are speaking to her, and that she finds it hard to process information: 'it takes me a while to understand what we have to do'.

Sophie related that 'my memory is awful – I can remember things from long ago, but short-term things, I just can't remember, and if I don't write things down, I wouldn't remember anything'. Confessing that she has a short attention span, she explained that she gets 'overwhelmed with information': 'I just can't remember my lines and I worry that I come across as someone who doesn't really care and hasn't done the work.'

Hollie stated that she cannot multi-task, and that her dyslexia assessment report pointed out that 'my working memory wasn't as good as I thought, and [. . .] they said I'd get the information, but I wouldn't be able to process it fast enough'.

What the Three Participants Stated They Found Problematic in the Gesture Identification Exercise

Sophie

In a written statement following the workshop, Sophie, as the director of the unit, recounted that they went through each action together as a group, but 'we found it very confusing, as what seemed simple to someone else makes our brains feel like we are having to do a thousand things at once'. Emphasizing memory weakness several times, Sophie said: 'I felt like it was too much for my brain to think about all at once and *found it hard to remember* what we had agreed as *my memory is bad* and got in a muddle.' Reiterating memory overload, Sophie went on: 'there were so many different elements to take in that we jut [her spelling] got confused and *couldn't remember* what we were doing. My brain felt very muddled. *Remembering* what each action was with the text on top was daunting, even though we kept asking, we couldn't get to grips with what was being asked of us' [my italics].

Elizabeth

In a written statement, Elizabeth imparted that she found it too hard to multi-task, doing actions in conjunction with 'speaking at the same time'. When having to use improvised words or sounds, she relayed that her brain became blocked and she panicked: 'I found it hard to explain what I wanted to say. I couldn't think fast enough on the spot, I knew what everything meant, but my brain wasn't letting me do it.' Elizabeth reported that she 'could not think of good words for the actions', she was bewildered by having to give titles to the actions, and 'couldn't get her head round any of it'. She explained that even when she knows something really well, sometimes she just cannot do it, either because *she cannot remember* or 'the words won't come out of my mouth. When pressurised or stressed, it all gets much worse' (my italics).

Hollie

Hollie stated:

> I found it extremely difficult having to think one thing, say another, and do an action all at the same time, to carry out the psychological or metaphorical gesture of imagery or emotion, saying a paraphrased version and having actions called out of what you are meant to do and thinking of where you are meant to be.

Conclusion about Action Research (Cycle Three) and Teaching Strategy Three

During this action research cycle, in my attempt to assist my participants in comprehending and anchoring the text, it appeared that I had achieved the opposite outcome with Elizabeth, Sophie, and Hollie; overloading their memory systems, exposing them to difficulties with dual-tasking, procedures, and the arrangement of information in their minds. I was also imposing on them a structure of external 'rules' by asking them to intellectually abstract and recall information from the text in a set sequence rather than originating their own personally devised responses. Their task demanded a substantial level of automaticity of procedure on several levels, with a high use of episodic and semantic memory. They were having to remember their identification of and naming of each type of gesture, their planned Stanislavski verbs and actions, the meaning of Shakespeare's words and their pronunciation, the characters' lines and their psychological and emotional journey, and the interplay between themselves and the character within the scene while keeping in the present moment of the world of the play. (See Chapter 14 for more information about prospective memory difficulties in dyslexics.)

Conversely, the other research participant, James, had not struggled with this exercise. He performed his section of the text with confidence, and explained his choice of gestures with a specificity of signification related to the meaning of the text and his character's perspective, showing comprehension for the rationale of the exercise. This demonstrates that each teaching situation can differ in its outcome according to the make-up of the individuals and group, and that this method may still be a useful experience for some with dyslexia.

Memory, Processing, and Dyslexia

Following this experience, in scrutinizing their interviews, I noticed how prominent the word *memory* is in their explanations of difficulties. The staggered Stanislavski exercise of *Actions*, although chunked into small components of distinct stages, demands the activation of several systems of memory, both long- and short-term, in meaning-making, process, and retention.

Memory weakness is an important focus running throughout my study, and is a principal component in my conclusive findings (see Chapter 14). In reviewing the literature, a weak working memory is frequently cited as a sign of dyslexia (Reid 2003; Gathercole & Packiam Alloway 2008; Mortimore 2008; Thomson 2009; Grant 2010; Nicolson & Fawcett 2010). McLoughlin et al. (1994: 17) refer to adults with dyslexia as having dual difficulties in memory and information processing. They list adults with dyslexia having difficulty with sequencing, organization, and working memory tasks such as remembering instructions or carrying them out in the right order (ibid.: 19–20). In a series of trialed tasks, Beneventi et al. (2010) carried out several tests on dyslexic and non-dyslexic children which gradually increased working memory loads. They then measured the activation in relevant parts of the brain using MRI scans. Recognizing that there was reduced activation in the prefrontal, parietal cortices, and the cerebellum in those they tested with dyslexia (and not in the group of non-dyslexics), they concluded that those with dyslexia did have a working memory deficit. They therefore recommended that provision for learners should ensure that there is a reduced working memory overload. Nicolson and Fawcett's *automatization deficit hypothesis* (2010: 67) focuses on procedural memory, claiming that those with dyslexia often have problems with making automatic a range of skills, such as dual-tasking and motor skills. They also propose that those with dyslexia have a *procedural learning difficulty, specific to the cerebellum*, suggesting that dyslexia reflects impairment in the procedural memory system (ibid.: 204; Nicolson 2015: 56). They assert that this can significantly affect learning.

Through introducing this exercise, I had contributed to their feelings of inadequacy and anxiety, situated as they were amongst the majority of the cohort who had mostly delivered the exercise with ease and enjoyment. However, it is through the testing out of ideas within an action research trial that the outcomes are observed, discussed, reflected on, analyzed, and then, most importantly, amended with the aim of improvement of practice. It is critical that teaching procedures which are *not* effective are also made explicit, shared, and written about, as it is through such mistakes and the reasons for them that we can learn.

Critical Friend Observation

My critical friend observed the workshop and compared the confusion experienced by the participants in doing this exercise with those who are not dyslexic.
He stated that, in his experience, individuals usually find the *Units and Actions*
exercise enabling as both a memory and sense aid. He introduced a psychological perspective of intrinsic motivation, remarking on the participants' behavior:

> It has become clear that some of the students with dyslexia are highly moti-
> vated and push themselves to succeed, whereas others may give up on tasks
> and feel they have a limit, which they cannot go beyond. As we have seen, the
> type of individual varies and therefore the outcomes are different in each case.

The danger of low self-esteem and a lack of feelings of self-efficacy influencing the progress of those with dyslexia is well documented (Mortimore 2008;
Thomson 2009; Grant 2010). Educational psychologist Robert Burden (2005)
has written on the implications of a damaged self-concept and learned helplessness affecting the motivation and educational success in those with dyslexia.
Burden emphasizes that 'behaviour can often be predicted better by their beliefs
about their capabilities than by what they know'. If those with dyslexia believe
that what happens to them is outside their control and unchangeable, they will
give up trying (ibid.: 21–22).

The Next Chapter

To gain a fuller understanding about these participants, it was necessary to examine their personal methods of entering the text. Three participants' creation of a
visual analogue of the written text is presented, revealing their individual methods as compensatory strategies. The analysis of the case studies is aligned with
modern and ancient theory on memory and processing.

KEY POINTS OF CHAPTER 11

- What it means to be entangled in the text
- Charles Peirce's theory of semiotic signs and David McNeill's gesture
  identification in grounding the significance in the text
- Action Research (Cycle three) and Teaching Strategy Three, trialing
  the identification of gesture type when applying Stanislavski-inspired
  actions on Shakespeare's text.
- The failure of the teaching strategy for three participants with dyslexia,
  and analysis of why it failed
- Memory overload and difficulties in multi-tasking in those with dyslexia

---

References

Alfreds, M. (2007). *Different Every Night*. London: Nick Hern.

Barton, J. (1984). *Playing Shakespeare*. London: Methuen.

Beneventi, H. et al. (2010). Working memory deficit in dyslexia: behavioural and MRI evidence. *International Journal of Neuroscience*, 120, pp. 51–59.

Blair, R. (2008). *The Actor, Image, and Action*. Oxford, UK: Routledge.

Burden, R. (2005). *Dyslexia and Self-concept*. London: Whurr.

Carey, D. & Clark Carey, R. (2010) *The Verbal Arts Workbook*. London: Methuen Drama.

Gathercole, S. & Packiam Alloway, T. (2008). *Working Memory and Learning*. London: SAGE Publications.

Grant, D. (2010). *That's the Way I Think*, 2nd ed. Oxford, UK: David Fulton.

Iser, W. (1978). *The Act of Reading; A Theory of Aesthetic Response*. Baltimore, MD: John Hopkins University Press.

McLoughlin, D., Fitzgibbon, G., & Young, V. (1994). *Adult Dyslexia: Assessment, Counselling and Training*. London: Whurr.

McNeill, D. (1992). *Hand and Mind: What Gestures Tell Us about Thought*. Chicago, IL: University of Chicago Press.

Mortimore, T. (2008) *Dyslexia and Learning Style*, 2nd ed. Chichester, UK: John Wiley & Sons.

Nicolson, R. (2015). *Positive Dyslexia*. Sheffield, UK: Rodin Books.

Nicolson, R. & Fawcett, A. (2010). *Dyslexia, Learning and the Brain*. London: MIT Press.

Reid, G. (2003). *Dyslexia: A Practitioner's Handbook*, 3rd ed. Chichester, UK: John Wiley.

Rodenburg, P. (2002). *Speaking Shakespeare*. London: Methuen Drama.

Rosenblatt, L. (2005). *Making Meaning with Texts*. Portsmouth, UK: Heinemann.

Tejera, V. (1988) *Semiotics from Peirce to Barthes*. Leiden, The Netherlands: Brill.

Thomson, M. (2009). *The Psychology of Dyslexia*, 2nd ed. Chichester, UK: Wiley-Blackwell.

Tompkins, J.P. (1980). *Reader-response Criticism*. London: John Hopkins University Press.

12

THE CREATION OF MNEMOTECHNICS TOWARDS A *MEMORIA RERUM* (MEMORY FOR THINGS AND IDEAS) AND *MEMORIA VERBORAM* (MEMORY FOR WORDS)

Case Studies: Sophie, James, and Hollie and Their Individual Methods of Entering the Text

In this chapter, three participants' visually diverse analogues of the written text are presented, demonstrating their individual methods as successful compensatory strategies in circumventing their dyslexia. Their choice of images might be literal translations of the word, but could also be freely associative, according to their idiosyncratic responses, creative stimulus, and dyslexia challenges. It is important to highlight that the strength of this work arises from this subjective resourcefulness, rather than having others' ideas for images or teaching conventions imposed upon them. This is demonstrated in this chapter, including my work with a participant on the choreographing of a physical storyboard, where his drawing of narrative proved to liberate his thinking and acting more successfully than the physical work.

Sophie's Use of Technology and PowerPoint

Sophie brought an original method to this investigation by using PowerPoint as her working medium. What is significant here is how Sophie molded the mediation of PowerPoint into a new activity in bypassing her dyslexia. This allowed a fostering of her abilities, which would have remained unrecognized in traditional teaching practices, therein increasing a sense of self-efficacy and enabling achievement of assured performance. PowerPoint is commonly utilized as an information communicator, but Sophie used it to remediate the written text into her own image sequences through its visually led affordances. Under her own incentive, Sophie utilized this visual genre to advance her engagement with, and her acting of, the written text during the Shakespeare unit. For all the key assessment points (the monologue presentation, the Voice sonnet presentation, and her acting scene with another actor), she created PowerPoint storyboards, mostly made up of photographs, pictures, or symbols she found on the internet, devising image ideographs representing her subjective construction of the text. Visually literate, they are impressive in their detail and imaginative allusion, requiring much effort in their compilation.

Two days before her Shakespeare monologue presentation, Sophie gave me a copy of a PowerPoint visual storyboard, signifying her monologue for Adrianna in *Comedy of Errors* (Shakespeare 1962: Act II, Scene ii). Sophie reported that she used the creation of a PowerPoint slideshow to work on the lines of the text at home. She took a considerable amount of time to find what she considered the 'right image' to supplant the words when building her pictorial sequences, explaining that:

> It does take a while to make but it helped me a lot, as I was making it, as I was absorbing and teaching myself and making discoveries from think-ing about the different meanings and looking up words I wasn't sure of. It made sure I didn't just browse over something I didn't understand, as I had to know what it meant to make the slide.

Once the slides were constructed, she used her visual text as a learning aid by speaking and acting the words of the text while watching the slide images run through their sequence on her computer. She relayed:

> [It] hooked the text into my brain as I had sectioned it out in manageable chunks. The added words reminded me of the structure and form that I had looked at, such as alliteration and the richness and meaning of some words.

By running through the automatic slideshow, Sophie's thoughts shifted freely with the images, while their visual arrangement became embedded into her long-term memory.

An Excerpt from Sophie's Monologue: Adrianna in Comedy of Errors (Act II, Scene ii)

> Ay, Ay, Antipholus look strange and frown,
> Some other mistress has thy sweet aspects;
> I am not Adriana, nor thy wife.

Description and Analysis of One Example from Sophie's PowerPoint Slides

As Sophie's PowerPoint slides are made up of images drawn from the internet, due to copyright reasons they cannot be shown here. However, here is a brief description of her Slide One, Representing the Phrase 'Ay, Ay, Antipholus look strange and frown'

Description

The text 'Ay Ay, Antipholus' is printed below two pictures, and the alliteration in the phrase is picked out by a blue coloring on the first letter A of the three words. Above the text, there is a photograph of a baby with huge eyes, using a visual rendition of the homophone 'Ay, Ay'. There is also a photograph of a woman's face with striking eyes, with a tense, frowning facial expression, looking 'strange'. What is notable is that sometimes the image representations do not make sense within the context of the piece, such as using pictures of eyes for the words 'Ay, Ay' where word meaning is 'yes, yes'.

My Comment

Throughout my study, I have been perplexed by the participants' mixed visual referents within the gestalt; the image anchors sometimes being particular to the word alone, and not making sense within the whole meaning (for example, using a picture of eyes for the homophone 'Ay, Ay' meaning in this case, 'yes, yes'). Sophie accentuates the power of inferring images from the verbal form, which then gain an additional layer of embedding in the mind when recoded back into words. She explained:

> I can imagine the images a lot easier in my mind than just the text, but obviously my brain has to work more into translating the images back into what I need to say for the text. When I try and imagine the text, I can see it in my mind as a block, but it is blurred and I can only see the first line, where as I can pretty much visualize the whole order of the PowerPoint without much trouble.

Therefore, Sophie uses literal images, directly illustrating the meaning of the word, but also creates images that work as vivid mnemonic symbols which require a certain amount of translating and recoding in her mind to revert to their original meaning within the context of the text. Sophie also describes a synesthetic approach to her graphics. There are conspicuous examples of connections being made using color, touch, taste, kinesthetic movement, and auditory sounds which feed directly into her acting and speaking. She explained:

> Some images I use provoke a feeling, such as the word 'welcome' I used an orange color writing as it provoked feistiness reminding me of the sexiness. Some images help me to bring the words to life, such as a picture of torn paper helps me to imagine the sound of paper tearing, so when I say the word it is sort of onomatopoeic. The pictures of spit and contaminated

boils on the skin help me to spit the words out, and also by thinking about the horrible pictures, it helps me feel and portray resentment and disgust.

Released from the inhibiting blocks of dyslexia, Sophie's technological mediation can cultivate what has been identified as the strengths of dyslexia in some individuals (Bacon & Handley 2010, 2014).

James and Macbeth's Soliloquy

In his scene in the Shakespeare unit, James played Macbeth (Act I, Scene vii). The scene begins with Macbeth's soliloquy:

> If it were done, when 'tis done, then t'were well
> It were done quickly: if th'assassination
> Could trammel up the consequence, and catch
> With his surcease success; that but thus blow
> Might be the be-all and the end-all − here,
> But here, upon this bank and shoal of time,
> We'd jump the life to come. − But in these cases,
> We still have judgement here; that we but teach
> Bloody instructions, which, being taught, return
> To plague th'inventor: this even-handed Justice
> Commends th'ingredience of our poison'd chalice
> To our own lips. He's here in double trust:
> First as I am his kinsman and his subject,
> Strong both against the deed; then, as his host,
> Who should against his murtherer shut the door,
> Not bear the knife myself. Besides, this Duncan
> Hath borne his faculties so meek, hath been
> So clear in his great office, that his virtues
> Will plead like angels, trumpet tongu'd, against
> The deep damnation of his taking off;
> And Pity, like a naked new-born babe,
> Striding the blast, or heaven's Cherubins, hors'd
> Upon the sightless couriers of the air,
> Shall blow the horrid deed in every eye,
> That tears shall drown the wind. − I have no spur
> To prick the sides of my intent, but only
> Vaulting ambition, which o'erleaps itself
> And falls on th' other −

In the first few rehearsals, James's communication of this speech was blurred into blocks of words that were broken up in the middle of phrases while spoken in a light, unconnected voice. James's strong talent as a performer was masked, and he appeared unable to follow the thoughts comprehensively or transform into the character of Macbeth. James revealed his lack of understanding of the content by skimming over or mispronouncing several of the words, running the thoughts of the speech together, with some strangely articulated words with a misplaced emphasis. When working through the monologue with him for meaning, I found that James had misunderstood much within it. He had forgotten what 'trammelled' meant (to catch in a net – he consistently pronounced the word 'trammer', and he always missed out the determiner 'the' before the word 'consequence'). He therefore did not know what Shakespeare might have been intending to communicate by 'trammel up the consequence', nor how to speak those words when inhabiting the character of Macbeth. He told me that he thought Duncan's surcease (his death through Macbeth's murder) was something about Duncan being a successful king. He thought that Duncan, rather than Macbeth and Lady Macbeth, would be the one 'jumping the life to come' by dying, not understanding that Macbeth is saying that he would evade the risk to come in the afterlife by risking his immortal soul (Bevington et al., in Shakespeare 2007: 78). In Macbeth's image-laden exposition, when painting the metaphoric picture about the horror of the reaction to Duncan's death – 'Pity like a new-born babe, / Striding the blast, or heaven's Cherubins, hors'd / Upon the sightless couriers of the air' – James thought that Duncan was Pity and that Duncan would be hors'd upon the sightless couriers of the air, rather than heaven's Cherubins.

In a previous voice class, I had already focused on the ten lines in this section of the text, beginning with 'Besides this Duncan' and finishing with 'and falls on the other'. These lines demonstrate Shakespeare's use of incredible imagery as an example of personification, metaphor, and simile, linked to clues given about Macbeth's growing hallucinatory state by the extravagance of the images in the language. During this discussion of the text in voice class, I had noticed that James's attention had wandered into 'zoning out' with a dream-like expression. James had already mentioned in his initial interview with me that this 'zoning out' is something that happens to him quite often. Gathercole and Packiam Alloway (2008) state that this is a sign of working memory overload. James therefore had not remembered the analytic explanation and breakdown on meaning and language that we had already examined in class on this text.

To attempt to get to grips with the meaning of the language, and to try to anchor it in James's memory, I asked him to devise a physical storyboard of the words (as Amelia and Callum had done with their Greek Chorus pieces described in Chapter 9). In class rehearsal, I worked through the whole monologue with James, ensuring that he created a physical action for the meaning of each phrase or word in the running sequence of the monologue. Imitating Amelia's and Callum's methods of establishing a spatially defined action-image for each word or chunk of text, running in a learned sequence, this work is similar to Carey and Clark Carey's *line painting* exercise, where individuals 'paint' imaginary images in the air with their hands as they read the text (Carey & Clarke Carey 2010: 37, 170). However, I was working towards an immersed whole-body commitment, with attention on the preciseness of movement related to word meanings to address the vagueness of James's understanding. In particular, I remember working with him to point out Shakespeare's riding images within the speech:

Phrase: 'I have no spur to prick the sides of my intent';
Action: James 'spurs' himself with his hands into his own body's sides.
Phrase: 'but only vaulting ambition'.
Action: James jumps as though a horse leaping over a jump.

At this point, I also asked James to devise a drawing storyboard of the speech as homework.

Following the creation of the physical storyboard, when he acted the speech, James's movements now became stuck in a literal demonstration of the meaning of the words rather than being natural gestures driven by Macbeth's psychological or emotional state. As he spoke the words of his monologue, I could perceive James's mind shuffling through the devised physical cues that we had created. His concentration of thoughts and energy withdrew into himself. Although greatly reduced from the large movements he had originally created into smaller physical suggestions, James appeared trapped in using these illustrative movements with each phrase. For example, as he acted the monologue, for the phrase 'for this blow' he would do a thrusting, hitting movement, for 'poison'd chalice' he would lift an invisible cup to his mouth, all enacting literal movements signifying the word meaning rather than a gesture underpinning psychological urge and thought.

I began to be concerned that in my desire to assist James with understanding the language and the articulation of the words with a realistic 'truth', I had blocked his connection to Macbeth's thoughts. He seemed unable to uncouple Macbeth's intrinsic thoughts within the language from the devised storyboard movements related to word meaning now embedded through his body. (This had been Callum's problem with his Greek tragedy storyboard. This relates to McLoughlin and Leather's assertion that those with dyslexia have problems with the function of the central executive component in memory, finding it 'hard to change a habitual manner of doing things, such as a set reading style'; 2013: 21.)

However, in the last couple of rehearsals and final performance, I was surprised, as there was an enormous improvement in James's acting. Suddenly James was acting with movements driven by a psychological realism, and he was no longer breaking the text up into inappropriate clauses. Amazed by his progress, I asked James what he had done to break out of his prior patterns of demonstrated actions, and he explained that he had used the process of drawing a storyboard of Macbeth's thoughts onto paper. He stated that it had been the drawing of the speech that had freed him.

After the Shakespeare unit concluded, I met with James so he could show me his drawing storyboard. At first glance, his drawings appeared to me to be undeveloped and child-like. However, as he talked me through them, I began to understand their serious value for James as a metacognitive tool of perception and thinking. Each drawing acted as a window, opening a container that held much larger chunks of information retained in his memory. James explained that artistic accomplishment was not the point of his drawings, saying:

> Leonardo De Vinci I am not, but it's got what it needs and as far as meaning and stuff, I can get it all from this. I get time to think about it and do it, which makes it a lot easier.

James had used three sheets of A4-size paper, which he had folded into four, making four separate picture spaces on the page (Figure 12.1). James described his storyboard as like 'little caricatures, which are just about capturing their feeling and the thoughts'. He said:

> I picture it slightly like a comic book almost, so I can picture each individual part and then I know the feeling and I know what's going on, so it's kind of every little bit of his mind injected into the pictures which is handy for me. I can learn that as a sequence of feelings a lot easier than if I read it.

Description

Picture one: 'if it were done, when tis done, then t'were well it were done quickly'

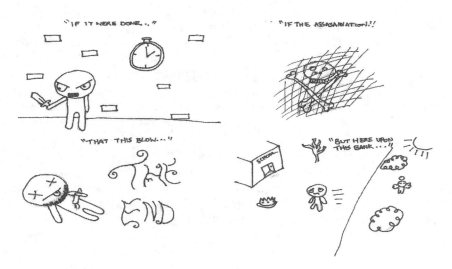

FIGURE 12.1 Example of James's pictures for *Macbeth*

James' explanation: The first one is a picture of little Macbeth with a dagger, and there's a stopwatch behind him to signify that they want it done as fast as possible.

Picture two: 'If the assignation could trammel up the consequence and catch with his surcease success'

James's explanation: it's a picture of a skull and cross bones and then netting over the skull and cross bones. The skull and cross bones is the consequence, so that's possibly his death – Macbeth's death if anyone finds out, the netting is the consequences being got rid of because they did it quickly, it's all over.

Picture three: 'That but this blow might be the be-all and the end-all – here'

James' explanation: We've got a picture of Duncan with a knife in him and the words 'the end', which signifies that's it, the end of everything.

Picture four: 'but here upon this bank and shoal of time'

James's explanation: I read somewhere that shoal was actually a word for school in Shakespeare's time and I've done a picture of heaven, and he is running away from heaven towards the crown and a more desolate area, but as long as he is king, he doesn't mind running away from that sort of thing.

My comment: James is correct here. The First Folio refers to 'school of time', but Block (2013: 360) reports that 'shoal' is now the usual word use.

James is a talented musician and singer. Fascinatingly, James reflected that he discovered a similarity between the creation of pictures and music. He compared the two, saying:

> the best metaphor for it is actually music, because with music you get so many tones, you can get jealousy with the darker tones, you can get anger from the minor chords, and then you can have the light, happy, melodic tunes, and it is exactly the same because you can encapsulate all, whether in the music or in the pictures.

Despite the difficulty James had in letting go of the movement/action work created in the physical storyboard, he still described it as 'useful'. He thought the physical actions should precede the drawing, but then the drawing work should follow, 'because that is the way for it to cement and stick in my mind'.

Hollie as Dorotea in Cardenio: Constructing a Macro and Micro Understanding, Improving Her Articulation of Words

Hollie had poor articulation, often skimming over the formation of the words so they remained indistinct, possibly reflecting a weak mapping of the phonological sounds to the alphabetic letters in the words, or revealing her imprecise cognition of the word itself in her reading of it. Before the Shakespeare unit began, I knew that a key goal for me would be to improve Hollie's communication of language and reading fluency.

It is valuable for voice teachers who work regularly with articulation and text to note that there are several theories that link weak articulation with dyslexia. Nicolson and Fawcett identify in dyslexics an *articulatory deficit*. They contend that 'there is considerable evidence that dyslexic children are impaired in articulatory skill, though it is not clear whether this is caused primarily by a phonological deficit or by a motor skill deficit arising from the cerebellar' (Nicolson & Fawcett 2010: 97). Griffiths and Frith carried out a trial which asked adults with dyslexia to repeat phonemes aloud, and then to identify a picture of the articulators which represented the physical position they formed to make the sound of the phoneme. They found that the dyslexics struggled to relate the sound to the articulators' shape and that 'dyslexics were significantly impaired in articulatory awareness' (Griffiths & Frith 2002).

Similarly to participants Jimmy and Richard in Chapter 8, Hollie related that when learning text, she breaks it into sections, giving each 'little pinpoint' an imagined picture, and then she highlights each 'pinpoint' with a different color. She uses this approach to make things 'more prominent in my head when I'd go back to it'. In lectures, she explained that she would:

> be thinking about it and listening, but I would be drawing the whole time. I'd understand all the things, I'd write a sentence down, and I'd doodle all over the sentence. I'd make certain characters different. It allows me to focus on that sentence a lot more, like a separate entity and I'd think, 'Ah, now I understand it a lot more.'

Hollie's Acting Scene

Hollie played Dorotea in *Cardenio* (Act I, Scene vi). *Cardenio* is cited as a 'lost re-imagined' play, compiled by director Gregory Doran and Spanish author Antonio Alamo, sourced from various play texts and possibly originally written by Shakespeare and John Fletcher (Doran and Alamo 2011: 5).

Some of the language in the scene is fairly cryptic, not only for the audience, but also for the actor speaking it. A short example of the complex meaning and word use, and long sentences in a speech within the scene is given below. Here Dorotea finds that she is being forced to give up her virginity by an over-ardent suitor.

Dorotea:

> If I were now between a lion's paws
> And were made certain sure of liberty
> If only I'd forsake my honour here,
> 'Twould prove all as impossible for me
> As for the lion to give his essence o'er.
> Then even as you have engirt me round

So likewise have I binded fast my mind
With virtuous and forcible desires
(All of which are wholly different from yours),
As you shall find if force you seek to use.

During rehearsals, I continually drew Hollie's attention to her pronunciation of consonants, vowels, and syllables. Although always in a state of flux, her diction improved tremendously. Gradually she began to give value to every word rather than delivering slurred clumps of indistinct meaning. As Cicely Berry stipulates, the weight given to the whole word not only communicates the *literal* meaning, but 'the meaning which is transmitted by the very sound of the words' (1993: 30). When working with Hollie on articulation exercises, I reminded her of her drawing techniques she had told me about in doodling over the words when listening to lectures or learning texts. I suggested to her that she might achieve a deeper assimilation with the language and her articulation of it if she developed her drawing techniques on her *Cardenio* text.

At the end of the Shakespeare unit, Hollie handed in her customized *Cardenio* text. In a written evaluation of her work, Hollie commented:

> As I was still struggling with the disjointed language of the piece during rehearsals, I began to explore ways to allow the language to become more flowing. I began illustrating the text visually to help celebrate each word in its own separate entirety, allowing me to feel, see and experience the word and it was during this exercise it allowed [me] to uncover the extent of how important the word 'honour' was to Dorotea. She is a determined, strong woman with the power to fight him with her formidable language, and this for me was only discovered as I began to illustrate and embrace her words.

Hollie's *Cardenio* text is interwoven with visual symbols (Figure 12.2). Adjacent to the customized text, she has drawn larger images capturing whole phrases and encapsulated meanings. In interview, Hollie explained her drawings to me.

Description and Analysis of Hollie's First Picture

Picture one: 'If I were now between a lion's paws
And were made certain sure of liberty,
If only I'd forsake my honour here'
Hollie's explanation: I drew a picture of two lion's paws (which represents Fernando) grabbing the word 'liberty' written in gold. Firstly, it's written in gold to highlight how important and precious her freedom is to Dorotea. Secondly, it represents her body being physically grabbed by Fernando.
My comment: These larger pictures have broken the text up into three units of action, capturing several lines within each image. They represent the action as

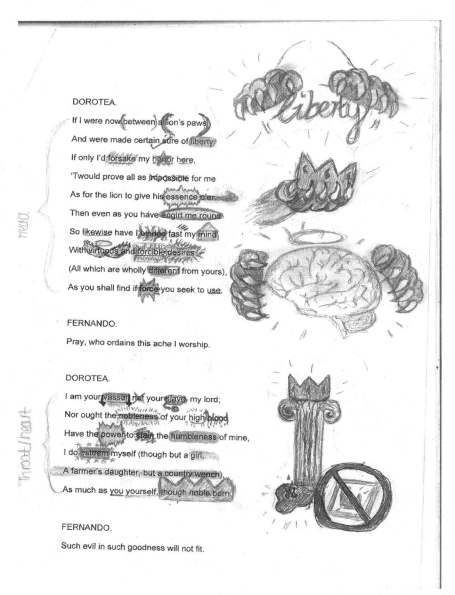

FIGURE 12.2 Example of Hollie's *Cardenio* text

described in the text while also containing an overall *psychological* understanding of what is happening to Dorotea from the actor's perspective.

Hollie gave the following explanation about four of her drawings onto the words of the text:

1) *forsake* is colored with grey strokes to illustrate the fast carelessness of her honor being thrown away
2) *honour* is starred with gold color to highlight its importance, and here is underlined to further reinforce how significant it is to Dorotea
3) *binded* has green vines interweaving round the letters as Fernando physically does to Dorotea
4) *desires* is in the center of gold and red-like flames of passion

Hollie explained the function of her drawing onto the words of the text in assisting her articulation, saying:

> The customized words on the text are for a different purpose than my drawings at the side of the text. When I draw onto the words, that's what the words look like and feel like in my head, making it also easier to articulate as I can see how the word feels or is meant to feel like. The drawing onto the words is to help with the pronunciation of the word and feeling, flow, and energy of the language. When I draw on the words, it helps me visualize the meaning of that word.

Consideration of the Participants' Methods Associated with Memory

An Ancient Perspective of Mnemotechnics

The methods used by Sophie, James, and Hollie correlate with the ancient Roman utilization of *mnemotechnics* for memorizing oratory speeches, such as the tactics endorsed by the unknown Roman author of the *Rhetorica ad Herennium* (Anon. 1954). The author announces that there are two types of memory: the natural memory, which flows with our thoughts, and the artificial memory, which must be trained (ibid.: 207). He introduces the idea of placing the thing that needs to be remembered as an image into a background, which must be 'small scale', so that they might be 'grasped' by the natural memory. The background the images are placed upon should be able to be run forwards or backwards in memory sequence, so that, 'reminded by the images, we can repeat orally what we committed to the backgrounds' (ibid.: 213). This reminds me of Sophie's PowerPoint pictures placed within their moving slide sequence and James's comic book genre storyboards.

The author makes much of the difference between images for 'things' (*memoria rerum*) and images for 'words' (*memoria verboram*). Yates (1966: 24) interprets that memory for 'things' is for the subject matter, 'the argument, a notion'. The memory for 'words' means that one must 'represent the words by means of images' (ibid.: 217). This reminds me of Hollie's drawings at the side of her text representing the ideas (*memoria rerum*) and her customizing of the words themselves (*memoria verboram*). Accentuating the subjective nature of the image, the Roman author expounds a constructivist philosophy, saying:

> One person is more struck by one likeness and another more by another. Often [. . .] when we declare that some form resembles another, we fail to receive universal assent because things seem different to different persons [. . .]. Everybody therefore should, in equipping himself with images, suit his own convenience.

A Contemporary Perspective

Psychologists Rod Nicolson and Angela Fawcett are prominent researchers into dyslexia, known for their cerebellar deficit hypothesis theory of dyslexia (Nicolson & Fawcett 2010). Although their theory is supported by some (Alvarez & Fiez 2018) and contested by others (Elliott & Grigorenko 2014: 82), they argue that an impairment of the cerebellum gives rise to difficulties in automatization of phonological and motor skills, articulation of speech, and information processing speeds. (These are all features involved in reading, speaking, and acting, where I have noted my acting students with dyslexia experiencing challenges.) Nicolson and Fawcett (2010: 68) have coined the term *conscious compensation*, describing the extra concentration and effort that dyslexic people sometimes undergo to achieve what might be automatic for some. In a personal interview with Nicolson, I asked what he thought might be underpinning the participants' remediation of the text. Nicolson suggested that it is likely that they are using a combination of several frameworks. He explained that there is an advantage gained from re-coding from one form to another which forces a deeper processing and therefore a better memory of it (Craik & Lockhart 1972). Directly relevant is the spread of encoding, where the more links one can make between an item and the rest of one's memory, the better the memory (Craik & Tulving 1975). Secondly, Nicolson highlights the idea of building a schema (Bartlett 1932), where it is easier to recall items if fitted into a relatively broad scheme of related meaningful associations and connections, which can include images, sound, smell, and feelings (Pritchard 2005: 26). Thirdly, Nicolson maintains that working memory can be facilitated by writing something on paper or on some other accessible format, so that all the items are presented as a unit. The visual representation can be used to circumvent the limitations of verbal working memory. Fourthly, utilizing an action sequence can function as a procedural learning system, which is independent of any declarative learning system of facts. Nicolson gives the example of a kinesthetic sequence such as 'tying shoe-laces where your hands know what to do, and in what sequence, although your mind might not have immediate access to the sequence'. Automatic processing, once learned in long-term memory, can function independently of the user's control and uses no working memory resources (Nicolson & Fawcett 2010: 60).

The Next Chapter

Throughout my three action research cycles, I have been assembling a fuller understanding of the range of problems met, the inclination towards certain working methods adopted by the research participants, and how and why those methods facilitate their challenges. In pulling the various threads together into a cohesive whole, I have harnessed these factors towards the formulation of another pedagogical facilitation. In the next chapter, I introduce Teaching Strategies Four and Five. I work with the same group of participants in their devised performance of Shakespeare's *Venus and Adonis* in my fourth and fifth Action Research Cycle to arrive at the findings of my study.

KEY POINTS OF CHAPTER 12

- The participants' own visually led methods in memorizing and expressing the written text
- Customizing the text to enable the muscular articulation of word
- Comprehending the function of the participants' compensatory methods through an examination of ancient and modern theories concerning memory

---

References

Alvarez, T.A. & Fiez, J.A. (2018). Current perspectives on the cerebellum and reading development. *Neuroscience and Biobehavioural Reviews*, 92, 55–66.

Anon. (1954). *Rhetorica ad Herennium*. Translation from the Latin by Caplan, H. Cambridge, MA: Harvard University Press.

Bacon, A. & Handley, S. (2010). Dyslexia, reasoning and the importance of visual-spatial processes. *In*: Alexander- Passe, N. (ed.) *Dyslexia and Creativity*. New York: Nova Science Publishers.

Bacon, A. & Handley, S. (2014). Reasoning and dyslexia: is visual memory a compensatory resource? *Dyslexia*, 20:1: 330–345.

Bartlett, F.C. (1932). *Remembering: A Study in Experimental and Social Psychology*. Cambridge, UK: Cambridge University Press.

Berry, C. (1993). *The Actor and the Text*. London: Virgin Books.

Block, G. (2013). *Speaking the Speech: An Actor's Guide to Shakespeare*. London: Nick Hern.

Carey, D. & Clark Carey, R. (2010) *The Verbal Arts Workbook*. London: Methuen Drama.

Craik, F.I.M. & Lockhart, R.S. (1972). Levels of processing: a framework for memory research. *Journal of Verbal Learning and Verbal Behaviour*, 11, pp. 671–684.

Craik, F.I.M. & Tulving, E. (1975). Depth of processing and the retention of words in episodic memory. *Journal of Experimental Psychology: General*, 104:3, pp. 268–294.

Doran, G. & Alamo, A. (2011) *Cardenio*. London: Nick Hern.

Elliott, J. G. & Grigorenko, E. (2014). *The Dyslexia Debate*. New York: Cambridge University Press.

Gathercole, S. & Packiam Alloway, T. (2008). *Working Memory and Learning*. London: SAGE Publications.

Griffiths, S. & Frith, U. (2002), Evidence for an articulatory awareness deficit in adult dyslexics. *Dyslexia*, 8, pp. 14–21.

McLoughlin, D. & Leather, C. (2013). *The Dyslexic Adult*, 2nd ed. Chichester, UK: Whurr.

Nicolson, R. & Fawcett, A. (2010). *Dyslexia, Learning and the Brain*. London: MIT Press.

Pritchard, A. (2005). *Ways of Learning*. London: David Fulton.

Shakespeare, W. (1962). *The Comedy of Errors*. Ed. Foakes, R.A. London: Arden Shakespeare.

Shakespeare, W. (2007). *Macbeth*. Ed. Bevington, D., Kahn, M., & Holland, P. London: Methuen Drama.

Yates, F. (1966). *The Art of Memory*. London: Routledge & Kegan Paul.

13

THE *MICRO AND MACRO STRATEGY* – DECONSTRUCTING AND RECONSTRUCTING MEANING AND SIGNIFICANCE IN SHAKESPEARE'S TEXT TOWARDS PERFORMANCE

Action Research (Cycles Four and Five) and Teaching Strategies Four and Five

Introduction

As has been demonstrated in the preceding chapters, it can be a slippery task for acting students with dyslexia to absorb the written words of Shakespeare, identify the meanings, recollect how it all links together, and speak the words with accuracy in the present moment of their character. This is not only testing for individuals with dyslexia, but can be demanding for any actor. The actor, in coming to 'own the text', must present an affinity with the words, a conviction in their communication, and an imagined and inwardly felt experience of the character they inhabit. To fulfill this objective, in this chapter I offer a teaching approach that can remove the initial discomfort in meeting the written words experienced by many of those with dyslexia, can anchor the text and individual interpretations, and harness and exhibit the individuals' strengths into performance while opening channels for a dissection of the textual layers and relishing of the words.

Action Research (Cycle Four) and Teaching Strategy Four

The work described in this chapter was undertaken during the Voice Storytelling Unit following the completion of the Shakespeare Unit. It involved the same participants as in Chapter 12: Sophie, Hollie, Elizabeth, and James.

The Macrostructure and Microstructure of the Text as the Foundation of the Teaching Strategy

To address the sometimes convoluted meanings embedded within Shakespeare's language (especially for my participants with dyslexia), I have drawn from reading comprehension theory in creating a simple framework and process as a teaching and working strategy. In reading comprehension theory (as discussed in the conclusion of Chapter 10), in the act of reading and meaning-making there needs to be an interplay between the bottom-up process (the *micro*) and the top-down process (the *macro*).

The *microstructure* is examining the individual words, such as decoding the symbols, recognizing the whole word, and analyzing the grammatical roles of the words. In Shakespeare, the microstructure would include recognition of unusual word meaning and use, the structural and literary form, and rich linguistic images such as personification and metaphor. For the actor, it would include the voiced sounding of the language, such as assonance, alliteration, rhythm, consonance, pauses, or tempo driven by caesura or punctuation, stimulating feeling, and auditory and kinesthetic memory.

The *macrostructure* relates to larger units of text, wherein the overall ideas and narrative arising from the whole piece can be identified. In Shakespeare, the macrostructure would include realizing and memorizing the storyline, impressions about characterization, and noting the characters' emotional and psychological needs and objectives.

Good comprehenders and fluent readers use both of these sources of information simultaneously as they read, while some readers with dyslexic difficulties may rely on one more than the other (such as guesswork of individual words based on story context), therefore comprehension can break down. Although those with dyslexia are often noted as possessing good comprehension skills, this comprehension can be undermined by a lack of automaticity in decoding skills (Thomson 2009: 193; Reid 2003: 122).

My Method – the Procedure in the Voice Class

As a preliminary exercise in a story-telling voice class, I divided the whole cohort of dyslexic and non-dyslexic acting students into small groups. At this early stage of the trial, group members were randomly selected. The dyslexic participants were not separated from the non-dyslexics, so the group's mix of individuals represented the common practice in a voice class. I gave each group a story and asked them to read through the text carefully and define the *Macro* overall narrative ideas arising from their understanding of the story. To stimulate their imaginations, I linked the *Macro* concept with an acting technique with which they were familiar. I aligned the *Macro* of the text with Bertolt Brecht's idea of *Gestus*, meaning in German 'the gist, gesture and point' (Willet 1977: 173). Brecht stated that the *Gestus* is a physical gesture or physical image which encapsulates an idea or message that the actor wishes to convey about the content of the play or their character to the audience. Although Brecht had meant the *Gestus* to be used as a device for breaking the fourth wall of psychological realism, it was also used for communication of ideas, a 'telling' through the body, which was my intention for the exercise.

First, I directed the students to individually draw some representations of their ideas for their *Macros* on paper, accompanied by a written title summing up the overall interpretation of the meaning/message of the story. When their sketches were complete, they could then share their drawings with their group, so their various interpretations could be debated together. The group members would then identify which *Macros* they wanted to use for their performance. The whole group would develop their ideas further by translating their drawings into physical group images – *tableaux vivants* (living pictures) as meaning anchors (like a still photograph). When taking up their physical group *Macro* positions, they were to speak their *Macro* titles aloud together with expression, so that they might deeply imprint their denotations through their visual/kinesthetic/spatial images of ideas, aural perceptions, and muscular memory of the body/mind. The physical group picture should strongly capture and communicate to the observer the overall message derived from the story.

Secondly, I directed them to isolate some key *Micro* words within the story: those that conjured up important word meanings, sensory responses, and images. I aligned the *Micro* with Stanislavski's idea of *Grasp* (Merlin 2003: 66), where he wanted his actors to really 'grasp' the material. Stanislavski said: 'grasp is what a bulldog has in his jaw. We actors must have the same power to seize with our eyes, ears and all our senses' (1980: 217). I instructed the students to particularly 'grasp' the *Micro* key words in the text. As with the *Macros*, they were to explore their mental images arising from the words in drawings, sketches, and scribbles, with the words written next to them. Then, having shared and discussed their *Micro* images with each other, the group should choose which they considered the most effective drawings for translating into their physical performance. They should then build group physical images of their *Micros* while they spoke the words aloud with expressive conviction. These *Micros* could then be developed further into physical movement or dance expressions, accompanied with the spoken word.

These living images are available to be analyzed by the whole group, and do not disadvantage those with difficulties with the written word. As a form of thinking-in and through-action, by the actors and the participating observers, the group tableaux are shared and can be reconfigured to encompass other interpretations, thereby providing an excellent thinking and creative tool. This use of *tableaux vivants* resonates with Augusto Boal's *Image Theatre* exercises, which he devised to explore social oppression. Boal said: 'The image speaks [. . .] the body thinks [. . .] think what the image thinks' (1992: 192). The students were introduced to this method as a class exercise. The groups were then asked to develop their story performance with their *Macro* and *Micro* drawings and tableaux outside of class time as homework, and then to perform their group interpretations of their stories at the next voice class. This experiment was successful in extending inventive interpretations of the text and performance in all of the students' work. Through a shared careful reading of the text in defining the *Micro* and *Macros*, their interpretations were amplified through a transmission of physical actions, informed by the language of drawing. Furthermore, it was noteworthy that the dyslexic participants within the mixed groups were wholly engaged in the exercise with an equality of opportunity, producing their drawings with enthusiasm, and performing with self-assurance.

The Function of the *Macro and Micro Strategy* Viewed through the *Indexical Hypothesis* (Glenberg 2011)

Psychologist Arthur Glenberg's research centers on the theory of embodied cognition and how words, when grounded through action, become meaningful to the reader (Glenberg 2011; Glenberg & Kaschak 2002). Glenberg's *Indexical Hypothesis* has an affinity with what my participants have been demonstrating, adding further insight into the workings of the *Macro* and *Micro* tableaux. Glenberg claims that those who find difficulty in making meaning derived directly from the symbols of written words can be assisted in comprehension by actually *doing in action* what is suggested in the words. Glenberg explains this through the *simulation theory of language*. It is proposed that when reading, the language is understood by the brain thinking into the equivalent perceptual, emotional, and active states the language describes, and is *simulated* in the brain as though in the real-life experience (Glenberg 2011: 6). I liken this *simulation theory* to exactly how the actor responds when working from the text. When acting the text, this process, once simulated in the brain, is then externalized through the body in vocal and physical expression. To further distinguish the components of language comprehension when reading, Glenberg's *Indexical Hypothesis* is configured into three stages. First, when encountering the written words in a phrase, they must be mapped (*indexed*) to a referent in the environment or imagination (possibly already encoded in memory, entailing aspects of emotion and action), thereby creating a mental model. At the second stage, Glenberg uses the term *affordances*, which is when a consideration and realization are formed about the manner in which the referent acts physically within the specific situation presented to achieve the goal of the phrase or sentence. At the third stage (titled *meshing*), the action takes place, and the pieces of the mental model all integrate together. These three stages create a *simulation* of the event contained within the words, as experienced within the reader's mind (Kaschak & Glenberg 2000: 510). Therefore, through the process of the *Macro and Micro Strategy*, the written word is mapped, simulated in the mind, and externalized through the body, supporting both working and long-term memory.

Making connections with my work, I surmise that the use of exaggerated, planned gestures and expressive actions will not only activate and cement the image with the word into long-term memory, but also enable an enhanced realization of it, and thus it will be embedded with more potency. In addition, as the articulators of speech are also connected with motor memory and an auditory feedback loop, the *Indexical Hypothesis* strongly supports the participants' articulation of the words.

Akin to gesturing, drawing utilizes both the mental and physical in a motor action to keep a concept alive in working memory. Artist Terry Rosenberg (2008: 109) describes the act of drawing as a thinking space in action, between the not yet formed and the formed. Thinking is set into action as the pencil strokes are made on the surface in a feedback loop of doing, seeing, and responding to what is seen. Significantly, Rosenberg uses the same verb I have quoted from Stanislavski for the *Micro* exercise: 'to grasp', wherein, Rosenberg elucidates, the hand can *grasp* the pencil, but also, through the drawing, the mind can *grasp* the idea; 'to *grasp* something is to know it' (ibid.: 111–112).

The *Venus and Adonis* Project (Action Research Cycle Five) and Teaching Strategy Five

To test the proficiency of my *Macro and Micro Strategy* for dyslexic acting students, I grouped my four dyslexic participants together for a voice performance, using a section of Shakespeare's poem *Venus and Adonis* (2007) as working material. As I had already trialed the strategy with the whole cohort (including dyslexics and non- dyslexics in the common working environment of a voice class), it was now important to place my focus on those with dyslexia. I aimed to record their individual experiences while nurturing their idiosyncratic methods. It was crucial at this stage to separate them from the non-dyslexics, to remove the pressure of trying to 'keep up' with the non-dyslexics and avoid the non-dyslexic methods influencing their choices. By drawing on constructivist teaching principles, in forming this small community of dyslexics with shared challenges I aimed to offer a social learning space. By working with each other, they would be able to learn from each other's dis/abilities and counteractions while also developing a subjective understanding of their own intuitive processes, learning styles, and strengths.

Inclusion of the Participants' Personal Methods of Processing Text as a Central Component of the Live Performance

This performance was self-directed by the participants. I asked the participants to utilize the *Micro and Macro* method in devising, rehearsal, and performance of *Venus and Adonis*. Crucially, as part of Teaching Strategy Five, I also asked the participants to include their personal modes of processing text as a principal component interwoven into their devised live performance.

Specifically, the following were to be included in the performance:

- Sophie to incorporate her PowerPoint image storyboards
- Hollie to include her drawing

- James to create some musical interpretations
- Elizabeth, who had not yet shown any personal methods, to explore ideas with the group

By giving credence and attention to the participants' personal methods of accessing the text, removing their fear of criticism for diverting from conventional performance style, I aimed to give them a sense of autonomy. I wanted them to use their individual modes that enhanced their abilities and displayed their distinctive strengths, rather than constraining or hiding them.

The Performance of Venus and Adonis

It is problematic to attempt to capture the ephemeral and corporal experience of live performance in written words, nor is this description meant to act as a review of the performance. Huxley and Witts underline that live performance leaves only a 'trace' of itself, so searching for the roots, methods, and reasons behind the creation is critical. They stipulate:

> To understand the diversity of performance one must consider the practice and the practical concerns that have engaged its creators. Performance means process as well as final artefact, and an engagement with process is essential to any full understanding of the form. [. . .] it is easier [. . .] to consider the traces – the drawings, photographs [. . .].
>
> *(Huxley & Witts 1996: 2)*

Description of the Participants' Performance

Although the text of *Venus and Adonis* is classical, the performance style was contemporary. To accommodate their interdisciplinary practice, the participants had set the stage with a large painting canvas, placed centrally up-stage, with painting utensils set at the base. Another large screen was placed stage left, for Sophie's PowerPoint slide show. James played Adonis, and the three female participants (Sophie, Hollie, and Elizabeth) all played Venus, speaking or reacting together, or individually.

Their rendition of *Venus and Adonis* was rich in individual contribution, acting ability, and performance ideas. During the performance, the inclusion of live painting on the large canvas, Sophie's evocative PowerPoint images moving across the screen in tandem with the spoken words, and the employment of the *Macro* and *Micro* physical imagery were all underpinned by James's composed music. The performance began with all participants taking up a physical *Macro* tableau, which they had titled, 'You always want what you can't get', referring to Venus's desire for Adonis (Figure 13.1).

At the start of the performance, following their initial presentation of their first *Macro* tableau, they set about conjuring up the world Shakespeare depicts

FIGURE 13.1   *Macro* tableau: 'You always want what you can't get'

at the beginning of the poem. Before speaking any of the lines, Elizabeth and James began a voiced soundscape of birdsong and atmospheric vocalization while both played the ukulele. Sophie set about painting a purple sky, the sun, green fields, and trees on the large backcloth (as Shakespeare describes it in the text). As Elizabeth spoke the first lines of the poem, Sophie's PowerPoint images, illustrating the text, echoing the words, began moving across the large screen:

> Even as the sun with purple coloured face
> Had ta'en his last leave of the weeping morn [. . .]

Hollie, embodying the horse Adonis is riding, wearing a model of a horse's head, appeared on the stage, galloping to the sound of horse's hooves, created by Elizabeth and Sophie banging coconut shells together as they spoke the lines:

> Rose cheeked Adonis hied him to the chase,
> Hunting he loved, but love he laughed to scorn [. . .]

Throughout the highly physical performance, the participants activated their *Micro* and *Macro* tableaux to underpin the words, communicating their interpretation of meaning and artistic expression (Figure 13.2–13.4). The poem proceeds as love-sick Venus approaches Adonis:

> Sick-thoughted Venus makes amain unto him,
> And like a bold-faced suitor 'gins to woo him.
> 'Thrice fairer than myself', thus she began,
> 'The field's chief flower, [...]'

A Consideration of the Function of the Drawings as Process towards Performance

I report here on some of the participants' drawings produced as part of their experiencing of the text during their rehearsal period, and I consider their function as hermeneutic tools towards an immersion in the text. Examples of their drawings and my analysis are distributed over the following pages of the chapter.

Sophie's *Micro* for 'that they have murdered this poor heart of mine' is shown in Figure 13.5.

James's *Micro* for 'She bathes in water yet her fire must burn' is shown in Figure 13.6.

FIGURE 13.2 Hollie's drawing of the *Micro* tableau for 'The field's chief flower'

Note: Here, Hollie's drawing of the metaphor 'the field's chief flower' is a literal translation from the words into picture form, creating a paired 'key word' mnemonic as a memorable semantic elaboration (Sadoski & Paivio 2013: 75).

FIGURE 13.3   *Micro* tableau for 'She feedeth on the steam as on a prey'

Hollie's *Macro* for 'You can't always get what you want' is shown in Figure 13.7.

Elizabeth's *Micros* for several phrases are shown in Figure 13.8.

A Brief Assessment of the Performance

This was an ensemble creation, bursting with feeling and energy in relaying the text, embodying the words through the mediations of live painting, PowerPoint, music, and their *Micro* and *Macro tableaux vivants* (living pictures). Generally, they produced a high quality of work, notably less undermined by aspects of their dyslexia. Appearing in command of the words and meaning, they spoke and acted with a mental and physical commitment, without signs of fear of failure. Overall, there was a tremendous improvement in their articulation and performance of the text, displaying freedom and confidence (as commented on by the audience, critical friend, and other validating observers).

Additionally, Sophie was dual-tasking in an extraordinary manner throughout the live performance. As she acted the text, she held the hand-controlled device that changed the slides on the PowerPoint. At each changing word, Sophie

FIGURE 13.4 Hollie's drawing of the *Micro* for 'She feedeth on the steam as on a prey'

Note: In Figure 13.3, it can be noted how the physical image of the action in the *Micro* tableau echoes the drawing of the bird of prey portrayed in Figure 13.4, while both genres capture the visceral content of Shakespeare's metaphor.

imperceptibly changed her PowerPoint pictures on the large screen at the back of the stage exactly on cue although her body and attention were focused on her acting performance. What was remarkable was how deeply Sophie had assimilated all her pictures, knowing exactly what piece of text they represented, so she was able to multi-task. Although immersed in the acting of the piece, her mental schema of images was running through its sequence as she clicked for each picture change with a synchronization of modes.

Analysis of the Effectiveness of the Strategy

Following the performance, I collected feedback from the participants. In semi-structured interview, I questioned whether working with the *Macro* and *Macro* exercises had assisted them with their dyslexia challenges or not. In my analysis,

FIGURE 13.5   Sophie's *Micro* for 'that they have murdered this poor heart of mine'

Note: This is an action-filled picture. In the eyes and the heart, the pencil strokes are swirling, full of movement. Lurid colors and strong black eyebrows add impact; the placement of the heart, as subject, is central, with the active verb *murdered* highlighted by the knife moving diagonally across the page, piercing the heart, the blood bursting from the wound. The graphics powerfully underpin the words and the pain Venus is suffering. Sophie's performance reflected all that is within this picture.

I re-read the interviews looking for identifiable themes. Their feedback affirmed that they believed that this exercise functions as a powerful tool to overcome or by-pass some of their prevailing difficulties while supporting their development in several areas. I have divided the themes into eight categories (see Figure 13.9).

Due to the themes' interconnecting relationship, where separation would have reduced their full meaning, I have merged them into four headings which I have laid out below. I include a brief analytical comment under each heading, including a selection of participant feedback.

Theme: Stress Relief, Sufficient Time, and Simplicity of Task

The *Macro and Micro Strategy* offers a structure that removes an initial confrontation with the text, eliminating the demand for an immediate 'correct' response.

FIGURE 13.6 James's *Micro* for 'She bathes in water yet her fire must burn'

Note: James's picture six has a naïve style, yet its design is dramatic. Venus, with voluptuous figure and flames of passion burning from her head and hands, cuts a spectacular figure. This representation amplifies her power, experienced by Adonis in Shakespeare's narrative, and James when acting the role of Adonis.

This reduces the risk of failure within the public arena of class/rehearsal. By approaching the text in a shared manner (with group discussion of meanings, interpretations, and pronunciation of words before performance), the danger of exposure and humiliation is lessened. With a simplicity of instruction in identifying the *Macro* and the *Micro*, there is a clarity of goals, allowing time for the realization of the words. Sophie explained:

> I often panic when I know that I will be asked to read a big chunk of text, but if my mind was taken up by this – by looking at the meaning first and deciding on the *Macros* and *Micros* – and then creating the physical actions – it is very helpful.

FIGURE 13.7 Hollie's *Macro*: 'You can't always get what you want'

Note: Hollie's drawing portrays Venus's longing for Adonis. The drawing functions as a *Psychological Gesture* for Hollie in her acting of Venus. Michael Chekhov's technique for assisting actors in exploring their character – *the Psychological Gesture* – acts as the 'imaginary body', 'calling up feelings, motions and will impulses' (1985: 133).

Hollie told us:

> I found this method easier to organize myself with the text and understand what the overall meaning is, what the characters are saying, and how the language is expressing this, as I can place it all on the page in drawings rather than doing lots of different things at the same time, such as in the Stanislavski verbs and actions method.

Theme: Depth of Processing, Drawing, and Visual Preference, Articulation

The strategy allows for multi-perspectives, abilities, and cognitive learning styles optimizing a more complex absorption of the text. The devising of images (physical, spatial, aural, and visual), where meaning can be mapped directly to word and captured into concrete forms, facilitates the embedding of mental models, supporting working memory and processing difficulties while also developing

FIGURE 13.8 Elizabeth's *Micros* for several phrases

Note: Elizabeth's drawings are impressionistic in nature, neatly capturing the word content. The image for the phrase 'bird tangled in the net' catches Shakespeare's metaphor of Adonis trapped by Venus, shown in the picture as a human figure with wings, encompassed by a net.

creative interpretations. The process of separating the various strands of the text and then synthesizing them back together enhances depth of comprehension, influencing fluency of reading and ability to articulate the words. Hollie reported:

> I found my own technique of drawing over the words of the text and the drawing of *Micros* help me memorize and express the text, as these were the images I mostly recalled when performing the text. The words no longer remain two-dimensional when speaking the text or visually on the page, but instead they evolved to become interactive, exciting and rich.

Elizabeth agreed, saying:

> I found this one of the most helpful exercises. It definitely helped me to understand the text but also made me look deeper into the meanings and

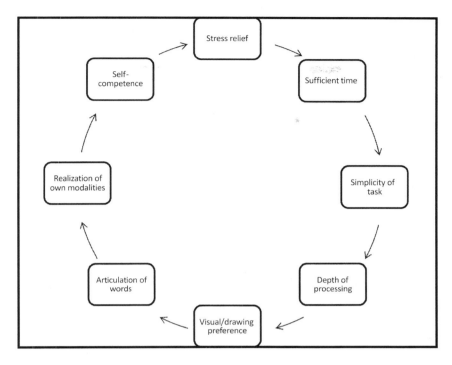

FIGURE 13.9 The Cycle of Themes

feelings of all the detail and individual lines. When learning the text, I could also visualize the pictures I had drawn. When learning my lines, I could picture the drawings and automatically feel something and connect with it when I spoke it.

Sophie wrote:

I never thought I could paint, but I see now how liberating and expressive drawing is. It was liberating to draw, because with my PowerPoints I know what the finished product will look like, but with drawing you never know where you will end up and your imagination creates things before you.

Theme: Realization of Own Modalities and Strategies

The action research aspect of this investigation meant that the participants became co-participants in it through an examination of themselves and each other, reflecting on their dyslexia and compensatory methods. Sophie explained: 'Through this research we have found that, by each of us sharing what helps us confront issues we struggle with, we created a collaborative piece where we taught and helped each other.' Considering her rationale for translating the text into illustrative PowerPoint slideshows, Sophie commented: 'I realized that most of my PowerPoint slides are *Micros* – picking out iconic details from the text, helping me to grasp what is going on and finding individual meaning.' James made some sense of his desire to interweave the text with music, clarifying:

> If I give a piece of music to a scene or a speech, and then I add the text into the lyrics of the music and then get the feeling from that, I then take away the music, take away the singing, I feel that the words become a lot more fluid and free. I can hear a piece of music and in my mind there will be a certain picture – an image – music is one way I can really express myself in the text – to give it a sense of me.

In recognizing her dominantly visual approach, Hollie said:

> the encouragement of drawing has really helped me when understanding or reading texts, also helped me learn the qualities of myself that I am a visual learner. It really helped me get into the text, and I loved discovering the sounds, textures, imagery, and colors within the language.

Theme: Self-competence

The utilization of the participants' personal modalities of working as valuable contributors to the performance encouraged a sense of competence and *self-actualization* (Maslow n.d.). In his model of human needs and motivation, Abraham Maslow's proposition of *self-actualization* is placed at the top of the pyramid of human needs, referring to 'a self-fulfilment [. . .] to become everything that one is capable of becoming' (ibid.: 19). Having removed many of the barriers that block those with dyslexia during this process, the individual is able to develop their abilities towards a self-actualization. Sophie underlined:

> I have learnt so much about myself. I found that half the challenge is about self-confidence. I have learnt that it is better to take your time with the text rather than panicking and rushing over it, and to make sure that I understand what I am saying. Now I can pick up a text and understand most of the language, and if I think about it, can work out most of the double meanings. I never thought that dyslexia and Shakespeare could go together, but now I could see myself performing Shakespeare with confidence, which for me is an achievement.

Conclusion

By joining concepts of acting methods with reading comprehension theory and Glenberg and Kaschak's *Indexical Hypothesis* (2002: 209), I have created a compensatory strategy with which to buttress my participants' talents and learning styles while circumventing deficiencies in reading, processing, comprehension, memorizing, and the attendant vulnerabilities found in those with dyslexia. This process is bolstered through shared discourse with others and exploration of modalities, so ideas in the text can be located and situated, overcoming any disequilibrium when encountering the text. Of huge importance is the inclusion of the participants' individual modes of entering the text, and an exhibition of their abilities through their practice and live performance. Commonly, these personally derived methods are a private process, and therefore remain unseen and unrecognized. When using the *Micro and Macro Strategy*, their methods emerge as principal tools in the creation of the work, interwoven into the language of their performance.

When debating the beneficial experience of mastery for those with learning difficulties such as dyslexia, Burden specifies that a sense of self-competence is not enough, but that there must be 'an improved understanding of how the application of knowledge or skill leads to successful outcomes together with a belief in one's own capability in making that application' (2005: 22). Here I offer strategies for studio teaching and performance that are not too demanding of time, underpinned by research into dyslexia, psychology, textual comprehension, and educational theory, led by a group of individuals with dyslexia, towards a self-mastery and generating evidence of capabilities. Although I acknowledge there is no typical dyslexic learner, and therefore no 'one size fits all', this is a method which can facilitate a wide range of individuals, including dyslexic and non-dyslexic learners. I have trialed this *Micro and Macro* procedure many times in class work with my dyslexic participants and other students. The practical results support the view that these strategies are effective in assisting individuals with dyslexia, neurodiversity, and across the student cohort. It provides a space for equality of opportunity that can be further developed using a multiplicity of texts beyond Shakespeare.

The Next Chapter

In the next chapter, I present my overall study findings, Action Research (Cycle Six) and Teaching Strategy Six, and offer my final recommendations.

KEY POINTS OF CHAPTER 13

- Introduction of the *Micro and Macro* approach, addressing dyslexia and supporting neurodiversity across the student cohort (Teaching Strategy Four)

(continued)

(continued)

- Description of the participants' individual methods of engaging with the written text, and introducing their methods as key elements of devised and live performance (Teaching Strategy Five)
- The use of *tableaux vivants* (living pictures) as meaning and memory anchors, extending performance style and grasp of the text
- Analysis of the effectiveness of the two strategies in building autonomy over the text
- The *Indexical Hypothesis*: the three stages of indexing, affordance, and meshing, combining together to form a mental simulation of the content extrapolated from the text

References

Boal, A. (1992). *Games for Actors and Non-actors*. London: Routledge.

Burden, R. (2005). *Dyslexia and Self-concept*. London: Whurr.

Chekhov, M. (1985). *Lessons for the Professional Actor*. New York: Performing Arts Journal Publications.

Glenberg, A. (2011). How reading comprehension is embodied and why that matters. *International Electronic Journal of Elementary Education*, 4: 1, pp. 5–8.

Glenberg, A. & Kaschak, M. (2002). Grounding language in action. *Psychonomic Bulletin & Review*, 9:3, 558–565.

Huxley, M. & Witts, N. (1996). *The Twentieth-century Performance Reader*. London: Routledge.

Kaschak, M. & Glenberg, A. (2000). Constructing meaning: the role of affordances and grammatical constructions in sentence comprehension. *Journal of Memory and Language*, 43, pp. 508–529.

Maslow, A.H. (n.d.). *A Theory of Human Motivation*. Floyd VA: Wilder Publications.

Merlin, B. (2003). *Konstantin Stanislavsky*. Abingdon, UK: Routledge.

Reid, G. (2003). *Dyslexia: A Practitioner's Handbook*, 3rd ed. Chichester, UK: John Wiley.

Rosenberg, T. (2008). New beginnings and monstrous births: notes towards an appreciation of ideational drawing. *In*: Garner, S. (ed.) *Writing on Drawing*. Bristol, UK: Intellect Books, pp. 109–124.

Sadoski, M. & Paivio, A. (2013). *Imagery and Text*. New York: Routledge.

Shakespeare, W. (2007). *Venus and Adonis*. *In*: Duncan-Jones, K, &Woudhuysen, H.R. (eds.) *Shakespeare's Poems*. London: Bloomsbury.

Stanislavski, C. (1980). *An Actor Prepares*. London: Methuen Drama.

Thomson, M. (2009). *The Psychology of Dyslexia*, 2nd ed. Chichester, UK: Wiley-Blackwell.

Willet, J. (1977). *The Theatre of Bertolt Brecht*. London: Eyre Methuen.

14

INTERPRETIVE MNEMONICS, DISTRIBUTED COGNITION, AND AUTHENTICITY OF SELF

The Research Findings, Action Research (Cycle Six) and Teaching Strategy Six

Introduction

In this concluding chapter, I offer another teaching strategy (Teaching Strategy Six) and consolidate the findings of my research, outlining the emerging answers. Throughout this study, I have sought to ascertain how dyslexia is characterized within the methods of actor training, to understand why many of my dyslexic acting students show a proclivity for processing the text through visually led and kinesthetic mediums, and to explore how the teacher might support the potential of the dyslexic individual.

In discussing the complex nature of dyslexia, the reading and language research scholar Maryanne Wolf has labeled dyslexia 'a mystery of the century' (2008: 192). She emphasizes that there is no one form of dyslexia, but a continuum of reading disabilities which reflect the many components involved in reading. However, Wolf's attention is primarily preoccupied with reading ability. During my study of the dyslexic participants described in this book, I have recognized that there is a connecting relationship of characteristics running between them which extend beyond reading skills. What I have noticed accords with what psychologists James Smith-Spark and John E. Fisk assert when they say: 'What is without doubt is that dyslexia is a condition that impinges strongly upon cognitive functioning, affecting performance across a wide range of domains' (Smith-Spark & Fisk 2007: 34). It is reiterated throughout much of the literature that those with dyslexia have problems with processing speed, working memory, and automatization of skills (Smith-Spark & Fisk 2003, 2004; Smith-Spark et al. 2007; Nicolson & Fawcett 2010; McLoughlin & Leather 2013; Reid 2016).[1] It is on these areas that much of my research has come to focus, and where I have arrived at some understanding of the causes, effects, and facilitation of my dyslexic participants' difficulties. (The role of working memory is presented in Chapter 4 when discussing the theories of dyslexia.) Briefly explained, working memory is the ability we have to hold and manipulate information in the mind over short periods of time. There is a limit to how much information can be held in working memory, and everyone's capacity will differ. Information can be lost very quickly through distraction or trying to dual-task (Gathercole & Packiam Alloway 2008).

My Overall Findings

Finding One

Working memory and processing difficulties can severely affect the progression and outcomes of dyslexic individuals' work, having as much detrimental impact on class work and performance as the reading difficulties connected to dyslexia. Therefore, teaching strategies when working on Shakespeare's text must consciously support the faculty of memory and reduce processing demands.

Working Memory Challenges

I have found that forms of memory aids were instrumental in assisting the participants' processing pathways and realization of Shakespeare's text into performance. Throughout this study, I have continually referred back to the participants' difficulties with memory weakness and problems with processing. I had noted the recurrence of the subject of memory weakness arising in the literature on dyslexia (Mortimore 2008; Thomson 2009; Grant 2010; Nicolson & Fawcett 2010) and the participants' own references to their weak memory. However, it was not until my second and third action research trials on the Stanislavski-inspired *Actions* sequence (described in Chapters 10 and 11) that I came to understand the impact of poor working memory, cognitive overload, and complications around the processing of information for the participants when connecting to the words in the text. To further my understanding of memory weakness, I returned to my initial interviews with my participants, searching for references that involved the subject of memory. By focusing on this area in my data coding, the exposure of memory problems as a major feature was revealed. All of the participants referred explicitly to their problems with memory, or highlighted their problems with blanking out, or experiencing a jumbled cognition.

My findings are supported by the work of cognitive psychologist James Smith-Spark and his fellow researchers, and their investigations concerning aspects of memory difficulties in those with dyslexia. Smith-Spark (2018) and Smith-Spark et al. (2016) have identified executive functioning deficits as an important element in dyslexia. Executive functioning is part of working memory, and includes cognitive functions such as planning, organization, dual-tasking, retaining task-relevant information in memory over the time for which it is required, and access to information in long-term memory. Currently, Smith-Spark is researching prospective memory and dyslexia, which is an area that has not yet been given much attention in dyslexic adults. Prospective memory is remembering the intentions that will need to be acted on in the future and when they need to happen. It also entails a retrospective component, as individuals have to remember the content and details about what they need to do in the planned future action (Smith-Spark 2018: 817).

When reflecting on the dyslexic participants' difficulties with the Stanislavski-inspired actions and verb sequencing exercise, challenges with executive functioning, prospective and retrospective memory can be recognized, as well as difficulties with reading the words. Likewise, it is clear that David's carefully choreographed actions, spatially designed locations, and elaborated card sequences in his rendition of *Sonnet 17* (described in Chapter 3) buttressed his prospective and retrospective memory through his interaction with his tools and environment.

Findings Two, Three, and Four

Finding Two

When reading Shakespeare's text, internal mental images of information arising from the text are created in the imagination. For those with dyslexia difficulties, the transmutation of these images into external concrete models (interpreted through the body or onto a surface) can provide stable representations and activations of individual schema structures and simulations which are constructed and mapped from the text. These external representations/activations support both memory weaknesses and difficulties with reading, overcoming the need to engage with the written text through a re-reading of the words. This apparently automatic default used by some individuals with dyslexia, can be further developed into methodologies of practice in voice and acting exercises.

Finding Three

The exploitation of what I have entitled *Interpretive Mnemonics* can aid the individual's comprehension, utterances, memory, and performance of Shakespeare. This representational and transformational mnemonic approach to the text can also serve as an acting method, not only as an aid to thinking and learning, but in unlocking creative forms of exposition.

Finding Four

When working on a complex text, the content should be organized into small units of focus in order to reduce cognitive overload, and then processed through structured frameworks which can guide a recognition of the hierarchical significance of the words and meaning.

Employment of Interpretive Mnemonic Aids

My data collected during this study has demonstrated that the participants relied very heavily on creating a parallel configuration of the words and content of the text, using a kinesthetic and visually processed bias. This parallel text often replaces the original written text as the primary base of reference, and is formed through the use of planned physical gestures and actions, or by creating a visual representation onto a surface, sometimes employing haptic and auditory elements in conjunction with the visual. Throughout this study, I have found that the function of this analogic text works as a:

a)   *Mnemonic tool*: The function of working memory facilitation is primary.
b)   *Hermeneutic tool*: This has a cognitive purpose, to enable thinking-through, analyzing, comprehending, simulation, and construction of meanings.
c)   *Artistic tool*: It can enhance the aesthetic ideas for performance and language prosody, and serve as a space for expression of feelings and perspectives.
d)   *Organizational tool*: It offers a space in which to sort information into orders and linear sequences.
e)   *Acting tool*: The psychological and emotional states and physical actions extrapolated from the text can be subjectively developed through sensory modes and embodied cognition.
f)   *Communicative tool*: The formulation of concepts, narrative story, and articulation of the structure of the words can be broken down, re-constructed, and rehearsed. This re-construction of creative interpretation and articulation is further communicated through the differing mediums of performance.

Findings Five and Six

Finding Five

There is a requirement for a scholarship of *inclusivity* in teaching and learning. There is a need for acting and voice teachers to possess not only a deep knowledge of their specialized subjects, including a broad knowledge of pedagogical theory in practice, but also, crucially, an informed knowledge about dyslexia and its multifarious manifestations. Pedagogical provision can be significantly improved if the teacher has studied the theories about dyslexia, drawing from experienced knowledge through their practical action in the field, rather than relying on received generic information, or the learning support tutor.

Finding Six

Humanistic approaches of pedagogy which emphasize nurturing of the individual and their differences, an empathetic understanding for their experience, and a fostering of their distinctive strengths are necessary to adequately enable and develop the potential of those with dyslexia.

Authenticity in and through Teaching, Promoting Autonomy and Self-authorship in Students with Dyslexia

Tanner has defined five types of failure that are experienced by dyslexics throughout their education (Tanner 2009). First, there is a *systems failure* when inappropriate educational opportunities are given, caused by a teacher's lack of knowledge about dyslexia and influenced by their attitude. Secondly, there is a *constructed failure*, when a narrow view is taken over what dyslexia is and the idea that it should be 'treated' outside of the teaching environment, without any adaptation of educational behavior (for example, relying on learning support staff outside of the class environment to 'fix it'). Thirdly, there is *public failure* (this is a prominent feature in actor training, where the individual's difficulties are publicly exhibited through methods in skills training, rehearsal, and performance). Fourthly, there is *family failure*, where some individuals retain a sense of guilt about failing the expectations of their parents, and finally, a *personal failure*. Dyslexics commonly harbor memories of perceived failures accumulated throughout their schooling, convincing them that they are inadequate in certain areas. These experiences of failure can result in strong feelings of fear. This can drive a learned helplessness, or a compulsion to over-achieve to prove their human value, as in Dweck's (2000) theories of self, where a view of a fixed intelligence/ability means that failure is seen as an indictment of themselves.

As demonstrated in the work with the dyslexic acting students in this book, these facets of failure can be ameliorated into experiences of success. The teacher's role is paramount here, and it is useful to consider what it might mean to be an *authentic* teacher, both *in* teaching and *through* teaching, in influencing students' progress towards a realization of their own authenticity. In Chapter 5, I discussed how the presence of dyslexia can severely interrupt the authentic expression of the individual with dyslexia, and what the word 'authentic' might mean in relation to voice, communication, and acting. (The concept of authenticity is a complex area to define. For a detailed analysis about teaching and authenticity in higher education, see Kreber 2013.) In a truncated consideration of what authenticity *in* teaching might be, it can be defined as teachers being true to themselves by confronting who they are, identifying their purpose, the areas they regard as important, what they believe to have value, and then living those beliefs through their teaching choices and actions. Authenticity *through* teaching is driven by teachers' modeling of their own authenticity, showing care for their students by ensuring their abilities and personhoods thrive, thereby encouraging their students to establish their own authenticity. This student authenticity can be recognized when they come to think for themselves, speak in their own voices, and express themselves in the manner that is appropriate for them, emerging as authors of themselves (Kreber 2013).

This attainment of authenticity and self-authorship is explicitly displayed through an achievement gained by my research participant Elizabeth (featured in Chapters 10, 11, and 13). Following the completion of her Acting degree at the Arts University, Elizabeth went on to complete an MA in Acting at the Royal Central School of Speech and Drama, where she gained an overall First in 2017. Elizabeth acknowledges the influence she took from the work she had previously done with me. She writes: 'Whitfield's research has supported most aspects of my research, rehearsal process and performance. I started my ideas from her pre-existing work' (Bartram 2017: 25). She stipulates:

> dyslexia is the main barrier to my acting [. . .] being dyslexic acts as a block from my brain to my mouth, so I may understand, but cannot find the right words to describe that this is the case. This seems prevalent for me when working on Shakespeare's text.
>
> *(ibid.: 3)*

For her MA practical project, Elizabeth chose to explore Imogen's monologue from *Cymbeline* (Shakespeare 1999: Act III, Scene v). She explained that she used her drawing work 'as a spring board, but I also wanted to look at other creative mediums, which enabled all the senses to connect'. She explored the physical handling of differing materials and their association with the words of the monologue, including feathers, pebbles, glitter, paper, paint, and confetti. She said: 'I began to rip, scratch, throw, drop or blow them to explore if I had a response with the words.' Elizabeth developed an original performance style, comparable in some ways with David's sonnet performance. For her live performance, she arranged her collected materials about the stage. As she acted the words of the monologue, Elizabeth physically interacted with her items, amplifying the words and their expression. This brief description can only skim over what was a sophisticated use of kinesthetic, aural, haptic, and visual processes in service of a thickly layered performance. Through my observation of her work, it is clear Elizabeth has gained an authenticity, an authorship of herself, and a management of her dyslexia.

Action Research Cycle Six and Teaching Strategy Six

In continuing my development of teaching ideas for a whole cohort of acting students, I have drawn from Elizabeth's multisensory approach, producing Teaching Strategy Six with the aim of facilitating and cultivating all of the students' cognitive and learning styles. In discussing dyslexia and defining the difference between cognitive or learning styles, Tilly Mortimore states that '*cognitive* style is seen as the spontaneous almost automatic way in which an individual processes incoming stimuli and *learning* style is seen more in terms of the strategies a student adopts to cope with learning tasks and situations' (2008: 6). Mortimore continues:

> if students can be made aware of their learning styles preferences, they will then be more able to recognise their strengths and become sensitive to their weaknesses. They will also become more aware of the demands of a particular context.
>
> *(ibid.: 98)*

I therefore offer this teaching strategy, with a firm foundation as its starting point. In my description of the outcome of its trial, I delineate areas that might be developed further to improve its facilitation across the student cohort.

Shakespeare Sonnets Examined and Performed through the VARK Learning Style Framework

Rationale

When reading Shakespeare's sonnets, it is apparent that his meanings are distributed throughout the text, induced through sensory elements, images, technical form, and a strong narrative. (See endnote 2 for recommended close readings of the sonnets.[2]). Shakespeare's employment of sensory signals that work beneath the surface of literal meaning is worth mining for in shaping acting approaches, stimulating psychological and emotional feeling, evoking the aesthetic and visceral through sounds, rhythms, and heightened language, while enhancing an understanding of grammatical functions.

As the inspiration behind my teaching strategy, I recognized that Shakespeare's emphasis on the senses invites an alignment with an individual's cognitive and learning style preferences. This advantage is not only in serving a pedagogic purpose, but also with the potential of enhancing artistic practice. The reader response theorist Louise Rosenblatt has coined two types of selective attention activated in a reader's transaction with the written text. There is the *efferent* (from the Latin word *efferre*, meaning to carry away) for collecting facts and information to be recalled after reading, and the *aesthetic*, which is the feelings and associations arising during the reading of the text (Rosenblatt 2005: 43). The VARK approach when reading Shakespeare provides an opportunity for activating both kinds of attention, in stirring up cognitive and affective consciousness. There are many differing learning style inventories (see Mortimore 2008; Waring & Evans 2015), but in my approach I coupled Shakespeare's evocation of the senses with the pedagogical Learning Styles model VARK (originating from Fleming and Mills 1992), based on principles of sensory perception, how we gather information from the world, and individual modal preferences for learning. The letters VARK stand for Visual, Aural, Reading (and Writing – in this case, I have linked it with Shakespeare's written technical form), and the Kinesthetic (VARK 2018).

Aims

- To support a mix of cognitive and learning styles preferences, thereby facilitating neurodiversity across the cohort
- To develop individuals' awareness of their cognitive processing strengths and their conscious application of learning styles towards their achievement of tasks
- To circumvent the challenges of dyslexia by offering another way into the text beyond class reading performance
- To offer a channel through which to connect strongly with the words, narrative and form of Shakespeare's text
- To build a social model of learning through ensemble creation and observation of each others' interpretations through the group performances
- To explore avenues of artistic creation into performance

Method

The Participants

There were twenty-six second-year Acting students involved in the Voice Unit as part of the Shakespeare Unit. In this sample, there were eight students (comprised of both genders) assessed as dyslexic by an educational psychologist. The students were already familiar with the concept of learning styles having undergone a computer-screening test which identified their preferred learning style when entering the university. However, it is important not to be rigid about this, as learning styles are malleable, multidimensional, and can change according to the context (Waring & Evans 2015: 64).

The Task

For their Voice presentation, the students were to perform a group presentation of a Shakespeare sonnet. Each group was to devise an interpretive performance of the sonnet, focusing on a specific sense, or the written form, which was dominant within the writing of the sonnet. This was to be student-led work, created outside of the voice classes, in preparation for their assessed performance. For the assessment, they would perform the sonnet twice: first, their devised version, where they had explored and heightened the dominant sense through choreographed interpretation, for which they were encouraged to use costumes, props, and any artefacts that amplified their sensory aspect, learning style and artistic performance. The second version was to be spoken simply for truth of thought and communication of meaning, with word phrases distributed amongst the group as a choral piece. This naturally spoken piece should retain an underlying awareness of the chosen sensory element.

Process

I broke the larger cohort into smaller groups, and each group chose a sense/mode from the VARK model that they wished to concentrate on, according to what they thought their learning style strength/dominance might be. Although the dyslexic students were mixed with the non-dyslexics, it was notable that the dyslexic individuals mostly chose to be in a Visual or Kinesthetic group, while one individual chose Aural and one chose Reading and Writing – the technical form. To help guide the students, I suggested sonnets they might use where Shakespeare's content leans heavily on a particular sense, or modal aspect (although they were free to choose other sonnets if they wished), for example: (1) Visual – *Sonnet 43* ('When most I wink, then do my eyes best see'), (2) Aural – *Sonnet 30*, where there is an accentuation of assonance, aspiration, and alliteration in communicating the speaker's grief ('When to the sessions of sweet, silent thought'), (3) Reading and Writing – *Sonnet 129*, where Shakespeare communicates the physical action, emotion, and thoughts of the speaker through enjambment, assonance, alliteration, caesura, antithesis, and rhythm ('Th'expense of spirit in a waste of shame'), and (4) Kinesthetic – *Sonnet 19*, which is filled with images and physical actions ('Devouring Time, blunt thou the lion's paws'). In preparation, I went through the texts in voice class with each group, eliciting meaning, the sensory elements, and the technical form.

Outcome

Across the cohort, most of the groups produced some extremely effective interpretations of their sonnet, using movement, musical instruments, song, expressive voice, artefacts, and painting. The focus on the prevailing sense/learning style provided a key into Shakespeare's figurative expressions, connotations, references, and metaphors, enabling the students' vision in devising. In accompanying reports, several of the students wrote that this learning style approach had been a revelation in noting how they processed generally, in extending their awareness in their reading of Shakespeare, and in influencing their future approaches to acting. The majority of the dyslexic students produced interesting, committed performances, clearly comfortable when working within their cognitive/learning style modalities. In taking a more critical view, one dyslexic individual in the Reading and Writing group, although throwing himself into the performance with gusto, appeared lost in his task of specifically marking the written technical form through physical interpretation. This indicated that more teacher guidance was needed, and that his dyslexia continued to block his connection with the writing and language 'rules'. Furthermore, the heightened expression through choreographed embodiment and utilization of artefacts revealed that there were some non-dyslexic students who had not understood the meaning of the text. If an individual can read aloud with skilled fluency, the teacher can assume that the speaker fully comprehends the content of the text. Additionally, the speaker is often not aware that they might have misinterpreted some of the content, so do not ask for clarification. Although this strategy encourages idiosyncratic interpretations, it is important that decisions are taken from a foundation of knowledge. This method makes explicit when fundamental meanings are misplaced, which suggests that a more concentrated analysis of the text with the teacher in advance of the performance would be valuable. Furthermore, some direction in devising skills would assist in enhancing awareness about the presentation of hierarchical information. Important meanings and words can be overshadowed by the distraction of over-elaboration on minor aspects of the text, so the central message of the sonnet can become lost, defeating the intention of the exercise.

Conclusion

Arriving at the end of this book, I return to the questions I posed at the beginning of Chapter 2. I asked:

- How might we, as teachers, abandon teaching methods that reinforce the dominant, normative perspectives that privilege some 'ableist' groups over others?
- How do we ensure our teaching practices do not 'disable' those who process differently?
- How might we scrutinize our own practices, ensuring that our values and pedagogical choices are ethical and socially just while fostering the potential abilities of every individual?

The work in this book has shown that opportunities that allow multisensory perception and multi-modal expression, that enable an offloading of memory and cognitive processing onto the environment through the utilization of objects and space, can remove the burden of reading the words from the page into spoken performance for those with dyslexia. This facilitation can be enhanced through encouraging intuitive practice and building social learning spaces. Moreover, developing inclusive teaching practices in actor training entails more than simply inserting a few additional exercises into habitual teaching routines. Most importantly, it involves paying close attention to our students with dyslexia and neurodiversity, noticing their capabilities, listening to what they are saying, and giving regard to and opportunities for development of their individual methods while attending to their difficulties. This involves an openness to changes in our teaching practices. These changes necessitate a student-led, research-based approach for the construction of a flexible, inclusive curriculum which can facilitate the disadvantages and cultivate the advantages of difference. Although it can be time-consuming in devising teaching ideas, challenging in investigating the research and theory about dyslexia and learning differences, and demanding in exploring practice, this should not impede a determination to remove inequitable barriers in our teaching for those with dis/abilities.

In writing this book, my purpose is to share my research and ideas with the teaching community and those with dyslexia, contributing to a body of knowledge and resources in the world of actor training (and possibly beyond). With the aim of improving dyslexic individuals' learning experiences and recognizing their diverse talents, this contribution to knowledge can prompt others to commence their own investigations and disseminate their findings. In learning from each other, and with our students as co-researchers, we can come to understand and embrace neurodiversity through our teaching. Although there are many acting students assessed as dyslexic enrolled in our actor training institutions, this remains an area where investigations into teaching practice remain under-researched. In the spheres of artistic expression, the new and original bring fresh insights, methodologies, and vision. As verified in the work recorded in this book, there is much that dyslexic individuals can contribute to this end, and that their teachers can learn from them.

KEY POINTS OF CHAPTER 14

- A presentation of my overall research findings regarding teaching some acting students with dyslexia
- A discussion concerning weak working memory and processing difficulties in those with dyslexia
- A presentation of current research in psychology that emphasizes problems with executive functioning and prospective and retrospective memory in those with dyslexia
- The various affordances of *interpretive mnemonics* for those with dyslexia
- The need for an authenticity *in* and *through* teaching, to promote development of authenticity in dyslexic students' work
- An example of a research participant's personal process when working with Shakespeare's text, her development of ideas in working with her dyslexia leading to achievement of self-authorship in her performance
- Action Research Cycle Six was trialed and Teaching Strategy Six was offered, combining Shakespeare's multisensory writing with the VARK learning styles framework to facilitate neurodiversity across the student cohort
- A call for student-led and research-based teaching and shared dissemination of findings concerning the removal of barriers embedded in our teaching for those with dyslexia and neurodiversity.

Notes

1 In his book on the psychology of dyslexia, Michael Thomson states that 'one of the key features of the dyslexic learner is problems with memory. In particular, these centre around short-term memory in its relationship to classroom instructions and organization and in particular to aspects of written language learning' (2009: 165). Dyslexia consultants David McLoughlin and Carol Leather underline that:

> Our practice in assessment, counselling, teaching and training has for some years been based on the assumption that all the behavioural difficulties experienced by dyslexic people stem from an inefficiency in working memory [. . .]. This view is based on the scientific literature, but also on our practical experience. It is reinforced by the feedback provided by our clients.
>
> *(2013: 19)*

2 See Caroline Spurgeon (1935) for a close reading of Shakespeare's images in his plays. For an advanced reading of the meanings and literary form of Shakespeare's sonnets, see Helen Vendler (1997). For a useful explanation of the meanings of the words, see Katharine Duncan-Jones (in Shakespeare 1997). For a personal response and critical commentary on meaning and the writing of each sonnet by another poet, see Don Paterson (2010).

References

Bartram, E. (2017). *When Looking at the Role of Imogen from Shakespeare's Cymbeline How Can Exploring the Use of Imagery, Sounds and Other Creative Mediums Help Me Understand and Connect to This Character, Along with Enhancing My Performance of Shakespeare's Text?* Special Independent Project (MA). Royal Central School of Speech and Drama, London.

Dweck, C.S. (2000). *Self-theories*. New York: Psychology Press.

Fleming, N.D. & Mills, C. (1992). Not another inventory, rather a catalyst for reflection. *To Improve the Academy*, 11:1, p. 137.

Gathercole, S. & Packiam Alloway, T. (2008). *Working Memory and Learning*. London: SAGE Publications.

Grant, D. (2010). *That's the Way I Think*, 2nd ed. Oxford, UK: David Fulton

Kreber, C. (2013). *Authenticity in and through Teaching in Higher Education: The Transformative Potential of the Scholarship of Teaching*. London: Routledge.

McLoughlin, D. & Leather, C. (2013). *The Dyslexic Adult*, 2nd ed. Chichester, UK: Whurr.

Mortimore, T. (2008). *Dyslexia and Learning Style*, 2nd ed. Chichester, UK: John Wiley & Sons.

Nicolson, R. & Fawcett, A. (2010). *Dyslexia, Learning and the Brain*. London: MIT Press.

Paterson, D. (2010). *Reading Shakespeare's Sonnets*. London: Faber & Faber.

Reid, G. (2016). *Dyslexia: A Practitioner's Handbook*, 5th ed. Chichester, UK: John Wiley & Sons.

Rosenblatt, L. (2005). *Making Meaning with Texts*. Portsmouth, UK: Heinemann.

Shakespeare, W. (1997). *Shakespeare Sonnets*. Ed. Duncan-Jones, K. London: Arden Shakespeare.

Shakespeare, W. (1999). *Cymbeline*. Ed. Nosworthy, J.M. London: Routledge.

Smith-Spark, J. (2018). A review of prospective memory impairments in developmental dyslexia: evidence, explanations, and future directions. *The Clinical Neuropsychologist*, 32:5, 816–835.

Smith-Spark, J. & Fisk, J. (2003). Investigating the central executive in adult dyslexics: evidence from phonological and visiospatial working memory performance. *European Journal of Cognitive Psychology*, 15:4, pp. 567–587.

Smith-Spark, J. & Fisk, J. (2007). Working memory functioning in developmental dyslexia. *Memory*, 12:2, pp. 174–182.

Smith-Spark, J., Fawcett, A., Nicolson, R., & Fisk, J. (2004). Dyslexic students have more everyday cognitive lapses. *Memory*, 12:2, pp. 174–182.

Smith-Spark, J., Henry, L., Messer, D., Edvardsdottir, E., & Zięcik, A. (2016). Executive functions in adults with developmental dyslexia. *Research in Developmental Disabilities*, 53, 323–341.

Spurgeon, C. (1935). *Shakespeare's Imagery*. Cambridge, UK: Cambridge University Press.

Tanner, K. (2009). Adult dyslexia and the 'conundrum of failure'. *Disability & Society*, 24:6, 785–797.

Thomson, M. (2009). *The Psychology of Dyslexia*, 2nd ed. Chichester, UK: Wiley-Blackwell.

VARK (2018). *VARK: A Guide to Learning Styles*. Available from: http://vark-learn.com/. Accessed 7 May 2019.

Vendler, H. (1997). *The Art of Shakespeare's Sonnets*. Cambridge, MA: Harvard University Press.

Waring, M. & Evans, C. (2015). *Understanding Pedagogy*. London: Routledge.

Wolf, M. (2008). *Proust and the Squid: The Story and Science of the Reading Brain*. Cambridge, UK: Icon Books.

INDEX